AMERICAN Familia

A MEMOIR OF PERSEVERANCE

David A. Morales

RIVER GROVE
BOOKS

This book is a memoir reflecting the author's present recollections of experiences over time. Its story and its words are the author's alone. Some details and characteristics may be changed, some events may be compressed, and some dialogue may be recreated. The names and identifying characteristics of persons referenced in this book have been changed to protect their privacy.

Published by River Grove Books
Austin, TX
www.rivergrovebooks.com

Distributed by River Grove Books

Design and composition by Greenleaf Book Group and Lindsay Starr
Cover design by Greenleaf Book Group and Lindsay Starr

Publisher's Cataloging-in-Publication data is available.

Print ISBN: 978-1-63299-450-9

eBook ISBN: 978-1-63299-451-6

First Edition

To my savior Jesus Christ, for blessing me with a loving and caring family, for renewing my heart daily and for blessing me with a purposeful life and vision. "Where there is no vision, the people perish" (Proverbs 29:18 KJV).

~~~

To my family: my father, Antonio Morales, for his service to our country and for his tangible representation of what it means to be a loving father and husband, and a real man. To my mother, Ana Morales, for her selflessness, fierceness, and her deep, unconditional love of her children. And to my siblings, Diana, Dan, and Dwayne, for their limitless love and support.

To my loving wife, Samanda, for her kindness, patience, forgiveness, and deep commitment to love me unconditionally regardless of my mistakes and many faults. She is a gift from God and the pillar of our family.

To my two sons, may this book serve as a reminder to them that God always comes first and that *He* has a plan for their lives: "plans to prosper them, not to harm them, and plans to give them hope and a future" (Jeremiah 29:11 NIV).

~~~

To all young men and women who dream of a better future.

CONTENTS

Chapter 1

I DIDN'T KNOW

*Be proud of who you are and
where we come from.*

ANTONIO MORALES

"What was it like to grow up poor, Dad?"

I looked at my younger son, dark eyelashes against honey skin, his eyebrows drawn inward in thought. Alexander was around the same age I had been when my family came to the United States, yet at eleven years old, he seemed much younger than I was at his age in many ways.

"I wasn't poor in Puerto Rico," I replied.

"What do you mean?" Anthony asked. My older son's long body folded in half as he leaned toward me, his elbows on his knees, as if studying a play for one of his basketball games. His expression was mature, wise—at thirteen, he was growing into a young man.

"I mean, I was poor compared to our life now," I said, gesturing at the sprawling living space of our family home. "But I didn't feel poor until we moved to the US."

Both boys looked at me. It was a rainy afternoon in April of 2018, and we were sitting in our living room in our house in Massachusetts. Alexander's head tipped toward his right shoulder, his features pensive. Anthony sat up straight, his hands on his knees. As they waited, I wondered: Is now the time? Should I finally share the details of my complicated life?

"It's a long story," I finally said.

"Tell us," Alexander said.

Anthony nodded. "Yeah, Dad."

I patted the couch, signaling for them to sit next to me. Anthony ignored my invitation and instead relaxed his body, leaned into his easy chair, and kicked his legs up on the coffee table between us as if settling in for a bedtime story. But Alexander joined me on the couch, sitting and curling his legs up to his chest the way he used to when he was a toddler. I hid a smile, remembering him when he was little, my sweet, gentle son. I had worried about him as a child in a way I hadn't worried about Anthony. I'd thought Alexander's softness would be a burden, that he'd suffer, that he'd become a follower instead of a leader. That he'd never make it out there in the real world. I didn't want to raise a weak man.

It turned out I was wrong. Alexander's gentleness made him strong and confident. He was open and curious. I had learned from him that being a strong man didn't have to look rough and angry.

"What, Dad?" Alexander said.

"Sorry," I said. I chuckled; I'd been staring. I couldn't help it sometimes. I looked at Anthony, who was on the brink of an eye roll. They were growing up too fast. I had missed too much. I wanted to rewind, take it all back, live my whole life the way I'd lived the last three years, when I gave up a prominent and affluent career as a healthcare executive to be the father I knew I needed to be for them. The moment everything in my life changed for the better.

I couldn't rewrite the past. It was impossible to revise the pain, violence, and poverty of my adolescence. There was no way to erase the education I'd received on the streets of Lynn, just outside of Boston. I couldn't scrub my mind of the shootings, drugs, sex workers, and all of the other things I'd witnessed growing up. I was unable to take back the anger I'd carried with me throughout my early career, and the people I'd hurt. And I definitely couldn't undo the pain I'd caused my wife for so much of our marriage. She was so patient with me—more patient than I was with myself. More than I deserved.

But I could tell my sons the story of where I came from, and what I had learned. Over the years, I had shared pieces of my personal history and anecdotes about my family in Puerto Rico, but never the full story. As I looked at Anthony and Alexander, so eager to listen, I decided this was the time. I would share the lessons of my youth with them, including the mistakes.

My boys would never understand what it was like to grow up a low-income Puerto Rican in urban America, born an American citizen but culturally rooted in Puerto Rico. Their reality was different than mine. And yet . . . *and yet*, they needed to know. Not just the hero tales and highlights but the real story, in all its gritty details.

I noticed them exchange a look: lifted eyebrows, bottom lips pursed upward in curiosity. Their expressions seemed to say, "Is he going to tell us now?"

I had imagined this moment a hundred times: this living room, my story. My family's story. *Their* story. Where we came from and what finally shook the Morales family from the grip of poverty. How we got out . . . and how so many have not.

The truth was that it wasn't just my story, or even my family's story. It was a story echoed by so many young men and families—*generations*—and a story that would continue to play out across the United States. I wanted my sons to understand all the complicated aspects of my life and the lives of so many other young men like me. Maybe my boys could learn from past mistakes, and now from my example. I took a deep, long breath. *Help me do this right, God,* I prayed.

"Well, you know I was born in Valparaiso, Indiana," I began, settling in to tell my sons the story of my life. A history that is mostly mine but also others' histories, too. A story of our family's perseverance and unity. Family, and faith in God, is at the core of our success and continued blessing in the United States, our home.

I set out to teach my sons. I didn't realize they would teach me too. Or that we'd spend the next several days, between their school and activities, talking about our family's past, my past, with the hope that it would influence their future.

In 1975, the year I was born, Valparaiso, Indiana, was a college town of about 20,000 people. While the town wasn't racially diverse, the Latino population was increasing.[1]

While I don't remember anything of the two years I lived in Valparaiso, my sister and brothers recall it as a good life. Diana, Dan, and Dwayne are older than me by ten, eight, and seven years, and they remember our middle-class existence. Bedrooms with matching furniture. Bicycles. Dad's decent-paying job. Mom taking care of the house and socializing with her extended family, who also lived in Valparaiso and in nearby Gary. Their journey from Puerto Rico to the steel mill of Gary will come later.

The US was all my siblings and I had ever known. Both my mom and dad moved to Indiana as teenagers from Puerto Rico and met in Indiana. They married and started a family. Several years and four kids later, our life was solid and safe.

But that all changed when Dad decided to move our family to Dorado, Puerto Rico, where he and my mom were born, because a family member told my dad there was work there. I would learn much later of my parents' financial troubles. Dad had given his home and mortgage to someone without a legal contract, and when the person stopped paying on the loan, the house was foreclosed on. Dad was going to be liable for the debt, so he did the only thing that made sense to him in what felt like a financially hopeless situation. He left the country. But I also wonder if part of him simply wanted to go home— to be with family and friends. I doubt he had any idea what was in store for us, or the personal and financial crises to come.

Dorado is located along the northern coast of Puerto Rico, about twenty miles west of San Juan. The town is divided into three parts: beach, valley, and mountains. We moved to a sector of the valley called Maguayo, which was known for its production of sugarcane. The island has sunshine and humidity all year round, with temperatures ranging from warm to hot, and an annual low of about 70 degrees.

We moved into a cement rental house across the street from a massive sugarcane plantation. The land was surrounded by barbed wire and extended as far as I could see. As a child, I imagined it like the ocean, with endless waves of sugarcane. Our street was heavily lined by trees, and I remember as a child of just five years old looking out the window and up at the looming trees, wishing I could climb them.

Our home was a standard government-contract cement house, a mirror of hundreds of other houses: a box-shaped structure with two bedrooms, a small kitchen, and a tiny bathroom. Two windows. Cement floors. Cement walls. Leaky roof. Musty. Dark. Surrounded by vegetation, chickens, and lizards.

I was happy in our Maguayo home. I shared a room with my two brothers, Dan and Dwayne, who were my heroes. I roughhoused with them and gnawed on stolen sugarcane. My dad would bring home freshly caught fish, eels, and sharks, and I'd watch him hang them from one of the big front yard trees, skin them, remove their oils, and prepare them for the family to enjoy. We had a chicken coop, and banana, mango, lemon, and *guanábana* trees everywhere. My parents would gather fruit daily from the trees surrounding our house and make fresh drinks, which I'd slurp greedily, savoring the mix of sweet and tart. I'd eat *jobo* fruit, letting the juice flow over my hands, not caring about the stickiness between my fingers. I was never hungry, because all I had to do was walk out of the front door and find a tree to harvest. The landscape was plentiful. We had fruit, eggs, and seafood readily available and free.

And *ñame*! We ate so many *ñame*, yams that my dad dug up in the woods near our home. I hated *ñame*.

Puerto Rican tradition is to always have plain bread, coffee, and cheese in the house, and those staples were almost always stocked. My parents bought other limited groceries and stuck with the cheapest items they could get. With our sparse ingredients, my brothers got creative, making delicacies like toasted bread with butter and *Quik*, a chocolate powdery drink mix.

Our weekly meal rotation went like this: White rice and eggs. White rice and corned beef. White rice and Spam. White rice with *bacalao*, which is cod fish. White rice with *ñame*. White rice with ketchup. Of course, most meals and snacks often included fruit and fruit juice. It might not have been the most diverse diet, but I got what I needed as a growing boy.

The jungle landscape offered endless entertainment. I loved having the wildness of the jungle as my playground, and a steep mountain behind my house to climb. I'd hunt for lizards and *ciempiés* (centipedes), and pretend I was my grandfather, fighting in the war as part of the American military. Grandpa had been recruited from his home in Puerto Rico like so many other Puerto Rican men during World War II and returned a hero in our community.

The area around my house was so leafy that if I stood in the right spots, I could barely see my home—which fed my imagination and transported me to other lands and time periods. When my brothers were home from school, I'd trail behind them. My brother Dan was always inventing stuff in the woods, and Dwayne was his sidekick, always sticking next to him. I wanted to follow them wherever they went, but they didn't always want their little brother around.

"*A dónde van?*" Where are you going? I'd ask when they'd set out for one of their multi-hour treks through the jungle. "*¡Espérame!*" Wait for me!

They'd mumble something to me like "*quedate en casa que nos regaña mami*"—stay home, or mom will yell at us. Then they'd scramble out the door, their long legs carrying them too far and too fast for me to catch up. I'd call after them again, "*¡Espérame!*"

When my brothers were out of sight and I was out of breath from chasing them, I'd wander into the jungle behind our house and hunt for bugs, fossilized shells, dinosaur bones, and Indian artifacts. More than once, I made monumental discoveries that I was sure would wow the entire scientific community. I tucked my precious finds in my pockets and set off to make archeological history. Later, I'd line my findings along the windowsill in our shared bedroom.

On weekends, my father would take us to beaches in Vega Alta, Manatí, or Dorado, all of which were about fifteen to twenty minutes from our home. I didn't like to swim, but I loved to hunt for shells and use the sticks and palm trees I'd find on the beach to make cities of sand. Sometimes I dug for *cangrejos* (crabs) or *caracoles* (hermit crabs). When I grew tired of sand play, I'd lay under the palm or almond trees and look up at the waving palms or abundant almonds, my face warm with afternoon rays, then turn my head to look over at my dad. He was often camped in a chair under a palm tree sitting next to a cooler, a Schaefer beer in one hand and *pollo frito* (fried chicken) or *molleja frita* (fried gizzard) in the other hand. He always looked relaxed, peaceful. I felt it too.

With a ripe imagination and full belly, I had no idea we were poor or that our family struggled to afford food, rent, and utilities.

To the rest of my family, Maguayo was a shock. We went from a comfortable life in Indiana to a basic cement home in Puerto Rico. My brothers and I slept on two mattresses on the floor of our shared bedroom. We had one bathroom between the six of us, with the sink held up by a wooden broom stick cut in half and a small shower my big brother Dan seemed to dwarf. Our living space was small; our kitchen was miniscule. Dad struggled to find work and patched together a meager income between several jobs. Mom got a full-time job to support us. Diana stepped up to raise us while Mom was away.

As an elementary-age child, though, small was big. A bathroom was just for unwanted showers, annoying teeth brushing, and begrudging use of the toilet. And who cared if I was sleeping on a mattress on the floor when I had my two big brothers in the room with me? Mom and Dad were gone most of the time working to provide for us, and they were fighting more and more when they were home, but I had my sister Diana, who was now a teenager and cared for me like a second mom. She made me feel loved. I was oblivious to her sacrifice and what it must have been like to be a forced mother to three wild boys, with no social life because of the demands of her role at home.

I was also shielded from my brothers' daily testing of manhood. To make it in Puerto Rican society, boys and men had to be not just tough but fierce. Impenetrable. Supermen. Ready to throw a punch *como hombre*, like a man. Boxing was huge in the early 1980s and Puerto Ricans were beyond proud of world super bantamweight boxing champion Wilfredo Gómez. If you didn't know how to box as a young kid, you'd soon learn from the punches you were likely to take on the street.

Over the first couple of years in Puerto Rico, my brother Dan had grown to be one of the most violent guys in town. By thirteen, he could box and brawl. He was skinny and tall, but he was known as a great street boxer. More than once, I watched guys walk up to our house to challenge Dan, but he didn't wait for them to hit first. *Boom, boom, boom.* It was over. Dan would walk back in the house, job done. I'd look at another nameless dude staggering out of our yard and feel proud. My brothers could fight, and I was going to be just like them.

I was happy and naïve to the struggles my family was facing. Just outside the periphery of my joy, my dad's alcoholism grew. My parents fought regularly, and even though there were yelling and crashing sounds many nights, it didn't impact me the way it impacted my siblings—I was the baby, and they protected me.

I also didn't grasp the rate of killings and violence around me in Puerto Rico.

The year I was born, death was already pulsing through the country. The drug trade and crime were rising.[2] People were getting hacked up with machetes. Every single day, the front page of the island's newspaper, *El Vocero*, displayed pictures of murdered people on the cover. Puerto Rican culture was tough, gritty, and often brutal. Men had to prove themselves to be *fuerte. Sin miedo*. Strong and fearless.

Women, though, were expected to be at home taking care of the family and doing chores. There was a clear assignment of gender roles in Puerto Rico: women cared for the house, and men worked and drank. Looking back, my mother never quite fit the cultural role assigned to women. She was highly outspoken at home and worked incessantly outside of the house, unlike most of my aunts. She wasn't going to rely on a man to take care of her and us kids. She made things happen for herself.

So there I was, a little kid in the thick of it, with no idea of what was going on around me. All in the world was good from my perspective. *Sí*, I stumbled across dead bodies in the jungle, one in a burned car, another on the side of the road; *sí*, I watched my dad nearly beat the life out of someone in our front yard; *sí*, my brothers were brawling on the streets and trying to toughen me up with what I thought of as daily good-natured beatings.

But even though I witnessed the death and fighting, and felt the blows from my brothers, I was still detached from the reality around me. It all seemed normal, not dangerous. I was in my make-believe land of *guayabas, mangos, ciempiés*, and *coquis*, small frogs native to Puerto Rico. I saw what I wanted to in the world my family created for me.

Soon, I started elementary school at Pedro Lopez Canino, which was about a ten- to fifteen-minute drive on La Número Dos, a road that mostly travels along the periphery of the entire island of Puerto Rico. Pedro Lopez Canino was a big public school that served a lot of outlying towns, and went from kindergarten through middle school. The administration did a good job of keeping sixth-grade and younger kids siloed from the older kids, in a separate area of the school. We had a pebble play area about fifty yards long where we could run back and forth during recess. And we ran! Every day, back and forth: tag, races, anything to keep us occupied and move our bodies. Lunch was provided every day, usually rice and beans with chicken or pork and a side of *ciruelas*, prunes dipped in sugar.

My classroom was bursting with students from kindergarten through second grade, and we were a rowdy group, mostly poor and multicolored. Interestingly, I don't remember skin color impacting how we treated each other, but I do remember we were all different skin tones. Looking back, I think teaching in classrooms like mine, with limited resources and support, full of kids from diverse backgrounds and homes, is the work of saints. There was no gymnasium for PE, science lab for experiments, or even a playground for us to swing and slide on during recess. These women (and they were all women) were given a simple classroom, basic curriculum and books, and supplies that required imagination—and had the task of raising up children in a world that wasn't safe outside the school walls. Of course, we didn't know that, but they did.

I don't remember much about kindergarten, but I do remember first grade because of Mrs. Barrientos. She was a beautiful lady, inside and out, with dark skin and a bright smile. Mrs. Barrientos was loving. She was kind to me and cared for each of her students. She also knew my mother from church and typically checked in on me during the day, which I thought was normal. I went home every day feeling nurtured, and while I was still undergoing daily well-intentioned beatings by Dan and Dwayne, who wanted to toughen me up to survive in Puerto Rico, I felt protected by my brothers. I had my sister, Diana, who took care of me and loved me. I had the jungle. I had enough to eat. I was happy.

By third grade, though, everything about school changed in Mrs. Camacho's class. Mrs. Camacho was a tough woman. If you so much as looked like you were going to disobey, she would get out her wooden stick. Back then, teachers in Puerto Rico were allowed to hit children—not just a whack, but aggressive, sometimes violent strikes and repeated as often as necessary to instill discipline and order. Painful hitting with objects like sticks or paddles that left welts and bruises was the norm. While I was used to getting beat up by my brothers, I wasn't used to being beaten at school. Mrs. Camacho's blows stung and throbbed, both physically and emotionally. I missed the safety and nurturing I'd received in Mrs. Barrientos's class.

But I also couldn't seem to learn from her corporal punishment. I got in trouble a lot for talking and goofing around with my friends. This made me Mrs. Camacho's favorite target, and she used to hit me violently.

One day, I had some rubber bands that I decided to covertly shoot at my friends when Mrs. Camacho turned her back to write on the chalkboard.

Ping. I shot Carlos. *Ping*, Hector. *Ping, ping*, Margarita, the cutest girl in the class. *Ping*, Miguel, and then: "*Ay!*"

I'd hit Miguel in the eye. My body went hot, then cold, as Mrs. Camacho spun around. She marched up to Miguel.

"Tell me what happened," she demanded.

Miguel looked down at his lap, then inadvertently darted his eyes toward me. My jaw tightened. That was all Mrs. Camacho needed. She launched in my direction and grabbed me by the arm, then dragged me to the front of the classroom, my feet slipping on the cement floor.

After retrieving a large stick from her desk drawer, she instructed me to place my hands on the edge of her desk, then hit my knuckles repeatedly until they bled. I cried from the pain, even though I tried hard not to, and that seemed to be enough for her. Humiliated at my tears, I sat down and rubbed my bloody, swelling knuckles.

By the end of the day, my knuckles were twice their normal size and crusted in blood. As I walked home, I thought of what I'd tell my sister. Could I hide my hands? I worried Diana and Mom would be angry that I'd gotten in trouble.

I opened our front door and looked around at the empty space. Realizing Diana must be in her bedroom, I quickly hung my backpack on the little stand next to the front door and scurried to my room, digging around in my closet for something to hide my hands. Nothing. Maybe I could stay in my room for the rest of the day, and slip off to school tomorrow without anyone noticing . . .

Tap, tap, tap. My sister knocked lightly on the closed door, then opened it without waiting for me to reply. I threw my hands behind my back, wincing as my knuckles bumped together.

"*Hola, gordito*," she said, using my least favorite term of endearment, little fat boy. "How was school?" she asked in Spanish. "Do you have homework?"

I shook my head no.

She eyed me suspiciously, then walked across the room and crouched down. "What's in your hands? Let me see."

I hesitated, but she wasn't budging. Finally, I put my hands out in front of me, palms down. Standing in front of her, they looked worse than I remembered, my knuckles swollen into little acorns, blood crusted on my finger joints; my thumbs, which I'd used to grip the underside of Mrs. Camacho's desk, were spared. I thought of all the cuts and bruises I'd come home with from school on my knees, elbows, and palms. I could see in Diana's tight lips and drawn brow that this was the worst yet.

And it hurt. Badly.

"*Ay, bendito.*" She gently took my hands in hers. "Let's get this cleaned up."

I followed my sister to the bathroom and let her wash my hands with soap, then clean them with something that made my eyes water and cuts sting. She washed her own hands and applied bandages to the wounds.

To my surprise, Diana never asked me what I'd done to deserve the punishment, or why I couldn't just behave like the rest of the kids: sit down, shut up, and do as I was told. I'd been scolded before by Diana for coming home with bruises or cuts from Mrs. Camacho, because marks from the teacher meant I was being bad. I kept wondering when she'd reprimand me, but the scolding I was bracing for never came. After dinner, she helped me do my homework, neatly writing in the answers for me as I cradled my hands in my lap. She placed my books and papers in my backpack and zipped it up, then showered me, placed new bandages on my knuckles, put on my pajamas, and tucked me in.

I saw her pause at the door that night, looking at me with a soft expression I'd seen on my mom's face countless times. Diana was the woman who loved and cared for me because my own mom had to be gone so much. I missed my mom, but I loved my sister, my second mom.

The next morning, Diana looked squarely at me across the breakfast table. "Mom called Mrs. Camacho at home, early."

My sleepy eyes popped open. I sat up straight. Scrambled egg fell out of my slack-jawed mouth. "*¿Qué?*"

"Mom said it was too much," she continued, her Spanish echoing in my disbelieving ears. "The teachers are allowed to hit you, not abuse you."

I said nothing. Fear pulsed through me. What was Mrs. Camacho going to do to me now?

Diana reached across the table and put a hand on my arm. "Don't worry. Mom took care of it. Tell us if she does anything like this again." When I said nothing, she added, "*¿Me entiendes?*" Do you understand?

I nodded, shoveling egg back into my mouth.

Later that day at school, Mrs. Camacho didn't call on me once or even look in my direction. What in the world had my mom said to her? That day, I kept my head down, mouth shut, and did as I was told. Unfortunately for Mrs. Camacho, my good behavior wouldn't last beyond that afternoon.

We moved from Maguayo to Kuilan, a sector of Dorado, when I was eight. Our new place was about fifteen minutes from our old place, but it felt like we moved to a completely new area. Our cement home was a little bit better: it had a fresh paint job and the roof didn't leak. Sunlight streamed through the windows in the morning, and the house was awash in natural light well into the evening. The electricity didn't go out as much, and we had a porch and covered parking. Best of all, we now had a front yard with a gate—the yard was all cement, but that was just fine by me.

Looking back, this move marked our transition from working poor to working class. My mom had gotten a job teaching English at our local school; my dad was a maintenance mechanic. Both were still gone most of the day earning money, and it seemed to be paying off, as the additional income afforded us a better place to live. For my parents, it was a big step up. For us kids, it meant more comfort and less chance we'd be doing homework by candlelight.

When I wasn't in school, I'd walk the few hundred feet to the top of the hill our house sat on. There were two bars there, which we called *puntos*, or points. My friend Jaime and I used to go to one of the two *puntos* to watch Bruce Lee movies for twenty-five cents at the makeshift cinema at the back of one of the bars. I paid for the movie with money from my grandfather, who always gave me a quarter or so every Sunday when we'd go to his house.

There were always groups of men at the bar with the movie theatre. The men would sit outside on metal chairs with a small, short table in the middle to hold their beers and hard drinks. Everyone knew Jaime and me by name, but often ignored us as we weaved through their conversations to the entrance of the bar, past men sitting alone at tables inside, and into the back room where a projector and six wooden seats made up the theatre. In the dark of that room, we were transported to the world of martial arts for an hour and a half. If we got bored of the movie or had more time to kill, we'd play pool, which cost another twenty-five cents.

The bars were a central hangout for us neighborhood kids, but at night they often turned deadly. Someone would say or do the wrong thing, and a gun would be pulled or someone would be jumped. It was a common part of my childhood to hear talk of serious injuries or death, and I don't remember it impacting me much. Death was a part of life in Puerto Rico. Even though I hung out at those bars and knew those people, they were on the periphery of my awareness. Their injuries and deaths had nothing to do with jungle exploration, penny candies, or Bruce Lee.

But one thing I couldn't ignore was Dad's heavy drinking.

I was forced to confront reality one night as I huddled in my shared bedroom with my siblings. I was nine years old, and Diana had her arms wrapped around me, the two of us sitting on the bed. Dwayne sat next to Diana, his knees hugged up to his chest. Dan sat against the door, his back rigid. He reminded me of a German Shepherd on watch, ready to fight if he needed to.

Outside of the bedroom, I heard another crash, then my dad's booming voice and mom's screaming, which sent shivers down the length of my body. I imagined my strong mother afraid and alone, and my dad overcome by rage and alcohol. I wondered what Dad looked like when he was like that, because my siblings had always swept me out of the house or into the safety of the bedroom during his rampages. What was happening out there? Why was my father so angry? Was my mother in danger?

Diana was wiping my face with her thumb, and I felt wetness streak across my face. I hadn't realized I was crying, but suddenly I began to weep, the tears overwhelming my body, my limbs collapsing into her. We sat like that for what felt like hours, and I couldn't hear anything through my sobs until my tears were interrupted by three crashes, each one louder than the one before. Finally, the front door slammed, and I stopped crying abruptly as I listened, straining my ears to hear my mother in the other room.

Why was it silent? Was she OK? Was it safe to go out there to check on her?

Dan met Diana's eyes. When she nodded, he carefully opened the door. The three of us waited in the bedroom, my body rigid, the silence of the room so thick I prayed for my breath to quiet down so I could hear my mother.

What was taking Dan so long?

Finally, the door opened wide, and there was Dan, my big hero of a brother, standing in the doorway.

"*Mami está bien*," he said. Mom is OK. I exhaled with relief, but Dan didn't seem to share in my reassurance. At just fifteen years old, he wore age and sadness on his face.

I stood, wiping my eyes and nose on my arm. "Can I see her?" I asked in shaky Spanish.

"Not tonight," Dan replied, just as my sister said, "It's time for bed."

Later that night, after my pajamas were on and teeth were brushed, I lied in my bed next to Dwayne, with Dan on his own mattress next to us, and tried to imagine my dad differently.

In my imagination, Dad was a superhero fighting bad guys in our living room, not a drunk who made my mom feel afraid. Did he hit her? I shook away the thought, because as bad as these episodes were, I didn't think he'd ever lay a hand on Mami.

I fell asleep that night with the sticky feeling of spent sobs, and dreamed of my dad. In my dream, my dad was no longer a superhero but instead a Puerto Rican Bruce Lee, protecting our entire community with Wing Chun, and saving our family from his drinking. But even in the innocence of nine-year-old dreams, I didn't believe my own fantasy.

Chapter 2

TAKE ME TO CHURCH

*The only person you are destined to
become is the person you decide to be.*

RALPH WALDO EMERSON

A few weeks after that huddled night with my siblings, I sat in the pew beside my mom, sweat inching down my back. The memory of Dad yelling was far from my mind; all I could think about was changing out of my church clothes and going to buy some *pio pio* at the corner store. My mouth salivated as I thought of the snack of ground corn and sugar, packaged in two-ounce bags and sold in local *bodegas* for twenty-five cents each. I tugged at my shirt collar. We were going on hour two at church, and thick, wet heat engulfed the space. The church had high ceilings, and the fans set high above were working overtime to distribute the ninety-plus-degree air. While I sweated through my church clothes, the adults seemed unfazed by the stifling tropical heat. This was our Sunday home, but I was itching to get outside, cool down, and play with my friends Willie and Carlos.

Church had been pretty much standard fare that Sunday: lots of singing, a sermon, a baptism, and the most dramatic point of any service, a woman writhing on the floor like a snake, speaking in tongues. The pastor had admonished the evil spirits inside of her and she'd been freed, plunking herself down into a pew, breathless and tired. We'd resumed church as normal.

Exorcisms were commonplace at our church's three- to four-hour services. I wasn't sure what to make of them, but they were at least entertaining—if not sometimes terrifying. With hundreds of people in attendance, there were sure to be at least a couple of exorcisms per service. After each occurrence, I'd pray hard that an evil spirit would never inhabit me.

Church played a big part in my life, even if I was often hot and bored. It represented order and discipline. I attended service from nine in the morning until sometimes as late as two in the afternoon. I was in the church choir, and my singing teacher was precise and strict; every Sunday morning, she lined us up, training our voices in preparation for singing during church. There was no goofing around in her choir. She had expectations, and you were to meet them. No exceptions. She was kind, too, and would sometimes invite all the choir kids to her house on Saturdays for cookouts—though the conversation always ended up being about music and practicing songs for Sunday worship.

Service took place in a beautiful white church in the *barrio* of Espinosa, about three miles from our home. Most often we drove, unless the car wasn't working, in which case we would walk. The church was large and glorious, with dozens of wooden pews made of *caoba*, or mahogany, and there were also intricate decorations in the front of the church. With a congregation of about two hundred in a rural area, nearly everyone we knew attended. The pastor was a powerful man in our community with a huge calling from God on his life. With so many in attendance, there were a lot of kids: about thirty of us, running around between breaks, playing in the church parking lot, or crossing the street to buy candy, *pio pio*, or an Old Colony pineapple flavored soda before service resumed.

The church sat at the main intersection of Ruta Numero Dos, across from a gas station and a popular bar that was well-frequented seven days a week, including by church members. During lunch breaks at church, my siblings and I would go to the bar to get sodas with money Grandpa had given us.

That day in church, I looked at my bored siblings to my left. Diana was sitting up straight but had a glossy look in her eyes; Dan and Dwayne sat slightly slumped, legs splayed. They looked to be on the edge of mischief, but I knew they wouldn't dare cause trouble or they'd have Diana and Mom to answer to.

I looked to my right, at my mom, whose honey skin was damp like mine. Mom was listening intently to the pastor, fanning herself with an *abanico,* a handheld fan. Nearly every woman in the church used an *abanico* to fan themselves during the church service. As I looked at my mom, it struck me that although she was tough—a hard worker, the reliable provider for our family—she was beautiful inside and out. That afternoon, she glowed with holiness as the waving fan rhythmically swayed her hair in midair.

My thoughts were interrupted by the driving sound of *panderetas* (tambourines), drums, guitar, and loud singing exploding in the church. The congregation jumped to its feet, and my siblings and I did too. I sang and clapped but was distracted as I watched my mom joyfully wave her hands and dance in place. Her floral cotton dress clung to her stomach as she sang in unison amid a packed church of believers singing *coritos* (hymns) like "Poderoso es Nuestro Dios" (Our God is Powerful), or "Jerusalén, Que Bonita Eres" (Jerusalem, How Beautiful You Are).

As the music and joyful singing carried on, I wondered about my dad. Was he at work? Drinking at one of the two bars close to home? Or at home, tinkering with one of the cars? Why was he sometimes not with us on Sundays?

My mother, my strong *ma'i,* stood next to me like a pillar. She sang with her entire body, as if God was standing right in front of her. To me, Mom represented solidity, stability, and faith. While our culture celebrated men for their masculinity and physical prowess, women were the strong ones. They held homes together. They were the ever-present backbone of the family. I was surrounded by these powerful women at home and at church, and they were a force to be reckoned with when it came to their families.

After church, we walked home in a processional, with my brothers off ahead, me scrambling after them, and Diana walking next to my mother, the two of them chatting about the sermon. When my brothers started running off ahead toward the house, I couldn't keep up, so I slowed down and waited for Mom and Diana. I walked the rest of the way with them, listening to talk of upcoming church events, which parishioners needed prayers, and what to bring to Grandma's house later in the afternoon.

At home, mom made me a Spam and cheese sandwich and I ate quickly, standing at the kitchen counter. I had already ripped off my church clothes and put on shorts and a T-shirt, both of which fit my growing body snugly. I wanted to get on with the day and into adventures, and my friend Jaime and I had agreed to meet outside at one-thirty. Two quarters jangled in my pocket and I planned to buy pocketsful of penny candies to share with my friend. Later that day, I knew, we'd be going to my grandparents' house for dinner, so there was no playtime to lose.

I finished my sandwich, left my plate on the table, and gave my mom a quick kiss on the cheek.

"*¡Nos vemos horita!*" I called over my shoulder, see you soon, running toward the door before my mom changed her mind. I threw the front door open and nearly collided with three women from church, all still in their Sunday best. They let out a collective burst of surprise as I skittered around them and hollered, "*¡Mami!*"

I wasn't about to stick around.

It seemed like a revolving group of church ladies came around every week, usually on Sundays but sometimes during the week too. I wasn't entirely sure what they did for all those hours together, but Diana said they mostly prayed, usually for several hours straight. I had once arrived home early to find five women, including my mom, all seated in a circle: they had pulled our kitchen chairs into our living room and were praying fiercely, Bibles sitting open in their laps and *abanicos* flapping back and forth in peaceful harmony. Startled, I'd stood for a long moment, staring. We were taught as kids that one was to never interrupt adults and that prayer was sacred and to be respected at all times, especially during the act of prayer itself. One woman was crying; another had her hands raised toward the ceiling; mom's head was bowed. It was like they had transported themselves to a different world. When I snapped to, I quietly walked out of the room, but as hard as I tried to escape that moment, I was chased by prayers for my father.

Querido Dios, please heal my husband. *Jesús*, please take alcoholism from this house. *Querido Padre Celestial*, please rid this home of pain. *Sana tu hijo, te pedimos por sanación y libramiento!*

Even as I tried to push that moment from my mind and pretend everything was fine, I wondered: Why did Mom have to beg God to heal Dad? Why did these women have to ask God so many times? Why didn't God just make my dad better?

Being just nine years old, I didn't understand the personal crisis my dad had undergone moving to Puerto Rico, and how that weighed on him. In Indiana, my parents had owned a middle-class home and two cars during the 1970s. Dad made eleven dollars an hour, enough to feed and care for us well. Mom was able to stay home with us, we had clothes that fit, got new toys on our birthdays, and the neighborhood was safe. Dad had been proud of what he was able to provide for our family. But then the financial challenges came, and we had to leave. Puerto Rico had felt like the only good option to my dad.

In Puerto Rico, Dad made $2.71 an hour. Mom sewed clothes for Diana and herself, and I never seemed to have clothes that fit me, my stomach bulging out the bottom of shirts or shorts that were too tight and riding up my backside. In emergency situations, I wore my sister Diana's hand-me-down underwear; I didn't own enough pairs to keep me clothed if the laundry didn't get done. It didn't help that I was heavy. It didn't help that Dad didn't make enough money to support our family.

We only brought one car with us from Indiana, a green Dodge station wagon with wood paneling that was always overheating or breaking down. My parents kept a few jugs of water in the car for when it overheated; we'd stop on the side of the road, and Mom or Dad would grab a jug of water and pour it over the radiator, let the car cool off, and we'd continue down the road. That was our ride. We were never able to afford a second car or to fix that car up enough so that it didn't break down all the time.

In Kuilan, our neighborhood, Mom was working, Dad was making closer to four dollars an hour, and things were getting better. Of course, being the youngest and having older siblings to look after me, I didn't realize all these financial struggles or the extent of my dad's alcoholism, except when he sometimes raged at my mom or brothers. I didn't recognize how bad things were, and my siblings didn't want me to know.

I also had no idea my dad was about to undergo a major personal transformation.

I paused storytelling and looked at my sons, partially in disbelief that they were still listening—neither of them had looked at their phones once in the past hour or so—and partially curious what they thought about all I'd shared so far. It was a lot to take in: our family's poverty, the violence and death I'd grown up around, and their grandpa's addiction.

"Any questions so far?" I asked, glancing over Anthony's head at the clock mounted on the wall a few feet behind him and to his right. It read 11:47 p.m., well past their bedtime on a school night.

"That doesn't sound like Grandpa," Alexander said. I looked at my youngest, who had retrieved a blanket at some point during the story and was now reclining on the sofa with his feet on my knees. His face was tight with concern, and he seemed to be processing what he'd learned. His grandpa was his hero and a pillar in his life, just like my grandpa had been to me. My dad was a hands-on grandfather who had taught Alexander how to use his hands and tools to make toys or wooden trinkets.

"He's a different person today," I said.

"Did he hurt Grandma?" Anthony asked, sitting up and leaning toward me.

"I don't think he hurt Grandma's body, but he hurt her heart. And he scared her."

"Did he hurt you?"

"He never hit me. But he scared me too."

"What about Tío Dan, Tío Dwayne, and Tía Diana?" Alexander asked.

"I don't know for sure," I said. "But I think Dan and Dwayne took the physical brunt of Dad's anger. And we were all afraid."

"What changed?" Alexander said.

"I've never even heard him yell," Anthony added.

"*He* changed," I said. "God changed his heart and saved him. All of the prayers your grandma and the church ladies asked for from God were answered. It's part of what makes faith so powerful. God answers prayers in His time and in His way."

My boys were quiet, lost in thought. When there were no more questions, I stood. "Time for bed," I said. When both boys groaned in protest, I added, "How about I tell you more tomorrow after school?"

As they made their way upstairs, I stood in the empty living room, thinking of how different their lives were than mine had been, and how blessed I was to be able to provide for them.

I slept well that night. The next morning I got up at five o'clock, like always. As I sat with my Bible and coffee, I considered what I'd say to them that afternoon. The boys slept in and rushed through breakfast and off to school.

As they hurried out the door, Anthony called over his shoulder, "Don't forget about telling us more of the story, Dad!"

When they arrived at home later that day, I was waiting for them. They went right to their same spots, with Alexander on the couch and Anthony on the chair. Their backpacks sat crumpled on the floor next to them.

"Do you have homework?" I asked with a grin.

"A little," Alexander said. "But can we do it after dinner? Please?"

I laughed. "Fine. Now where were we . . ."

Back in Puerto Rico, Sunday late afternoons were spent at my paternal grandparents' home. Always. No exceptions.

In my mind, my grandparents were like millionaires. Grandma was the heart and soul of the entire community. She was full of love, grace, kindness, and compassion. Grandpa was a proud member of the Greatest Generation, Americans who grew up during the Great Depression and fought in World War II. At a solid five foot five, he was deeply respected by everyone in our area. Both my grandparents were loved by all. Looking back, I think what compelled this respect was that they represented the American dream: the ability to live a peaceful life filled with family, good neighbors, faith, and moments to share all of God's provision with your loved ones. "Ahora Seremos

Felices," a song written by Rafael Hernández Marín, captured warmly the Puerto Rican dream and nostalgia.

My grandparents were also givers. They shared their time volunteering at church and hosted the family at their home, where they prepared massive meals for us and anyone who showed up—any day of the week. My grandfather kept his yard and home immaculate and my grandmother gave her shirt off her back to anyone in need. Both were selfless and would come to the aid of their family or church members at a moment's call.

My grandparents shaped my view of my American dream. They worked hard to keep the extended family—aunts, uncles, and cousins—close and united. We were one large family sharing the fruits of our labor, regardless of position in life or income. Everyone was welcome. It was my grandparents' way. My grandfather was especially adamant about sharing and giving, but he made it clear to all of us kids: you have to study and work. No excuses. In fact, my grandfather would go out of his way to tell anyone who would listen that nothing was given to him and he had to earn his way through life. *Con trabajo y esfuerzo se llega lejos!* With work and effort, you get far!

Like most Puerto Rican men his age, Grandpa had left Puerto Rico to serve in the Army, fighting in World War II. When he returned, one of his brothers encouraged him to go to Indiana to work, saying, "There's money everywhere!" Or as the old Puerto Rican saying goes, *Los chavos se consiguen dondequiera, hasta se le dan con los pies*, meaning: money is so abundant, you can kick it with your feet on the streets. Jobs are plentiful, my grandpa was told, and you'll make tons of money. With profound poverty and economic challenges in Puerto Rico, the possibility of financial stability was enticing.

So Grandpa went. About five years later, he sent for my grandmother and my father. For the rest of his working adult life, he stayed in Indiana, worked in the steel industry, and saved his money wisely. When he retired, Inland Steel, the company he'd worked at for years, gifted him with an Omega watch, a luxury brand that cost several thousand dollars at the time. Grandpa had just a sixth-grade education, but poured his soul into his work. Our family still has that watch, and it serves as a reminder and a testament to my grandfather's legacy and his impact on the entire family—and on my life.

With a pension and savings, my grandparents returned to Puerto Rico and, with the difference in cost of living, were able to purchase a respectable home. They bought a dark blue Oldsmobile sedan with leather seats. Grandpa's pride, though, was my grandmother. He'd stroll through town with her, his face relaxed with the happiness of a man in love. Grandma always wore nice clothes and looked graceful and polished. It was obvious Grandpa knew he was a lucky man.

Grandpa was the epitome of what nearly every Puerto Rican male in our community wanted to accomplish, and Grandma represented the same for women. They were financially stable, had a strong marriage, were active in the church, and never lacked a thing. They weren't wealthy, but they retired smart in a lower cost of living area, where Grandpa's pension and social security income contributed to a stable and admirable lifestyle.

On the other side of the island, in Moca, was my mom's family. We'd go there once a month to visit my grandmother in her modest cement home, where she lived with her mom, my great-grandmother. My great aunt, Grandmother's sister, would come over to eat with us. Behind Grandma's rural home was a soggy sugar plantation where we would fetch bananas and plantains for free; across the street was another small farm run by a farmer named Mingo. Every time we visited, my grandma would take a chicken from her backyard, swing it around by its head, and then chop its head off with a machete, remove its feathers, and boil it. We'd eat it with plantains or green bananas and a warm loaf of bread that my parents would buy at the local *panadería* before we arrived at her house.

I didn't know much about the history of these three women, but I knew there had been trauma and issues with men. They'd fled Puerto Rico; they'd returned. And they, like my mom, represented immense strength. They were pillars. I admired them, but as a young child, I didn't much enjoy visiting because I was usually bored at their house. After our monthly visit, I'd hug them goodbye, happy to have seen them but eager to leave. We'd drive the hour and twenty minutes home, and then I'd burst out of the car, ready to retreat into imaginary games.

I was never bored at my dad's parents' home. Every Sunday was like a party, with my cousins and everyone from our community invited. My grandparents lived on La Laguna off the Número Dos, and my dad's entire family lived within ten or fifteen minutes by car. There was always a feast prepared by my grandmother with the help of the other women in my family, and barley soda called *malta* and candy flowed like a river of sweet heavenly deliciousness, at least in my young mind. There was laughter and music and people coming and going.

My cousins Estela, Rodolfo, Sandra, Mildred, Axel, and Papito always came over, and we'd play and explore the area around our grandparents' home. I could escape with my cousins into the surrounding vegetation without adults noticing we'd been gone. And then there was my extended family: Tía Chin, Tía Lourdes, Tía Luz, Tío Anibal, Tío Edelmiro, and my grandpa's siblings, Tío Gelin and Tía Lydia.

Each Sunday, the men would congregate in the *balcón* (porch) to escape the kitchen's tropical heat, where they'd sit on aluminum seats and drink, while the ladies would hang with my grandmother in the kitchen, waiting for her to finish cooking and helping when Grandma would let them. The moms would discuss the plot of the latest *telenovelas* (soap operas), catch up about family, or share the latest *bochinche* (gossip), while the dads were busy drinking and talking about boxing and local politics. My dad always seemed happy and at ease at *Mamá's* house. All the cousins would hang out, waiting for a hot meal of *arroz con habichuelas y patitas* (pig feet) or *pollo frito y tostones* (fried chicken and plantains). We'd all eat together sitting in groups: the men with the men, the ladies with the ladies, and the kids with the kids. I loved being around my family. They were funny and loud and a lot of fun.

Grandma cooked everything from scratch and, to this day, her food is still the best I've ever tasted. She would feed anybody: if a homeless guy walked by the house, Grandma would be outside offering him a meal or *cafecito* (coffee).

After dinner, we'd have dessert and then go to our respective houses. Every time I left my grandparents' home, I couldn't wait to go back again. Lucky for me, we had holiday and family parties outside of our Sunday gatherings, so I got to spend a lot of time at their house. I loved it there, and I loved them.

My grandparents represented stability to me. While I felt loved and had a happy childhood in spite of the violence around and within my home, it often felt like the floor was shifting underneath my feet. Would the power go out? Would we be able to afford new clothes for school? Dad was drinking nearly every night and his episodes had grown in frequency, now happening every week or two. Each day, I wondered what he would be like. Would I get my loving *pa'i* who took me to the beach, or the raging man I barely recognized?

In the midst of my parents struggling to earn a living, my grandparents were steady providers. Grandpa was a war hero but also gentle and kind; Grandma was loving and affectionate. While Grandpa was just over five-and-a-half feet tall, to me he was a warrior, and I saw the way other men looked at him with deference. I felt safe with my grandparents, and every Sunday was reassurance of this anchor in my immediate family's stormy sea. If we needed something, they'd show up. If my dad started screaming or throwing things in the middle of the night, Grandma and Grandpa were our 911.

They were important to me, to us. They became even more important in 1983, when once again, everything changed for my family—and especially for my father.

I was young, too young, to understand all that was happening inside my dad. At nine, my father was my hero, flaws and all. In spite of his challenges, he was my example and someone I looked up to and admired. He was tough, strong, and quiet, with muscular arms and a short fuse that more than anything, no one dared to light. My siblings protected me from the worst of his episodes, and in my young mind, the loving, warm side of my father overshadowed his alcoholism. But my dad was chasing away his demons, and alcohol and cigarettes weren't working. They were just driving him deeper into hopelessness and depression.

It wasn't until just recently, as an adult, that I learned what happened to my father, my strong *pa'i*, that broke him in two that year, and ultimately saved our family.

There was a church service. It was one of the few Sundays that Dad attended. Mom and Diana were there; I'm not sure where my brothers were. I remember that day vividly. A man stood in front of the congregation, baring his soul, sharing his testimony of how God saved him. My father actually listened, opening his heart as the man shared his story.

The man had been an electrician; he'd been at work when a power surge shot through his body while he changed a transformer, nearly killing him. He'd lost parts of his arms and had undergone countless surgeries to reconstruct the significant burns across his body. He'd suffered. The man removed his shirt to show holes that had healed across his torso, where the electricity had burst through his skin. He had been in a coma, and told us about his near-death experience: what he believed had been a meeting with Christ. He was still in bodily pain, but he said he had been made spiritually whole. His story was raw and painful, but hope shone in his face as he spoke.

Something in my dad broke wide open that day. He wept, moved by this man's testimony. When the pastor called for people to come forward and give their life to Christ, my dad walked to the front of the church and knelt before the cross. He begged for forgiveness, promising to be a better man, and turned his life over to God.

That afternoon, he threw all of his cigarettes, beer, and liquor away. And he made a promise to himself: he would build a better future for our family.

For Mom, it was an answer to years of prayers. Her husband had made a major transformation. He'd started going to church. There would be no more screaming, no more drunk outbursts, no more of our measly income spent on alcohol. Her husband was back. *Por fin.* At last. *Gracias a Dios.*

As a child, I didn't understand all that had happened within my father, except that our shelves were suddenly bare of the things I knew were bad for him. Dad was home more. He was sober. He smiled a lot. There was no more screaming or yelling.

Dad even started attending the men's group at church. When I saw Dad walk into the church during choir practice one weeknight for the group meeting, all I could think was, Wow. Dad's here!

When he called our family together a few weeks after his experience at church, I wasn't sure what to expect.

We sat around the kitchen table, all six of us. It was Sunday afternoon, and we'd just returned from my grandparents' house. We'd had a relaxed day, and I was full from my grandmother's cooking and the dozen-plus pieces of candy I'd eaten when adults weren't watching. But I quickly recovered from my sugar high when I saw the expression on my dad's face.

"*Mis hijos,*" he began, looking at my mother, then at each of us. He cleared his throat and placed his left hand on top of my mother's right. I stared at their hands on the tabletop, waiting. "I have to leave. It's only for a short time, and then you'll be able to join me."

His words hung in the room, a tangle of Spanish and disbelief. My siblings and I were silent. Dad was leaving us?

Dwayne spoke first. "Where are you going?"

"To the United States," my mother answered for my father, placing her other hand on top of his and patting it twice. "To Texas."

"Why?" I asked.

"I'm going to find work," Dad said. He looked at Dan. "Dan will join me after he graduates from high school. Together we'll save enough money to move the family to Texas."

Diana and Dan were silent, and I could tell from their faces that they already knew.

"What about Diana?" I asked, panic starting to bubble in my stomach. Diana was my second mom. She couldn't leave me.

"Diana will stay," my mom said. "She's going to finish college here in Puerto Rico and then join us afterward. She'll live with your grandparents after we leave."

I looked at my dad. His face was pained and proud. "I'll miss you, *Papi,*" I said.

He said nothing but held my mom's hand for several minutes. I noticed redness forming around his eyes and felt the emotion he couldn't communicate.

It would only be a short time, I told myself. My family will be back together again soon. Dad said so.

Our entire family sat there for a long while until my dad finally said to me, "I promise I'll bring you as soon as I can. Don't worry, son."

That night, I lay in bed thinking of my dad, and wondering what his life would be like in the United States. How long would it take for him to send for me? Would he miss us? What if he liked life better without us—no. I shook away the thought. Dad loved us. I knew he did. He'd send for us and life would be better for my siblings and me.

But better how? We had everything we needed. To me, life was full and perfect now that my dad was himself again. He'd stopped drinking, smoking, and screaming. We had food and clothing, I had friends; we had my grandparents. What could the United States offer that we couldn't get in Puerto Rico?

The US, I would soon learn, was nothing I could have ever expected.

My dad, I'm told, carried a picture with him to America. It's of me: I'm smiling, my teeth overtaking my face. I'm standing full-front to the camera, with my hands dangling by my side. My clothes are tight; my shorts are like spandex, my stomach spilling over the elastic waist band. My shirt is short, hitting just below my belly button.

I was happy in that photo. I had no idea that it would drive my dad to provide for our family, because when he looked at it, he saw all that he couldn't provide.

My clothes: he couldn't afford to buy me clothes that fit my growing body.

My shoes: worn, ugly, mega-discount brand with holes beginning to grow along the big toe on each.

And my smile: he knew, deep down in his heart, the pain that he'd caused my family. I was the baby, the youngest. He would make things right for me.

As my dad flew across the Atlantic Ocean, that photo remained tucked carefully in his breast pocket, and later it would find a safe spot in the top drawer of his dresser in America. When he was tired from working, or feeling lonely, he would take out that picture of me and it would encourage him forward. I missed my *pa'i*, and he missed me just as much. And little David, with his protruding belly and giant smile, became the symbol of what he could change for the future of our family.

In Puerto Rico, the violence continued in my community and at school. I grew, and now at ten years old, I was molding every day into a young man who wanted nothing more than to be like my tough brothers. They were fierce and strong; they were becoming men. I wanted to be a man too.

Violence, and a need to test and prove manhood, was everywhere. When I left for school each morning, I knew I needed to be alert and prepared. I accepted this ever-alertness as part of life. It was normal. I didn't feel on edge, scared, or stressed. I was ready to brawl.

At recess, or even in class, if we were playing and someone got stupid, it was on. There were fights almost daily. My childhood grew more and more physical: blows from my peers, smacks from my teachers, beatings from my brothers. Before Dan left for the US, they'd worked together to toughen me up, joining forces to punch and kick me, telling me to fight back as they delivered a blow to my stomach or cheek. They seemed to feel it was their duty to knock the wuss out of me, and it was working. I was learning how to fight.

Once Dan left, it seemed Dwayne was twice as hard on me. I knew he was doing it to prepare me for what life would be like when I got older and was expected to be a man. Dwayne saw me as soft and babied. He believed it was his job to harden me so I could make it in Puerto Rico. He was the man of the house now, and as the man, he needed to make sure I could take care of myself.

The blows and bruises—while they stung—didn't faze me. I was still my happy self, just tougher. I also didn't think anything of the violence around me. Every morning, the daily newspaper, *El Vocero*, splashed at least two deaths across the front page, but I hardly noticed. At the local *puntos*, violence punctuated everything. Somebody said something stupid, machete. Dumb comment, gunshot. Piss someone off, beat to death.

Every single day.

This was part of daily living. I became numb to death. I wasn't afraid; I didn't have my guard up all the time. I accepted the culture and community for what it was, and who I had to be. Who I had to be was tough and violent. Me, the little boy with the belly hanging out of his shirt, the baby of the family, the apple of my parents' eye. I was being raised to survive, to dominate, to be a machine—even as an elementary schooler.

I felt I had a glorious childhood. I didn't realize it was abnormal to be numb to gunshots. My brothers were fighting all the time, and I was being groomed to do that as well. They were confident and at ease with themselves, and I emulated their confidence. If I didn't, I knew I'd be eaten alive outside the walls of my home.

Mom and Diana did their best to care for us, but they also lived within the reality of the poverty, hopelessness, and violent culture around them. My mother checked in on us by asking what my brothers were up to, but because of her work schedule she was not around to truly know the lives my brothers were living on the street. The message to Mom was that we were good boys, we were playing after school, and we were home by nighttime. Diana knew the truth: I was typically home by 6:30 each evening after a few hours of running around the neighborhood, including excursions to the bars and *la cancha* (the basketball court), while my brothers were somewhere farther away from home until 10:00 p.m. on weekdays, doing who knows what to survive.

The Morales boys grew up on the street, numb to the daily violence and crime that permeated our community. Violence was part of the fabric of my childhood, interwoven into our games of make-believe and Bruce Lee movies and mango juice and wilderness treks and beach Saturdays. And violence was becoming a part of me too.

But inside, I was still gentle. I wrote poems to my father, telling him how much I missed him, how desperately I wanted to be reunited. I missed my dad with an ache I couldn't articulate, and I had no one to talk to about my pain. My brother Dwayne was facing his own challenges and beginning to act out through drinking, fighting, and excursions far from home; my sister Diana was an overwhelmed nineteen-year-old trying to mother us and go to college at the same time; my mom was gone all the time, either working or at church. When she was home, she seemed too exhausted for me to share my feelings with her. I stuffed my heartache deep within myself, and often cried at night in my bed. I missed my dad. I wanted our family to be together again.

Over in the US, I didn't know my dad and Dan were facing their own pain and struggles. While Texas hadn't worked out, my dad had heard there was work in Massachusetts, and found a steady job there. He rented a studio apartment on Franklin Street in Lynn for the two of them and saved enough money to buy an old baby blue Ford Pinto. Dan had forgone college to join my dad and work to bring us to the United States. They worked day and night; Dan flipped burgers and bounced at bars while Dad worked at a tool factory in Saugus, Massachusetts. They only spent money on the basics: food, shelter, utilities. They were lonely and exhausted, but they kept working incessantly for us. And I kept working for my dad too, writing poems and saying prayers that we would be reunited.

I took a deep breath and remembered the pain of that time. I felt it viscerally, even now, more than four decades later. The room was quiet for several minutes, my sons and I lost in thoughts of our family's history.

"I don't get it, Pa," Anthony said, breaking the silence. He had transitioned into teenage philosopher mode, his brow tight in thought. At some point during my storytelling, he had moved to the floor and was laying down, staring at the ceiling, his head on his backpack like a pillow. He propped himself up on his right elbow to look at me. "Why didn't they just get jobs in Puerto Rico? Or better jobs in the US? If I were in that situation, I would just find a better job."

"Yeah, and couldn't they have just moved somewhere else in Puerto Rico?" Alexander added. "Kuilan seems . . . not good." He had reclined on the couch with his arms behind his head and legs folded up, reminding me of how he used to lay in our lawn and stare at the clouds when he was a young boy.

I looked at my sons, sitting on a couch that cost more than I used to pay for annual rent. While they had a much humbler childhood in Lynn, now they were growing up in a five-bedroom, three-bath home in Lynnfield, Massachusetts, where we had a sprawling lawn for our golden retriever, Bella, to run around in. My sons—of Puerto Rican and Dominican American heritage—were born in Lynn and raised early on in a modest apartment grounded by a mix of American and Latino culture. However, they were definitely far removed from my rural, low-income experience in Puerto Rico.

"It was hard for men," my wife chimed in from the adjacent sunroom, where—although the sun had long since set—she had been reading. I was grateful to her in that moment for giving me time to think about my reply.

"What do you mean, Mom?" Alexander asked.

My wife slid a bookmark into her book, set it on the coffee table, and walked into the living room, carrying with her the grace and beauty that had attracted me to her all those years ago.

"Puerto Rico had gone through a lot of turmoil not that long before your grandpa came to the United States. Men were trying to find their place in a society that changed virtually overnight." She paused in thought. "Well, a lot of men still are. They're trying to figure out how to be men."

Our sons looked confused.

"How to be men?" Alexander said. "That's weird."

"Not so weird," my wife replied.

"What do you mean?"

I spoke up. "I'll give you a little history lesson about Puerto Rico to answer your question."

The boys groaned. Anthony laid back down and looked up at the ceiling again as if ready to be bored.

"Trust me," I said. "You'll understand our family better."

My wife sat in the easy chair and my boys waited as I continued the story. As a kid, I hadn't understood how the Puerto Rican experience lived on in my family. To help them understand our family's history, they needed to understand Puerto Rico's history first.

—

The United States took over the island of Puerto Rico from Spain in 1898 as a result of the Spanish-American War. In 1917, Congress granted US citizenship to all Puerto Ricans, but the island remained an unincorporated territory. A couple of decades later, from 1939 to the late 1950s, the government of Puerto Rico and the US government implemented decades of government-sponsored programs to modernize and industrialize Puerto Rico's economy through investments in manufacturing and out-migration to the US mainland. The economy of Puerto Rico shifted from agriculture to industry virtually overnight, and Operation Bootstrap included provisions for farm workers to be transported from Puerto Rico to American farms. From 1940 to 1960, well over half a million Puerto Ricans—mostly poor, non-English speakers—migrated to the US as part of relocation programs for farm labor, or in search of work in urban cities.[1] Decades of government policies to "modernize" the island's economy did more than reshape Puerto Rico's agricultural-dependent economy. It upended the fabric of traditional Puerto Rican family norms.

With a flip of a switch, two-thirds of Puerto Rican families were displaced from an agrarian subsistence; men no longer had sugarcane or coffee plantations to farm, and they were left with no way to provide for their families. There were basically two options: enlist in the Army, or go work in factories or on farms in the United States.

When this happened, men lost their place in society. Suddenly, men were no longer farmers and field workers; they lost part of their identity as providers in the home. They couldn't provide for their families. *Boricuas*, fierce workers who placed loyalty to their family above all else—that's who they were. But not anymore.

From 1943 to 1953, almost one-third of the island's population left for the United States to work in factories in New York, New Jersey, Chicago, and Springfield.[2] The men who left for the US struggled. These were largely uneducated people, mostly farmers, who had sixth- and seventh-grade educations, and were now going into the largest metropolises in the world, cities of cement and tenements, or remote farms where they would labor for menial pay in a new, often hostile society. After three hundred years of Spanish colonial rule and agrarian lifestyles, they were placed in the most advanced cities in the world—places like New York City, Chicago, and Hartford—with no resources or education beyond primary school and were told, "Go."

What does a man do in that situation? He adapts. He figures it out. But the emotional and socioeconomic impact has carried far past their displacement more than seventy years ago. This social displacement and collapse of the family structure and norms continues to perpetuate itself in many cities across the United States, like Boston and Springfield, Massachusetts, where Puerto Ricans are among the poorest population.

As men lost their identities, they tried to find new ones. Demonstrating *machismo*—acting proud, strong, aggressive, and excessively masculine—became the status quo for Puerto Rican men. That was true in Puerto Rico and also in the United States. They were grasping at their identities as men with violence and aggression. They also began looking for their identity in bars. Titles of songs sung by one of the most famous singers of Puerto Rican music during the 1950s and 1960s, Felipe Rodriguez, serve as reminders of the new identity that Puerto Rican men were adopting as they navigated life in a foreign culture with wildly different norms: "Quiero Beber" (I Want to Drink), "La Ultima Copa" (The Last Drink), "Debo y Pagaré" (I Owe and I Will Pay), "Cárcel Sin Rejas" (Jail Cell Without Bars), "La Gitana" (The Gypsy), "Amor Terrible" (Terrible Love), "La Cama Vacia" (The Empty Bed), "Copas y Amigos" (Drinks and Friends), "Sigue Lloviendo" (It Keeps on Raining), "Aunque Me Maten" (Even if They Kill Me), "Te Voy Hacer Llorar" (I'm Going to Make You Cry), and "El Retrato" (The Picture).

Puerto Rican men went from a rural and farming subsistence to unemployment, menial work, violence, and drinking in just a decade, both in Puerto Rico and in the US. They were trying to find their place. The destabilization of Puerto Rico's agrarian society contributed to the destruction of the traditional family. Puerto Ricans are still feeling the effects of this disruption and the ensuing years of ineffective social policy today.

My dad was part of the next generation of men who were grappling with finding their place, raised by men and women who had experienced the traumatic upheaval of life in Puerto Rico. For Dad, the options to escape poverty in Puerto Rico were equally limited: stay in Puerto Rico and live on insufficient income to support the family, or find work in the US, earning little money but enough to eventually bring over the family. Thankfully for us, Dad decided his present would not be his future. He changed: stopped drinking, stopped yelling. Started fighting for our family.

Even though I didn't live through that upheaval, I felt it. My grandpa was a good man, and treated my grandmother well. But my father was raised within a culture that treated women badly. The men around him turned to vices like alcohol and tobacco to numb the pain and loss of identity. I watched my dad—my proud father, my hero—lose himself and find himself again.

I wish I had learned my lesson through watching him—but I didn't. I would need to lose myself too. But that would come later.

Back then, now at age eleven, I was eager to join two of my heroes in the United States. I had no idea what to expect in the US—this was way before smartphones and social media, and all I had to go on was pictures I found in books at school about Nueva York or Estados Unidos, or American TV shows with Spanish voice-overs like *El Gran Héroe Americano* (*The Greatest American Hero* with Ralph Hinkley); *La Mujer Maravilla* (*Wonder Woman* with Lynda Carter); *Los Pitufos* (*The Smurfs*); or *CHiPs*, the police show with Erik Estrada. Sometimes I'd sit in a quiet classroom, when all my friends had gone out to recess, an encyclopedia spread open in front of me displaying a map of Los Estados Unidos. I knew my friends were waiting for me to come play, but I didn't care. I was too busy thinking about what it would be like to fly like the Greatest American Hero in a large city like Boston.

I'd find Massachusetts, with its funny shape that reminded me of a toucan, then draw my index finger along the slick page, landing on Boston, which I knew was right near where my dad lived. Sometimes

I'd even make my index and thumb fingers into legs and pretend I was walking around the streets of Massachusetts with my dad. I wondered if he worked all the time, and if he missed me, and if he was saving money like he said he was so we could be together again.

Sometimes I would stare at the glossy map, as if looking hard enough could reunite us. Then I'd close the book and head to recess and join my friends on the stone and cement steps of my life in Puerto Rico, remembering Mom's promise that we would be with Dad soon.

Chapter 3

QUERIDO PA'I

It is a man's responsibility to provide values to his family and others. The very best way for you to provide values is by embodying them and living your values in the presence of those around you.

LTG (RET.) WILLIAM G. BOYKIN,
FROM HIS BOOK *MAN TO MAN*

I looked out the window of the airplane as we descended into Boston Logan International Airport on Eastern Airlines. I'd gotten the window seat, Dwayne sat in the middle, and my mom sat in the aisle. Since I couldn't remember my first plane ride from Indiana, I'd been especially excited about the flight, but now the thrill of flying was replaced with the anticipation of seeing my dad. With my face smashed against the glass, I looked down at the tiny buildings and even smaller cars, and imagined my dad racing to the airport with a big smile on his face.

It had taken my dad nearly two years to get us here. I'd seen him twice when he visited Puerto Rico, and we'd talked on the phone at least once a week, but those years were long and stretching, and I missed my *pa'i*. He told me he missed me too.

I leaned back slightly to run my hand over my front pant pocket to make sure my carefully folded poem to my dad was still there. I didn't dare take it out with Dwayne sitting next to me. I knew he'd just make fun of me. Instead, I pressed my nose back onto the window as the plane made its final descent, the wheels hit the runway, and we bump-bump-bumped into a safe landing.

The plane erupted in applause and cheers. Not sure why, I started clapping my hands too and looked at my mom.

"Why are we clapping?" I said, lifting my voice to carry my Spanish over the noise.

"Puerto Ricans clap every time a plane lands," she explained. "We arrived safely!" Mom smiled, her face bright. I noticed she'd taken extra care on her hair that day and had worn her church clothes.

Dwayne nudged me. "Stop clapping."

"Why?"

"Everyone else stopped already," he said.

I stopped mid-clap and looked around. He was right. I slid my hands under my thighs in embarrassment.

"What do you think Dad will be like?" I asked him.

"What do you mean?" he said.

"Well, it's been a long time . . . maybe he has a beard. Or a belly."

Dwayne laughed. "I don't think so. Dad's been working hard. I bet he's ripped."

I burst out laughing, imagining my dad walking in with a Hulk body, his Lycra sleeves bulging with massive biceps. Wouldn't that be awesome!

"Shhh," my mom said, leaning her body into the aisle. "Calm down. We're going to see your dad in a few minutes."

We waited as passengers made their way off the plane. Mom had us stay in our seats until the aircraft was nearly empty, and once there was a clear spot, she pulled down three pieces of carry-on luggage from the overhead bins. All of our most precious items were in those suitcases. She motioned for me to take the handle of the one in front, then handed Dwayne the handle of the second piece, and followed behind us, rolling the third suitcase. I bumped mine on a seat and looked back at mom, Dwayne nearly colliding with me.

"*Cuida'o*," she said, her voice sharp. Careful.

We exited the plane one by one and came together in a little cluster on the covered hallway ramp to the airport. My stomach had erupted with excited butterflies, and I wanted to sprint down the hallway to find my dad. But I remembered the luggage with breakables and walked slowly, pulling it behind me.

Finally, we made it to the airport entrance. As we exited the hall-way, I craned my head wildly, searching for my dad. Where was he? I looked up at my mom, who was scanning the crowd too, her brows knotted together in concern. The butterflies dropped to the bottom of my stomach when I didn't see him, and I stood there wondering, Where is *Papi*? Where is Dan?

What if they don't come? What if they don't want us anymore?

The seconds stretched into minutes. Dwayne looked worried. Mom looked worried too, and maybe a little mad.

Suddenly: "*¡Ay bendito!*" my dad's voice rang over the noise of the airport and we finally spotted him. He was running down the hallway toward us, waving his hand to get our attention.

I had never in my life seen my dad so happy. Since I couldn't run with the suitcase, I set it upright next to me and began jumping up and down in place, waiting for my dad to make it across the airport to us. When he arrived, I stopped jumping and hugged him tightly, squeezing his torso and burying my head into his chest.

Dwayne was next, and I realized my cool older brother had glossy eyes as he hugged my father. When it was my mother's turn, she was weeping. My parents embraced for a long time.

"Never again," Dad said, looking at all three of us, one by one. His Spanish was stilted with emotion. "We'll never be apart again." He grabbed the handles of Dwayne's and my bags, and we made our way toward baggage claim.

Finally, I asked what I'd been wondering. "Where's Dan?"

"He couldn't fit in the car with all of us," Dad said. "And he's work-ing today."

"Oh," was all I could say. I hoped he'd be waiting at the house when we got there.

After we collected our two big bags from baggage claim, we made our way into the airport parking lot. The late September air was crisp, and I hugged my arms to my body, not used to the cold. I'd already peppered my dad with questions by the time we reached his baby blue Ford Pinto in the parking lot. My first thought looking at our sweet ride was, Whoa, we're rich.

Dad used the key to open the trunk, and the three of us watched as he shoved the two large bags and one of the small bags into the minis-cule trunk as if he was assembling a complicated puzzle. The other two bags went between Dwayne and me in the back seat, blocking Dad's view out the back window. I shivered in the cold car but said nothing. As we drove to our new home, I surveyed the inside of the Pinto. It was the nicest vehicle we'd ever owned.

Wow, I thought, we're millionaires.

Half an hour later, we pulled up to 22 Henry Avenue in Lynn, Massachusetts. As we parked on the street next to an old oak tree, I looked through openings in its leaves at the towering three-story building in front of me, my face pushed up against the car glass like in the airplane. It was a beige wooden triple-decker, a towering build-ing on an urban street. I was used to single-story cement box houses, rural life, and jungles. This house looked like the ones in the movies! I giggled to myself, wondering if Bruce Lee would pop out from behind our building. Dwayne jabbed me in the ribs with his elbow to be quiet.

"Up there," Dad said, pointing to the top floor. "That's our place."

"We live here?" I said in awe. "At the top?" Even better!

Dad unloaded a couple of bags from the car, and I followed behind Dwayne and him as they made their way up two flights of stairs. Dad unlocked our apartment and brought the bags inside, followed by Dwayne, then Mom. I could hardly contain myself waiting for all of them to file into the apartment.

To me, the apartment was huge. In reality, it was a modest two-bedroom place, shaped like a rectangle. I walked from room to room, touching walls and turning on lights. There was a living room with a couch and a small TV. A kitchen with linoleum floors and a table. A bathroom. ("¡*Que revolú!*" my mom said under her breath, what a mess!) There was a bedroom for Dan, Dwayne, and me, and one for Mom and Dad, with a small balcony that faced the street.

We really *are* rich, I thought. We made it!

I felt warmth spread from the top of my head to my pinky toes. My family was together and we were wealthy. Could it get any better than this?

Standing in the grandest apartment I'd ever seen, I suddenly missed my sister and grandparents. I knew Diana would love this place. It would be hard to be away from my extended family, but Mom had told me we would go back to see them as often as we could. Diana would join us as soon as she finished college in Puerto Rico. I hoped time would go by quickly so I could be with her again.

Later that night, Dan arrived home from work. He wore a Wendy's uniform and a gigantic smile on his face. When I saw him, I gave him the biggest, longest hug. He laughed and mussed my hair, then punched me lightly in the stomach. We ate dinner that night, the five of us, and I felt the happiest I'd ever felt in my entire young life. The only thing missing was Diana.

I fell asleep fast and hard that night, crashing from the exhaustion of a full day of travel and the intense emotions I'd felt that day. In my dream, Diana was there, and we were holding hands as I walked her through the apartment, showing her each room and telling her we were rich now and she didn't need to worry. She had her own room in this dream house, with silk sheets on her bed and a rug made of woven gold. Diana laughed, and I laughed too, happy to be together in the United States.

Two mornings later, my mom woke me up early. She shook me gently over and over, but my eyes refused to open, no matter how hard I tried, and finally she pulled on my shoulders to sit me up and opened the blinds to let light stream in.

"*Levántate,*" she said. Get up. "We need to go sign you up for school today."

Even though my body begged for rest, I got out of bed, leaving the blankets a mess of sleep. She had set clothes on the edge of the bed for me, and I dressed, glaring at Dwayne's sleeping body with jealousy. When my clothes were on, I walked to the kitchen, rummaged in the small pantry for cereal, and retrieved a carton of milk from the fridge. I opened several cabinets before finding the bowls, and drawer after drawer looking for a spoon.

Finally, I sat down to eat. Mom came in, hair done, wearing a dress and her walking shoes, a sensible black pair of sneakers. She stopped as she walked past me and licked a finger to smooth down my hair.

"Así noooo," I said, yanking my head away. She grabbed the crown of my head and continued smoothing anyway. When she was done, I flattened both hands over my hair to wipe her spit away, then resumed eating breakfast. After I'd eaten, Mom told me to brush my teeth and get on my shoes and coat, adding *"¡Avanza!"* for motivation. Hurry!

Dan and my dad were already gone to work, so Mom poked her head into Dwayne's and my room. He must have been awake, because I heard muffled voices. As my mom left the bedroom, she called, "Don't leave the apartment for any reason!" Then she added, "There's a phone on the wall. Emergency is 911, just in case."

Soon we were on the street outside our building, the biting morning air nipping the tips of my ears. I hugged my coat around me as I chattered to Mom about everything I saw around us. The corner store reminded me of *bodegas* back home. People stood around outside just like back home too, though something felt different about the way they looked at us. In Puerto Rico, where it was hot and humid, men lounged at outdoor bars, leaning on their cars or sitting on chairs circling small tables; here, men stood, huddling together on corners wearing big coats. They kept glancing in our direction and seemed uneasy, even wary, but I wasn't sure why. I reached out for my mom's hand, her warm palm reassuring me as I kept on chattering about this and that. We walked up Washington Street to Broad Street to Franklin Street, passing corner shops, liquor stores, and a funeral home. I surveyed the aged homes. Some had porches with old televisions and easy chairs with ripped upholstery; others were dilapidated and shuttered.

I suddenly lurched forward, a sharp pain in my right lower back. As I whipped around, a rock hit my mom's leg and she yelped. Another rock hit my left bicep, but the padding on my coat shielded me from pain. Mom screamed. She gripped my hand and said, *"¡Corre, David!"* just as several boys' voices broke out.

"Get them!"

"Hit the kid!"

The two of us broke into a run, my short legs struggling to keep up with my mom's gait, her hand grasping mine so tightly I wondered if it would break off. I heard laughter. Cruel, horrible cackles chased us as we scrambled away. My breath was fast. Shallow. Mom was breathing heavily.

I heard a rock hit her, but she didn't cry out, so I hoped her coat had absorbed the impact. Suddenly, a voice boomed in front of us. A man leapt off a porch and began chasing the three boys, who scrambled away almost as fast as they'd appeared. Mom pulled me close, her arms wrapped around me like armor. I watched the man round a corner and heard him yelling, but I didn't understand anything he said except that his voice was loud and scary and the boys were gone. Blood rushed through my ears and my heart thumped so loudly I put a hand on my chest to keep it there. Mom stood still and silent, as if she didn't dare move as the man walked back in our direction.

"Are you all right?" he asked. He had a shock of red hair poking out under an American flag bandana, and wore a loose T-shirt and sagging jeans.

"Yes, thank you," Mom said.

"Little assholes," he said. "Always causing trouble."

The three of us stood there for several seconds, the silence stretching between us, Mom and me catching our breath and saying nothing. The man squatted down to meet my eyes.

"You all right?" he said.

I looked up at Mom to understand what he was saying. My mother nodded at him as if to say, "We're OK." But I didn't feel OK. What had just happened?

The man stood and jutted his hand toward my mom. "Ronan. You new here?"

She nodded. "Thank you for helping us."

"No problem."

I stood there, the blood still pulsing noisily through my body, not hearing anything else they said. Finally, I felt a tug on my arm from Mom. It was time to go.

We said goodbye, and when we were halfway down the street, Ronan called out, "Look, be careful, OK? This neighborhood can be tough."

Mom waved as we kept walking, her hands on my shoulders to turn me forward as I craned my neck back to look at Ronan, who was still standing there. When I looked back a few seconds later, he was gone. He had disappeared just like those boys.

We walked in silence all the way to the school. I wanted to ask my mom about what had happened, but it felt like my tongue was stuck to the roof of my mouth, my lips sealed shut. Thoughts swirled in confusion. Why had they done that? Who were those boys? Were they just messing with us, or were they really trying to hurt us?

I didn't talk for the rest of the walk. My throat was tight in thought, my mind working at full speed trying to make sense of this new place and new life in America. It had been different in Puerto Rico—I'd never felt unsafe walking down the street, or worried about my mom's safety. I knew from my brothers the importance of being ready to brawl. I understood that as a man, I needed to know how to fight. But I'd never felt the need to be on guard, to protect my mother.

I had been helpless. Mom could have gotten hurt.

I enrolled in school that day, and on the way back, we took a different route, giving a wide berth to the street where the boys with rocks had been. When we got home, I said nothing to Dwayne, but later that night, I heard Mom and Dad talking in their bedroom and guessed she was telling him what had happened. I wondered if Dad was disappointed in me for not being able to protect Mom.

I was just a kid, an eleven-year-old boy in a new country who didn't speak the language well yet. But inside of me was a storm of confusion as I tried to sort through what had happened that day. While Mom and I never spoke about it again, something had changed within me.

Still, I had school to look forward to. I'd start the next day as a fifth-grader at Harrington Elementary, and I couldn't wait.

The following morning, I was up and dressed without Mom having to wake me, and I poured myself cereal while I waited for her to walk me to school. I missed my friends and my cousins back in Puerto Rico, but I had always made friends easily, and I figured this would be no different. I couldn't wait to meet my teacher and the other students. Would there be other Puerto Ricans? I wondered. Could I learn to speak English well, the way Mom and Dad were constantly urging me to?

Mom dropped me off with a hug and a *pórtate bien* (behave) as I entered my fifth-grade classroom. I didn't realize it at the time, but she had signed me up for a bilingual class, which meant a lot of the kids spoke Spanish like me. The other kids were still playing outside, waiting for the bell to ring, but my teacher said they'd be coming in soon so I might as well wait in the classroom. I stood, looking out the window, still wearing my backpack, wondering what the kids would be like.

"You can set your backpack by your desk," Ms. Flores, my teacher, said from her desk at the front of the classroom. She smiled and stood, walking over to a desk in the middle of the room. "Don't worry, I didn't put you up front. I'll get you a locker assignment soon."

"*Graci*—I mean, thank you," I said. I blushed. English, I reminded myself.

"*De nada*," she said, smiling again.

Soon, the bell went off and students seemed to pour in one on top of another. I counted as they walked in: twenty-seven kids, including me. Some of them looked like me. Others were pale with red or blonde hair, or dark skinned with black hair, a spectrum of skin tones and hair colors just like back in Puerto Rico. But what impressed me was their clothes. Some were wearing brands I had never seen before; others had on brands of sneakers or jackets that my brothers had fantasized about back home. I had never seen such a wide range of nice-looking shoes and clothes, and I was fascinated.

"What the hell are you looking at?" a kid said as he took the desk to my right.

I quickly looked down at my lap.

"Good morning, everyone!" Ms. Flores called. When the class didn't settle, she clapped her hands rhythmically three times. About half of the class did the same, copying her rhythm. "Let's try again," she said. This time, all but a few of the boys repeated her rhythm. The class quieted.

"We have a new student today!" she said, her voice bright. I looked up from my lap. "Let's welcome David Morales! He just moved here from Puerto Rico."

I heard a few kids say "Hi, David" and a few snickers. When I turned to find the laughter, I noticed two boys a few rows back who were much darker with curly hair. Why were they laughing?

The first hour was a blur, a continuation of the previous day's lesson, and I found myself staring out the window and wishing I could be home with my mom and dad. Finally, it was time for PE, and we lined up at the door. I stood silently, waiting for the teacher to take us outside. We had no gymnasium, so PE took place outdoors on a long, rectangular field of black tar surrounded by six-foot-high steel gates all around. We filed onto the tar courtyard and waited to be dismissed from standing in line. I squinted my eyes, trying to find trees or any form of nature, when I heard a voice behind me.

"Fucking spic."

I turned around to find a pair of eyes staring hard at me. It was one of the two curly haired boys from earlier, standing right behind me; the other boy was just behind him. Both were much taller than me.

"What?" I said. Maybe I'd heard him wrong.

"I said, you fucking spic," he repeated. He was about three inches taller than me, and straightened his body to look even taller. I had no clue at the time, but the two boys were from the Dominican Republic. They had a flair of confidence about them that I would soon learn to adopt.

"You piece of shit," his friend said. "Go back to where you came from."

When the teacher turned her back to us, the bigger one shoved me, hard. Luckily I caught myself enough to stumble to the right and not into the kid in front of me in line. I scrambled back into line before Ms. Flores noticed. I knew better than to fight back during class, especially on the first day of school. I turned around to face the front, now on alert. My ears burned with embarrassment and anger. My stomach clenched. Was I going to have to fight on the first day of school?

I stayed away from the two boys during PE and for the rest of the morning, but after lunch was recess, and I doubted I could avoid them. While I wasn't going to look for trouble, I was ready to fight if I needed to.

At recess, I stood near the edge of the playground, watching kids kick balls back and forth and climb on the jungle gym. All of a sudden, a pair of hands shoved me in the mid-back and I stumbled forward.

I turned around and it was the big kid. He towered over me, his chin lifted; his buddy circled to stand behind me. I backed away, not wanting to start something, and as I did so, the smaller kid swung, punching me in the back, and the bigger kid shoved me to the ground. He popped me in the mouth, sending pain shooting through the right side of my jaw. I jumped to my feet and swung, delivering a hard punch to the bigger kid's stomach. He doubled over as a teacher came running across the playground.

"Stop that! Now!" he said, grabbing the two boys by the elbow. "Come with me. Are you OK?" When I nodded, the teacher pointed to a bench and told me to sit. He'd come check on me later.

I watched the teacher take the boys into the building, glad he'd seen that I hadn't started the fight. My father had told me to never start a fight, but if I had to fight, to make sure that I punished whoever started it. And if there were too many people to handle, to make sure I took one down with me. I wondered if the rest of my life at school was going to be like this, one fight after another, defending myself against nothing. At least in Puerto Rico fights happened because someone ran their mouth or did something dumb. I hadn't done anything.

I was watching the other kids play when I heard a voice to my right: "¿Mano, estás bien?" Are you ok?

I turned to see two boys who looked just like the guys I had fought. They radiated confidence. As I surveyed their friendly smiles and noticed their *piel canela*, or cinnamon-colored skin, I nodded, wondering what they wanted.

"I'm Franklin," the one standing closest to me said as he sat down to my right. "This is David." David sat next to him.

"I'm David too," I said. "I'm new."

"Yeah, we know, man," David said. "We're in your class. We're from the Dominican Republic. They are too, but they're stupid." I was impressed by their dominance of the English language. I would later learn that some Hispanic students who spoke fluent English were placed in bilingual classes because teachers often didn't know where to put them for numerous reasons.

"Listen, let me give you some advice," Franklin said. "You have to look like you belong here. You have to look confident. And you have to be ready to fight at any time. Those guys are going to rip you apart next time they get a chance, so be ready."

"Don't let anybody push you around, bro," David said. "Somebody hits you, you hit them. Somebody pushes you, you hit them first. Don't wait for them to hit you or you won't make it here."

I rubbed my jaw and winced, the pain still fresh. I nodded. Lesson received. I wouldn't make that mistake again.

After a few moments of silence, I asked them what a spic was. They both laughed and told me it was what "white people" called Puerto Ricans and Dominicans.

Anthony and Alexander stared at me across the breakfast table, their mostly empty plates in front of them. We had talked late into the night and resumed early that morning over the waffles and eggs my wife had made. Both boys had risen early—nine o'clock instead of their normal eleven or later on the weekend—and immediately asked to hear more. I could tell by Alexander's wide eyes, and the fact that Anthony had stopped eating, that my elementary school run-in had shocked them.

"Whoa," Alexander began. "So you fought on your first day of elementary school?" My son, who is blessed to attend an exceptional public school, had been in only a handful of fights in his entire life, and they were nothing like the ones I had been in as a kid. Kids at his school cried when they got shoved too hard on the basketball court during a game.

"That's right," I said. "But we didn't know any different."

"What do you mean?" Anthony asked.

"The kids in bilingual education classes were treated like dirt by the other kids at the school," I said, trying to think of the best way to explain this to my two American sons, who grew up with love, family, and abundance, and spoke fluent English with no Hispanic accent. "We were in a special classroom learning English. Most of us were poor or working-class poor. Many had recently come from developing countries from Latin America or the Caribbean, or lived in tough neighborhoods. Some were growing up in broken homes with parents who did drugs, drank, or were violent. Basically, we were used to violence. And since some were treated badly, we treated each other that way because that's what we knew."

"But that doesn't make sense," Alexander said. My philosopher wasn't accepting my explanation. "If you were all treated badly by adults and other kids at school, wouldn't you want to be extra nice to each other?"

"That seems logical," I said. "But it doesn't work that way."

"Why not?" Anthony asked.

"Popular culture tends to lump all Hispanics together, as if we are all the same—homogeneous. Actually, our entire culture still does that today. It tries to identify people by their race or ethnicity, not by character or work ethic. So we had Dominicans, Mexicans, Puerto Ricans, Guatemalans, Colombians . . . all nationalities in one room. We were poor, and most of us didn't speak English fluently, so the school put us together as part of the 'Latino community,' even though that label fails to capture the rich diversity and complexity of Hispanics. There are many countries and cultures that make up the Latino community. Puerto Ricans and Guatemalans are very different; Dominicans and Ecuadorians are different. As kids, we thought, 'What the hell are we doing here?' We didn't get why we were being grouped together.

"As poor kids from poor countries or poor areas of the US, we only knew what we had seen. So if someone's dad drank and yelled and threw things, like Grandpa used to do, we thought that yelling and violence was the way to be a man, to handle things."

When neither of my sons spoke, I went on. "The girls were tough too—they brawled just like us—but I think the boys got the brunt of the cultural expectation of toughness. Both the girls and boys were getting messages at school saying, 'You're not like the rest of the kids: you look different, and sound different, so we are going to lump you all together and call it bilingual education.' And as confused kids in a new place, often with bad role models at home, we reenacted what we saw at home, on the street, or on TV. It was a group of kids trying to figure out life. We were all learning how to get along together with no family structures or discipline to provide us crucial guard rails for daily living and interpersonal relationships.

"I was lucky, because I had a loving mother at home who deeply cared for me, and a father who had been transformed and was doing everything in his power to provide a better life for us. I had family, discipline, and a nurturing environment that pushed me to do better.

"At the same time, I watched your Uncle Dwayne continue fighting like he had in Puerto Rico, and I admired him. I wanted to be just like him and Dan; I wanted to be a man. But I didn't really understand what a real man was back then. I thought a man was rugged, tough, and violent. So I acted that way on the outside, but inside I wasn't that way. The problem is that my outward behavior, the violence and toughness I brought to the playground, started to work its way into my heart."

The boys sat thoughtfully. It was rare that they didn't have some quip or question, so I let them think and looked over at my wife, who mouthed, "I love you." I stood, walked over to her, and placed a hand on her right shoulder, giving it a gentle squeeze. She placed her hand on mine.

"What do you say we clean up and I can tell you more?" I finally said.

"Let's do it, Pa," Anthony said. Alexander nodded in agreement.

When the dishes were done, we gathered in our sunroom, the light streaming through the windows. Outside the walls of glass, I admired the springtime growth in our garden and on our tall trees in the yard. When everyone had settled onto the wicker furniture, I picked up the story where I'd left off: the streets of Lynn.

It didn't take long at our new triple-decker to know I needed to avoid the first-floor family: their glazed eyes, and random people constantly staggering in and out of their apartment, told me to keep my distance. The second floor was occupied by a Greek family who seemed nice enough but didn't say much to us. Across the street from our building lived a Haitian American family and next to them, a Dominican family. At the top of the street was a corner store, and next to it was a funeral home.

The diversity of our block was new to me. Back home, I had been a Puerto Rican in Puerto Rico. My world had been homogeneous with lots of vegetation. Now my neighborhood was full of multiethnic and multiracial families: African American, Puerto Rican, Dominican, Greek, Irish, Haitian—a mix of ethnicities, backgrounds, and cultures. We subsisted in informal and unspoken ways on a long street supported by noise, tar, cement, and very few trees.

I learned my dad's work schedule and waited with excitement every evening for him to come home from work. Mom had gotten a job in the school district's bilingual department, which was just down the street from Harrington Elementary, so we walked together to and from school each day, rain or snow, always avoiding the street where we'd been attacked. Since Mom had been away so much back in Puerto Rico earning money to support us, I cherished all this newfound time with her, but I also felt the gap where my big sister had been.

Diana was still finishing college, living with Grandma and Grandpa, and we were all counting the days until she could join us in the United States. I wondered what Diana's life in Puerto Rico was like, and if she was happy. I didn't think so. Diana had always disliked living in Puerto Rico. I bet she couldn't wait to finish college and join us in Lynn.

Dwayne was figuring himself out—skipping school, getting into trouble, and testing his manhood on the streets of Lynn like he had back in Puerto Rico. Dan was working, going to the gym a lot, and trying to shape his future. I noticed that Dan was always learning new skills and devising different ways of earning money. Dad and Mom still worked a lot, but it didn't matter to me. What mattered was that my family was together.

I did miss my extended family—my grandparents, my cousins, my aunts and uncles—and neighborhood friends in Puerto Rico. Each Sunday, I'd wonder what they were doing. Were they all eating and laughing without us? What jungle discoveries had my cousins made without me? Did Grandpa and Grandma miss me? I hoped we would get to go visit them soon. Who was Jaime spending his time with? Was Bruce Lee still beating up bad guys at the bar cinema? A piece of me was always back in Puerto Rico, even as I tried to adapt to life in the United States.

Sometimes, when Mom would pour orange juice from a carton in the fridge, I'd remember the fresh juice we drank every day in Puerto

Rico. Life had been hard there, but it had been simple. And to my young mind, it had even been sweet.

As we started to get into a new rhythm of life, fifth grade went on. My parents had started speaking more English at home a week after we moved to the United States, at the encouragement of our bilingual teacher so I could learn the language faster. Since both of my parents had grown up in the US and were fluent, and Mom had taught English back in Puerto Rico, they were aggressive in teaching me. They knew I had to learn, and fast. If I didn't, I would struggle for the rest of my education.

Mom especially drilled in the message: "You're American. You're going to learn English. English is the key to succeeding in America. You don't forget Spanish, but English is the key. ¡Aprende a dominar los dos idiomas!" Learn to master both languages!

At school, the bilingual education approach was to teach us English using our native language. Basically, a bunch of us non-native English speakers were crammed together and taught English through our first language of Spanish. This approach goes against everything experts now know about language acquisition. Language is best learned through immersion, so separating us from the other kids slowed our ability to learn English. It also made integrating into American society more difficult.

A few years later, bilingual education would be eradicated in Massachusetts because it didn't work well, but back then it was the norm. I was fortunate that my parents both spoke English, and that they insisted we speak the language at home. Many of my classmates didn't have the same opportunity to practice English at home with their families, and it showed in the classroom.

I accepted my parents' persistence in teaching me English because I wanted to learn too. Part of me was self-conscious. I saw how some of the other Hispanic kids, especially the Dominican kids, were treated by non-Latino kids and adults (both white and black), and I didn't want to be treated that way. I worked hard to learn how to speak English clearly and eloquently. I focused on getting good grades. I would show my teachers that I was just as capable as anyone else—faster, better, smarter. And I knew speaking fluent English was part of that process.

I also began noticing how skin colors were treated differently in the schoolyard. Many of the kids in my class had dark skin, and with my lighter brown skin, I seemed to be less "other" to the white kids in the mainstream classroom. I saw it and felt it. At recess, I watched the Hispanic students keep to themselves, and noticed that the white girls and boys wouldn't go near them much. Looking back, I think all of us probably didn't understand each other: there was a language barrier, and a you-look-different-than-me barrier. Still, I noticed the separation—whites versus others—and I didn't like it.

I went out of my way to make sure I wasn't treated differently. I was David Morales, not a nameless Hispanic in the bilingual classroom. Part of being treated the same as everyone else was speaking English, and speaking it well. I also continued demonstrating strength and confidence on the playground. If I thought a kid was looking at me wrong or staring at me with an attitude, I'd confront them with a hard glare or a "you got a problem?" as my brother Dwayne had coached me to do. Over time, I didn't have any problems at Harrington. The kids got to know me and I got to know many of them, bilingual or not. I had decided not to cower or slink back, and to not separate myself into the bilingual group. I'd talk to whoever I wanted to, when I wanted to; I didn't buy into the idea that I had to only hang out with kids who looked like me.

Another factor that helped my transition was that a few months after I started school, my mother switched me from bilingual to regular classes. She aggressively pushed to get me out of bilingual education as she grew concerned about my progress and my playground altercations. Although inside I was still loving and gentle, on the outside I demonstrated toughness, manliness—don't-mess-with-me-ness. It was the only way I knew how to navigate and adapt to the new social rules of my environment.

Back on Henry Avenue, I became friends with Delwin, a Dominican kid who lived in my neighborhood. The two of us began riding bikes around the block or hanging out at one of our houses. Delwin attended Cobbet Elementary, where my mom said I would be transferring to for sixth grade. I'd be closer to home and in a mainstream classroom where I'd have to make new friends and figure things out all over again.

Delwin and his family were warm and kind to me. He had a brother and two sisters, and his mother and stepfather were wonderful. His mother would prepare Dominican fare like *mangú*, a traditional Dominican dish made up of boiled ripe or green plantains with fried eggs, cheese, onions, salami, and olive oil. His stepfather reminded me a lot of my uncles. He was handsome, sang beautifully, and always dressed like a gentleman with his *guayabera*, a traditional button-up linen shirt with several pockets and two sewn pleats running down the front. On Sundays, you could hear him playing Puerto Rican and Dominican *boleros* from the 1960s by Trio Los Panchos, Juan Lockward, Trio San Juan, Gilberto Monroig, Felipe Pirela, and many others. Like my father and my grandparents, he helped keep the flame of my Latino roots and music alive in my soul, as well as the nostalgia of Puerto Rico. One song he played frequently was "En Mi Viejo San Juan," by Noel Estrada.

Another song he sang often, "Linda Quisqueya," was written by one of Puerto Rico's most prolific songwriters, Rafael Hernández, about the Dominican Republic. I always got one of the verses stuck in my head.

While Delwin and I had a lot of fun getting to know each other and our families and riding bikes, Delwin was always complaining to me about this guy, Greg, who picked on him at school. Greg was a big Greek kid who had been bullying Delwin at recess, relentlessly. This guy wouldn't leave Delwin alone. I told Delwin, "Don't worry. As soon as I get there, I'll take care of it."

Fifth grade ended, and Delwin and I put aside Greg's bullying and all our school troubles. During the summer before sixth grade, we were just two kids riding bikes, playing basketball, exploring our neighborhood, learning about our ethnic cultures, and wondering what our lives would be like as we entered sixth grade.

Chapter 4

IN THE MIDDLE

*The specific circumstances you are facing may be out
of your control, but the way you respond to those
circumstances is 100 percent up to you.*

KRIS "TANTO" PARONTO,
FROM HIS BOOK, *THE PATRIOT'S CREED*

Soon it was the last weekend of summer, and Delwin and I were sitting on the bottom step of the stairs of my triple-decker. We'd be
starting sixth grade the next day at Cobbet Elementary. As we sat
there, Delwin leaning back on his elbows, me grinding a rock under
my shoe in a circular pattern, we talked about Greg, Delwin's bully,
and what we'd say to him at school the next day. I promised Delwin
I'd handle it.

Sixth grade would be different for him. We'd be the tough guys this
time. No one would mess with us.

The next morning, I rose early, dressed, and ate my cereal, waiting
for Mom to finish getting ready so we could walk the short distance
together to school. Cobbet was just a few blocks from my house instead
of the miles-long trek to Harrington, and while I'd insisted I could go
with Delwin, Mom said it was my first day of school, and she'd take
me. When she was finally ready, I slung my backpack over my shoulder, smoothed my hair under the palm of my hand, and walked out
the door. I felt both nervous and excited about my new school. What
would it be like? And would it be similar to Harrington: rough, gritty,
and all cement?

Cobbet, Mom had told me, was supposed to be a better school for me. Since I'd made so much progress in English, I didn't need to be at Harrington or in a bilingual classroom and could be with the other students. I knew this meant there would be kids from my neighborhood in my new school that I had yet to meet.

When I met my teacher, Mr. Fiste, I liked him right away. He was Greek, had a big personality, and was loud, confident, and vociferous. He smiled warmly at me, said hello, and shook my mom's hand. As Mom said goodbye, she kissed me on the top of my head even though I'd asked her not to. I quickly smoothed my hair again and waved goodbye as she left my classroom to continue her walk to the school department. Mr. Fiste pointed to my seat. Sitting at a desk directly in front of me was the one person I was looking for: Greg. I recognized him instantly based on the many descriptions Delwin had given me. As I took my seat, I tapped him on the shoulder. He turned around in his chair, eyeing me.

Tough guy, I thought. You just wait.

"Hey, are you Greg?" I said.

"Yeah, why?"

Mr. Fiste called our attention then, and Greg spun back around. I said nothing more. All morning, I thought of recess and what I was going to say to him.

As soon as we were outside, I walked up to Greg.

"So you're Greg," I said.

"What about it?" he said. He crossed his arms and looked me up and down.

"You the one picking on my bro, Delwin?" I pointed with my thumb over my shoulder at Delwin, who was several yards away and unaware of our exchange, then dropped my arm and started clenching my fists. I drew my face so close to his that our noses almost touched.

Greg's eyes widened and I could tell he was deciding what to do. "How do you know Delwin?" he said. His shaking voice betrayed his attempt at sounding tough. He was scared. I knew I had him.

"You're gonna stop picking on him, or I'll fuck you up," I said, my voice affirmative and growling. I tilted my chin up and met his eyes. "You won't pick on Delwin anymore, you hear me?" I tapped him in the chest, hard. I felt my nostrils flare and kept clenching my hands. I let all the anger I'd accumulated on Delwin's behalf flood my body, and I was ready to hit Greg if he challenged me.

Greg's eyes grew even wider and he stepped back. I could tell he'd never been confronted like this before. He was used to bullying people, and now someone was putting him in his place. After several seconds, he finally put his hands up, waving me off.

"I don't pick on him. It's all in fun," he said. "But I won't do it again."

I stared at him for several seconds. Satisfied I'd made my point, I walked off to find Delwin. "You don't need to worry about Greg anymore," I told him.

Delwin whooped and slapped my arm. Finally, he was rid of his bully.

But that wasn't the end of Greg. Actually, it was only the beginning.

Greg and I didn't fight that day, or ever. We didn't even have another verbal altercation or glare in each other's directions. Instead, we became friends. Great friends.

That day on the playground had made an impression on Greg. Greg had earned my respect. While he never apologized to Delwin, the two forgave and forgot without ever exchanging words. Soon, the three of us joined forces, a motley crew of boys trying to find their way through sixth grade. Even though we lived in very different neighborhoods, and came from different economic backgrounds, we found a way to get along: a Greek, a Dominican, and a Puerto Rican, all united in America. Greg's family owned a couple of pizza shops in Boston and he came to school with cash, sometimes lots of it! Delwin and I came to school with no cash. But regardless, we hung tight and became a force on the playground—rough guys, ready to fight if someone looked at us the wrong way.

Among my peers I was Morales, the tough kid, don't mess with him. In the classroom, I was a near-perfect student, always doing my best work, listening and trying to win Mr. Fiste's approval. Mr. Fiste was a great teacher: hilarious yet strict. We all respected him immensely. And overall, things were good for me. My English was getting much better; I had an accent, but my fluency was strong. I was doing well in school. I had two great friends.

But something inside me was starting to shift, not just the defensive layer I put between the world and me—that had been developing for some time—but an awareness that I was poor.

In Puerto Rico, I had never noticed my family's poverty. We had what we needed, even if our house was made of cement and my clothes were old and didn't fit. While I was always hungry as a growing boy, I never went hungry. We ate Spam and bread, *plátanos*, *batata*, and *bacalao*. We feasted on the wild fruit that grew on our street, and the vegetables my dad foraged, and the fish he caught fresh and brought home to cook. I had wealthy grandparents (at least in my mind), and we had a car that mostly ran, as long as we kept a jug of water for the radiator in the trunk.

Everyone around me was the same. All my friends were poor. And as far as I knew, none of us had a clue or thought about race or socioeconomics.

In Puerto Rico, I viewed poverty as living in an aluminum house with a *letrina*, an outhouse. I thought of being poor as only getting to eat once a day, or having to beg on the streets, or being homeless. I knew the poor suffered, and that being poor in Puerto Rico was hell, and I thanked God as a child that we were fortunate to have everything we needed. Since we were not *that* kind of poor, I always thought of our family as well-off.

In the United States, though, poor meant something different. Dad didn't have steady work, Mom was trying to make ends meet with her job, and they were doing their best to figure out how to provide for our needs: food, shelter, utilities, transportation. But we had a roof over our heads and food in our bellies. And to me, compared with Puerto Rico, we had abundance in the United States. We weren't poor—we were wealthy! I knew it the moment I laid eyes on that triple-decker at 22 Henry Avenue. My family would be OK, because we were suddenly rich! We were living on the *third floor* of a wooden home. We had the *coolest* car. I thought we were set. Living the American dream.

But I started to question my perception. I noticed other kids like Greg, who had twenty-dollar bills that flowed like water out of his backpack, and the kids who lived in Pine Hill—a well-to-do area of Lynn—in single-family homes with trees and a beautiful public park.

Rather than renting an apartment on the third floor, they owned a single-family house with two entire floors to themselves, sometimes even a basement. Their parents owned two cars that were a lot nicer than our two-door Ford Pinto. The kids had fresh haircuts, Adidas sneakers, and new backpacks. They did special sports clubs on the weekends their parents paid extra money for. They had Nike shorts and CB Sports ski jackets that looked new and fit well. I had hand-me-down T-shirts, loose jeans with elastic waistbands, and no-name Velcro sneakers from Zayre, a discount department store that was like a low-income Target. When I did get new clothes, they were from the sale racks at JCPenney, Woolworth, or Zayre.

When I started seventh grade, these differences became apparent. I attended Breed Junior High School for seventh and eighth grades. The kids at Breed were nothing like the kids from my neighborhood. Some of the kids would tease me in gym class or on the bus, especially two Latina girls that I befriended, Natalie and Ive. They'd say things like, "Where'd you get that shirt, D?" and "What brand are those shoes?" When girls made fun of me, I'd laugh it off. When boys did, I'd fight them or tell them to shut the f-- up or else. Still, their comments stung.

When other kids point out the fact that you're poor, believe me, you get it. And it burns deep inside.

The first few months of seventh grade were like waking up to a new day, when things that were always there become glaringly obvious. Suddenly, I looked around the world I'd regarded as wealthy—our family's American lifestyle that seemed luxurious compared to Puerto Rico—and realized we were working-class poor. *Damn, bro.*

There I was: thirteen years old, overweight, puffy hair, hand-me-down clothes, and a chip forming on my shoulder. One that would really take shape in junior high.

The sun was high in the sky now, and our sunroom was growing warm.

"What do you say we go for a walk?" I said to my family.

"Good idea," my wife said. Alexander, who had been laying on the floor, reached his arms up like a mummy, beckoning my wife to help him up.

She laughed and walked over to him, tugging him off the floor. Anthony stood too, giving Alexander a shove for no clear reason. Brothers, I thought.

A few minutes later, we had Bella on a leash and were walking the wide sidewalks of our neighborhood. The tall oaks and pine trees around us were cloaked in bright greens; some of the smaller trees had flowered with vibrant purples and pinks.

"So Pa," Anthony began, "you didn't realize you were poor until you were twelve or thirteen years old?" He looked confused. "I don't get it."

"Wouldn't you have noticed that you weren't wearing clothes that fit you?" Alexander added. "And that you lived in a triple-decker instead of a house, and stuff like that?"

Bella pulled at the leash in my hand and began barking at a squirrel. I tugged gently on the leash to quiet her down as the squirrel ran up a tree in terror.

"You guys live incredible lives today," my wife said once the barking stopped. "When you're a child, and you're poor, you don't know any different. You don't know other kids have more than you." She'd had her own challenging upbringing in the Dominican Republic, and I knew we'd get to that soon.

"Exactly," I said. "You don't know any different until you get old enough to start comparing, or when others call out the things they have versus what you don't have. Once I left the bilingual classroom, with all the other kids who were poor like me, I started to see the difference between me and some of the kids in my new school."

I knew my sons could never completely understand. Because while we had a lot less money when they were younger, they never lacked. I would make sure they never would be poor. But I would also ensure they developed empathy and a deep understanding for kids who grew up like me, looking at kids like them with a sort of awed curiosity.

"OK, so sixth grade was when you started to notice the difference?" Anthony asked.

"That's right," I said.

"And seventh grade was when you started to *really* notice?" he added.

"Yep. I was coming of age. I was becoming a young man."

"Was that weird?" Alexander asked. "I mean, dealing with all the normal growing up stuff *and* also realizing in the middle of it that you're poor?"

"Poor is relative," I said. "In Puerto Rico, I wasn't poor. In America, I actually wasn't poor either, not really. But American poor is very different from Puerto Rican poor. And I began to shift the way I thought, and started to recognize that I was different from some of the other kids." I thought back on that experience, and how it stung to go to school every day knowing that the kids looked at me differently because of my skin color, my clothes, my accent . . . my everything.

"So what happened in seventh grade?" Anthony said.

"Yeah," Alexander added, "tell us."

"All right," I replied. Seventh grade was a big year for me, and I wanted them to understand why. As we walked, I went on.

In seventh grade, the chip on my shoulder deepened. While Breed Junior High School was outside our district, Mom had pushed for me to go to the school because she knew I'd get a good education there. The school was largely populated by white students from the Pine Hill area, and suddenly I was surrounded by Anglo kids who had a lot more money than my family. And the girls—there were so many beautiful girls. I had never been around so many blonde, light-skinned girls in my life, and I was dumbstruck by how well they dressed. They reminded me of the girls I used to see on American shows I had watched in Puerto Rico. But now they were in front of me speaking in English, not in subtitles on a TV screen. But it didn't matter, because I knew there was a dividing line between the white girls and me. They had homes in Pine Hill. I lived in a triple-decker on Henry Avenue.

Two moments define that year for me: getting teased by girls I liked, and my dad telling me I was fat. Those experiences would stick with me for the rest of my education, even my life.

The teasing was good-natured, usually by Natalie and Ive, the two Latina girls I'd become friends with that year. Natalie's family was from Colombia and she had a sharp sense of humor; Ive was Dominican and followed Natalie's lead in teasing and poking. But even though they probably thought their teasing was harmless, and I laughed it off and dished it right back, inside I was embarrassed. And pissed off.

One morning, I boarded the bus and found my seat, excited to pull out the Walkman stereo tape player my brother Dan had given me. I'd seen all the kids on the bus listening to music on the way to school, and now I could be like them with my music too. I sat down, dug into my oversized pant pocket, and pulled out my tape player, which already had my cassette in it. I felt cool as I put on my headphones. The bus rolled on, and I lost myself in my Frankie Ruiz cassette, tapping my fingers on my knees and staring out the window. I jumped when I felt a tap on my right shoulder.

I turned around, and when no one was there, I turned to my left. Natalie was leaning over the back of my seat, laughing at having fooled me, and I pushed pause on my tape player. The play button popped up with a *click*, and I removed my headphones.

"Yo," I said, returning her smile. I loved attention from girls, even if there was a risk of teasing with Natalie.

"What is that crap?" she said.

"What crap?" I had no idea what she was talking about.

"That shit you're listening to."

"My Walkman?"

"Yeah, that's like, three years old."

Ive, who I hadn't noticed was low in the seat next to Natalie, sat up and leaned forward. "And what are you wearing?" She tugged on my sleeve and pointed to my shoes.

I looked down at my T-shirt. It was baggy to hide my weight, a hand-me-down from Dwayne. Across the front was a small frog with a Puerto Rican flag and the words *Boricua*. I wore huge jeans with the widest legs I could find. I thought I looked cool and slimmer than I was.

Natalie mussed my hair. "And your hair. What are you, fresh off the boat?"

I quickly ran my hand over my hair and laughed. "I know you like it. Admit it."

She giggled and exchanged a look with Ive. This was a daily ritual with them: find Morales, make fun of him. I knew it was good-natured.

Had a guy said something, it would have been on. When cute girls made fun of me, I went with it.

But underneath the joking was the truth. I let them tease me, and laughed off their jokes, but inside, I was like, damn. Do I look poor? Do they think I'm fat? Why can't I just be cool? It was like waking up to a new reality. I was paying attention to their words, beginning to better understand how different I was than the other kids. They teased my style, my weight, my backpack, and apparently my awesome Walkman.

By seventh grade, Mom let me start walking home from school. All of the kids would walk in a big mass, heading toward the general direction of our houses. On the way, the group would reach the street to Pine Hill, where the wealthy Anglo kids lived; there were no people of color up there, except I'd heard this one ethnic kid, John Sasso, lived in that area. While I wouldn't get to know John until eighth grade, the fact that he lived there blew my mind. Delwin and I would walk with the cute girls and popular guys who were heading in our same direction, and we'd say goodbye as they'd all turn toward Pine Hill and we'd continue home to Henry Avenue. One day, they asked where we were headed, and when we told them, a tall, blonde soccer player named Alyssa replied, "Oh, you're going to the ghetto." Delwin and I walked home that day in near silence, thinking about what she'd said. I kept running her words over and over in my head.

So that's where I lived. The ghetto. I didn't live in a mansion as a millionaire; our triple-decker on Henry Avenue was not a palace. I lived in the ghetto, the poor part of town, where the beautiful girls and popular guys would never, ever go. There was an unspoken rule that we weren't allowed in Pine Hill either. That's where the rich white kids hung out, not us. At least that's what we perceived.

Awareness had continued to grow like a flame inside of me, burning the chip on my shoulder deeper and deeper until it nearly struck bone. I was quietly building rage, fury against being poor. I knew, deep within me, that I wanted out. I didn't want to be teased anymore; I didn't want to be different. And I definitely didn't want to become like the guys I saw on the street corners, the ones who had gone to the same school I did and had big dreams and a lot of talent, only to become "used-to-be's"—our term for all the dudes who used to be amazing athletes and ended up high on crack, hanging out at Lynn Common or in public parks in West Lynn.

All through seventh grade, I observed the kids and adults around me, forming my ideas about who I was and who I would be. I refused to accept the path that was laid out for me as a kid from the ghetto. Screw that. I would make something of myself. I'd show them.

I'm getting out of this, I told myself. I'm never going to be like those used-to-be's.

Toward the middle of seventh grade, this chip on my shoulder grew even larger. One night I was hanging with my brother Dwayne, each of us sitting on our beds in our shared bedroom, talking about his escapades, when my dad walked in holding one of my T-shirts. He looked pissed.

"This was in my drawer," he said loudly, holding the shirt by the shoulders and out toward me. "It's a freaking tent."

I looked at the shirt in front of me, the light blue fabric spread wide. His entrance was so abrupt and his volume so unexpected, I had to quickly make sense of what was happening. My dad had made comments about my body in the past, but what had made him so instantly mad? Why was my dad yelling?

"You need to start losing weight," he yelled. Then his voice dropped low. His tone dripped with disgust. "What the hell is wrong with you? Do you want to be fat your entire life?" He crumpled the shirt into a ball and threw it at me, then walked out. The pressure of the fabric hitting my chest lingered on my skin. It hadn't hurt physically, but I felt the pain emotionally.

So that's why. He was yelling at me for being fat.

I was stunned. Dwayne said nothing. We both sat in silence, each of us uncomfortable. Embarrassed. For all the times Dwayne had teased me, or had cracked a joke to ease tense situations, he couldn't find any words in that moment. I looked down at my body. Dad was right—I was fat. I had weighed myself recently: 170 pounds on my five-foot-two frame.

A tent. I needed a freaking tent to clothe my huge body.

I knew I was big. I wasn't blind. I recognized my size in relation to the kids around me. And I knew Dad noticed too, but I'd never known my body repulsed him. Until that day, I'd never felt such deep pain and shame. His words, and the way he'd said them to me . . . they ached. I knew Dad loved me, but the way he spoke to me hurt.

The rest of the evening was spent mostly in my own head, processing what Dad had said to me. I avoided him and didn't say much at dinner, poking my food around the plate as I replayed the scene over and over in my mind. When Mom asked if I was OK, I avoided Dad's eyes and gave her enough of a smile to convince her I was fine.

"I'm good," I assured her.

After dinner, I shut myself in the bathroom and removed my shirt, turning side to side, lifting my belly and dropping it, wondering how to get rid of my bulk of a body. I felt ashamed of my own skin. I wanted to trim myself away.

I am fat, I thought. What the hell *is* wrong with me?

I thought back to sixth-grade basketball, when I had started to notice my weight. I had been given a T-shirt to wear for games that was too small for me, and each game I'd have to put that tiny shirt on, my gut protruding from the bottom. There were no bigger sizes; I'd have to wear that one. My shorts were tight too, like mesh spandex, and rode up in the back. Each time I put the game shirt on, the guys would help me pull it down, but it was no use—a few minutes into the game, it'd ride up and my gut was out again. I'd play that way the entire game, my body fighting to burst through the shirt, my belly escaping out the bottom. There was a Puerto Rican girl, Tricia, who would come to games. I knew she liked me, and I liked her too. When each play stopped, I'd tug the shirt down as far as I could and avoid looking toward Tricia. My ears burned hot.

I'd worn that shirt every game. *Every single game.* And I'd cried most nights after playing, remembering Tricia in the stands, and feeling angry at my own body. My chest had heaved with embarrassment.

My dad's words were the first time I felt like someone else was disgusted with my body too. I still own that basketball shirt as a reminder of my past.

I knew the problem. I ate a lot of junk: sugar-based products like juice and candy, and a lot of fried foods. The most movement I got in a day was PE or basketball. And while I didn't know much about how to lose weight, I did know the fundamentals. Eat healthy food. Exercise. That's what I'd do. Yet even those terms, "healthy food" and "exercise" were ambiguous to me. I wasn't sure exactly what they meant or how to make sure I did them more so I wouldn't look like this.

That night, my head was too foggy to think more about it anyway. I crawled into bed, feeling heavier and sadder than I'd ever felt, and I sobbed quietly, careful Dwayne wouldn't hear me. If he did hear me, he didn't say anything. As I lay on my back in the dark of my room, tears streaming down the sides of my face and pooling in my ears, I shut my eyes tight and imagined myself light, free of my weight. I envisioned walking into school a different David and pictured my dad smiling at me, proud of his strong, fit son. But when I opened my eyes and stared into the dark of my room, I was back to my old self again: my heavy body, the fat version of me. I wanted to peel away layers of fat and sadness and emerge a man.

I'm invisible, I thought. I'm poor, I'm fat, I'm invisible, and I'm going to fix this. I'm going to do something about my body and people are going to respect me. They're going to respect my name; they're going to respect my family. And my dad—I'll show him. He'll see.

We made it back from our walk and were now sitting on our back patio. Alexander and Anthony both reclined on our two loungers in the sunshine. Bella sat to Anthony's right, in the shade of his chair and body, and he was aimlessly stroking her soft ears. I sat on a couch across from them, happy they were still here, wanting to hear more of my story. My wife had left to take care of some items for the women's group she leads at church, so it was just the three of us. She'd be back in time to make dinner together that evening.

No one spoke as we each processed our thoughts. We listened at length to the birds chirping in the trees above us. A lawn mower roared to life. A car started.

"That sounds crazy, Pa," Alexander finally said. His eyes were half-moons, and I could see that he felt for me. Anthony sat silently next to him.

Alexander is my artist, my intellectual. Anthony is my athlete. Both are slim and tall, and have never once in their entire lives had to worry about weight. I could tell it was hard for them to understand what I went through, and to reconcile this poor, fat, invisible, sad father with the one they knew today.

"Pa?" Alexander said. I had lost myself in thought.

I smiled sadly at him. "It *was* crazy."

"And you really had to wear that shirt to every game?" Anthony asked. I guessed he was thinking of his own basketball games, and what it would be like to live through the shame I'd experienced.

"Every game," I said. "It was awful."

"And when *abuelo* said that to you . . ." Anthony trailed off.

" . . . what did you do?" Alexander finished for him.

"Well, I asked Grandma not to buy me any more junk food. I decided not to eat candy or ice cream anymore. I still ate it sometimes, but not every day like I had been."

"And did you lose weight fast?" Alexander asked.

"No. It took a long time," I said. "Every day, when I put on the elastic waist stretchy jeans and XL shirts Grandma had bought me at JCPenney earlier in the year, it was a reminder that I didn't want to be fat anymore. I'd hid under my clothes my entire life, and I didn't want to hide any longer."

No one said anything for several seconds. For a moment, I felt transported back to that point in time: that body, that feeling. Adolescence will always bring pain, it's a human fact, but I was glad my sons' pain had to do with girls, friends, and sports. They would never know the deep pain, shame, and anger I had felt as a kid. Never.

"What happened next?" Anthony finally said.

And so I told them.

For the rest of seventh grade, I tried to figure out what to do about my weight. I had stopped eating as much junk food, I got more involved in sports, and I also began riding my bike more—not to lose weight, but for the freedom of roaming the streets.

I started having regular dreams that I had lost weight. I'd wake from these dreams and, for a happy moment, think I was thinner. My entire body would be awash in joy as I'd think, I'm not fat anymore! But then I'd feel my stomach, and reality would hit me in the early morning light. I'd lift up the covers to see my still-heavy body.

I was sleeping over at Delwin's house one night when I had one of these dreams. I woke him up and asked him to tell me if I'd lost weight. Was I skinny now?

"You're still fat, man," he said. I was crushed.

These dreams motivated me to keep working to lose weight. Along with watching what I ate, I also observed the popular kids to see what they were doing to be so thin and strong. I noticed a lot of them were involved in sports. They played baseball, which was a sport the rich white kids did and something I only had access to during in-school intermural sports. But you didn't have to be rich to play basketball, so I followed their example and was always on the basketball court with my buddies Delwin and George, and other kids from the neighborhood. Along with intramural basketball, we played all sorts of games at school.

After school, I would go home and play basketball on the streets with Delwin and our neighbors Jamal and Seneca. There was a basketball court at the top of our street, and we would also venture into Marian Gardens, a low-income housing development a few blocks from Henry Avenue. I was playing basketball with blacks, Latinos, and low-income white kids down there, and on Western Avenue with the poor white kids. It was always Delwin and me on our bikes, searching for a game. Sometimes other neighborhood kids would join us on their bikes as we rode around, searching for a court and some guys to play ball with.

We weren't playing the organized basketball games our middle-to upper-class friends played. They practiced in gyms and well-kept outdoor basketball courts, with coaches to teach them the fundamentals. They wore Adidas shorts and special court shoes that didn't leave black marks on the pristine indoor gym floors. Their parents waited for them with orange slices and water bottles after a game. We played street ball—and it was brutal and bloody. When you're hungry, and all you care about is getting your hands on the basketball and being the best on the street, you'll whoop someone's ass to win. The grit we brought to the court was a world away from the grit the Pine Hill kids brought to their fancy leagues.

My friends and I played with older kids too. We were all talking trash, and it was on. Fights broke out nearly every game: you hit someone the wrong way during a play, either run or be ready to fight. I didn't fear anyone or anything. The basketball court was a testing ground for my manhood, just like the streets of Puerto Rico had been for Dan and Dwayne.

I used sports and my bike as therapy to lose weight. That's all I wanted: to not be fat anymore. The weight started to come off slowly, pound by pound.

I also started getting in trouble. By the end of seventh grade, I had racked up three suspensions. The first time I got suspended was for fighting, and the conversation with my dad was quick and simple.

"Did you start it?" he asked.

"No, I didn't."

"Did you finish it?"

"Yes, I did."

"OK." Conversation done. Over before it really began. I got the lesson: don't go around looking for fights, but if someone starts a fight, make sure you end it. I needed to win the fight and make a point so no one would ever want to fight me again.

The second suspension was different. I was caught stealing at school and was sent home for the day. I had to walk because the afternoon school bus service wasn't running yet, and the entire walk home, I imagined what would happen when I got there. I guessed Dad would still be at work, but what about Mom? Since she worked at the school district, Mom usually came home much earlier than she had in Puerto Rico but wasn't home at this time of day. Had the school phoned her? Would she have left early and be waiting for me? The walk home was long, probably three or four miles, and my dread grew with each step. When I opened the door to our apartment, Dad was waiting for me on the couch. I nearly passed out from fear.

"What did you steal?" he asked before I had even shut the door behind me. He stood and walked toward me, his huge hands and arms spread wide as if in disbelief and shock. I could see anger simmering behind his eyes. His face was tight and his mouth a hard line.

"I stole a carton of milk," I said. His eyes narrowed as I spoke. "There was a truck parked at the back of the school delivering milk, and me and this other kid each stole a carton."

When I stopped talking, Dad went haywire.

"Milk? Milk!" he hollered. "I didn't teach you to steal! I work my ass off to provide for you!" He was screaming at the top of his lungs, his face red, his arms gyrating with each sentence. I waited, my body tight, for him to smack me. "We don't go hungry. You don't need any-thing. And you don't steal—ever!"

Dad didn't hit me that day, but his words did. He yelled for another fifteen minutes as I sat in a chair, slumped over in shame. The next day, he took me to school and sat me down with the principal. Dad told him that if I ever did something stupid again, he had full author-ity to punish me. And that included hitting me, if need be.

Well, it wasn't long before I did something stupid again and got my third suspension. I'd had another fight at school. Toward the end of the fight, a knife had fallen out of my pocket, and suddenly everything had stopped and the crowd that had collected stepped back in unison. The person I'd been fighting backed away too, and I'd stared at the knife, shocked. I'd been carrying it to feel tough but never planned to use it. We all stood there for several seconds until suddenly the principal grabbed me by the arm and swung me like a rag doll. All I remember was the world spinning and all the students stepping back in horror.

When we got back to the principal's office, he shut the door while I sat and—*pow*. He knocked me out of my chair and I flew across the room, then scrambled up. He smacked me hard across my head and I fell to the floor again. I knew not to hit back. I couldn't punch my principal. He started screaming at me, standing over me and yelling at the top of his lungs about my family, my mother, my father. The sac-rifices they were making to live like good Americans. When he finally stopped screaming, he walked to sit behind his desk. I pulled myself off the floor and sat in the chair opposite him.

His voice was gruff and low as he said something powerful to me that I have never forgotten. "Don't become another statistic," he said, meeting my eyes. "There are plenty of bad guys in the world. Don't be one. You have a loving mother and father. Honor them."

Then he called my dad on speaker and told him about the fight.

"Did you hit him?" my dad asked.

"Yeah."

"Good."

They hung up, and I sat there in his office, processing what had happened. I'd just gotten my ass beat by my principal and learned a life lesson I would not forget.

My head stung and my gut ached, the principal's words fresh on my mind: *Don't become another statistic. There are plenty of bad guys in the world. Don't be one. You have a loving mother and father. Honor them.* I understood: cause trouble, get trouble. I didn't want that anymore, and I especially did not want to let my parents down or dishonor them.

I think part of seventh grade was about testing the "bad" path and seeing if it was for me. Did I want to be the kind of kid who carried knives and was constantly in trouble? Did I want to join a gang or start doing drugs?

No, that life wasn't for me. Seventh grade was the end of deviance, at least the kind that landed me in the principal's office. I wasn't going to be a punk, a used-to-be. I didn't want to get whooped in my principal's office, or by any adult for that matter. I didn't want my dad screaming at me anymore. I didn't want to let my family down.

What I wanted more than anything was to be liked. Accepted. To fit in and be popular. And with summer soon approaching, I was set on emerging from those few months, and into eighth grade, a changed David. They'd see: Natalie, Ive, the popular guys, the principal, my dad. They'd see what David Morales could do, who he could be.

Sitting on the hard wooden chair in the principal's office, I felt the fire inside burn hotter, and I decided I would show him. I'd show everyone.

You just wait and see, I thought to myself. You just wait.

Chapter 5

CAMBIO

Things do not change; we change.

—HENRY DAVID THOREAU

On my cheap-ass white Sigma bike with white wheels, I pushed boundaries and ventured into every corner of my area of Lynn. I was free. I could roam, untethered, accountable to no one. Ride past the used-to-be's smoking crack on the corner. Park my bike at the basketball courts and join a game with the older kids, the guys everyone else was afraid of, but not me. Pedal up and down streets where drug dealers would stare, hazy-eyed, and sometimes nod at me, Dwayne Morales's little brother. And venture farther and farther away from my block, into places my mother would never, ever allow me to be.

All summer between the seventh and eighth grades, I rode my bicycle. Delwin and I, and sometimes other neighborhood boys, biked all over the place. My bicycle became part of my weight loss therapy. I was active, moving constantly, instead of watching TV or eating. We rode all day and into the evening, until we knew our mothers or grandmothers wanted us home for dinner. And as I rode, my body started to melt away. My baby fat began to give way to a lean, strong body.

While I was changing physically, I was toughening emotionally. I had been exposed to so much already in seventh grade; junior high was a whole new experience, and I was only halfway through. Fights, girls, my weight . . . it was a transformational time. Outside, I was growing stronger, slimmer, more attractive to girls—especially, I hoped, to the Pine Hill girls. While I still had some of my baby fat, I was becoming a machine, and shaping into a future athlete. Inside, I was growing angrier, and the chip on my shoulder was getting deeper and deeper.

By the start of eighth grade, I began realizing there was a whole world out there beyond Henry Avenue and my junior high. I started going farther from home, riding my bike to places I hadn't dared over the summer. I branched out from my street, touring the city of Lynn, not limiting myself to my small section of the city, and learning new worlds.

One day toward the beginning of eighth grade, Delwin and I rode our bikes the farthest we'd ever ridden, to our friend Tommy's house about two miles away. Tommy lived close to Pine Hill, just a street below and right on the border. Tommy was a white kid from a working-class family who was home alone a lot, and that afternoon at his place, we felt like we'd ventured to another country.

Tommy lived in a single-family home with two stories. He had a Sega video game console, baseball cards, a ton of food in the fridge, and a huge coin collection. There were so many things to play with that Delwin and I spent what seemed like hours in awe and shock at the abundance of stuff.

For Delwin and I it was a thrill to be off our own turf, and by the time we made it back home, we couldn't believe we'd pulled off this grand adventure. That evening, we realized we could go anywhere and do anything as long as we were back by dinnertime. On the ride home, we talked about having money when we were older to buy Sega video games and real basketball hoops for our yards, instead of the milk crate we used in Delwin's backyard, which his brother had nailed to a tree so we could play.

That night, my mom asked where I'd been that day.

"Just riding around the neighborhood with Delwin," I said quickly. "Played basketball up the street."

"That's nice, David," Mom said. She had no clue where I was going, the people I was hanging around, or the things I saw while out on my bicycle. I felt an instant dagger of guilt at betraying her trust.

Mom didn't know that earlier that week I'd been hanging around at King's Lynne, a tough area far from home. Or that Delwin and I planned to ride to Curwin Circle that weekend to play basketball with kids from school, in a part of the city that was full of drugs and drug-related shootings. On my bicycle I was fearless, venturing into the toughest areas, talking to anyone I wanted to and playing ball with whoever would play. I went places most boys my age wouldn't dare go, but there I was on my Sigma bike, riding up to play ball. If I ever got into a situation, I'd fight my way through it and it was done. Getting pummeled by my brothers growing up had taught me to fight, and I used my fists to earn respect in all the different pockets of the city. After I would take a kid out, everyone else would be cool to me because they'd see I was one of them.

There we were, Delwin and me, a Dominican kid and a Puerto Rican kid, just trying to figure out the world. We had responsible parents who weren't home because they were working to provide for us. Delwin's mom was never around because of her work schedule as a nurse aide, so we were often home by ourselves or roaming the streets on our bikes. I was deathly afraid that my parents would find out about this new life I was living on my bicycle: who I was hanging out with, where I was going, the trouble I was getting into with fights, the drugs and guns I was around every day. While I walked a straight line at school, attended church with my parents, and didn't use drugs, I was growing up in a tough environment and being exposed to things that would shock and horrify my parents. Fighting was how I navigated my way through a lot of the problems I encountered—but frankly, it was normal back then where I grew up.

Exploration and intellectual curiosity were in my DNA. I'd get on my bike and go. With the exception of Pine Hill, there were no boundaries. When Delwin would protest, saying we might get beat up if we went to certain areas, I'd say, Don't worry. Everything will be fine. Let's go!

To Mom, I was David, her golden child. By eighth grade, I was done with suspensions and had solid report cards. Most teachers loved me, and Mom heard their praise first-hand, because she knew many of them through her job in the school district. I was the baby of the family. Mom told me every day that I was smart, that I was going places. I got As and Bs at school, and everything was good in her world. I was going to bring honor to our family's name, she told me.

But Mom was oblivious to the life I lived outside of home and school. On the streets, I was fierce, angry, and violent. This reactive part of me was a side I never wanted my parents to know about, especially my mom. It would kill me to disappoint her.

I was wracked with guilt over this double life I was living: golden boy at home, brawler on the street.

But the fact was, the streets were my reality. I lived in a tough area, and my tough area was surrounded by tougher areas and even tougher people. Every morning on my walk to the bus stop, I'd witness things my Pine Hill friends would probably never see in their entire lives. Poverty, prostitution, drugs, crime, death—it was all there, right around my block. I'd see guys on the street corners in their baggy clothes, with big coats full of drugs and guns tucked into their waistbands. Everyone knew who they were, and these guys were an accepted part of life in Lynn. I could name all the drug dealers and rode past them every day on my bike. They all knew who I was because I was Dwayne's little brother. Dwayne had earned a reputation on the streets, and the dealers knew not to mess with me, or Dwayne would mess them up.

The reality of life in Lynn was normal, part of my everyday reality. I wasn't afraid of anything or anyone. But inside I was deeply afraid of two things: disappointing my parents and living in poverty.

As Delwin and I rode bikes around the city, I observed the community. I noticed the single-parent homes and knew my intact family was rare. I saw the strained relationship between Delwin and his stepdad, and compared that to the love I got from my mom and attention I received at home from my family. Delwin and his stepdad clashed—they had nothing in common. Delwin was always on the streets or at my house. Some of my friends had entire families of criminals and no one at home to encourage them. Many of their moms and dads, if they were even around anymore, were strung out or hustling. Addiction and violence permeated the homes of many of the families around us. There were a few families who were poor but not broken, and some families like mine, who had healed and had fathers and mothers who cared deeply about their children's futures. We weren't perfect but there was love, and my mom especially went out of her way to keep us together. She worked hard on weekends to care for us at home. I knew I was fortunate to have her effort and care in my life.

At school, on the other hand, were teachers who routinely told Greg and I that we'd flip cheeseburgers at McDonald's for the rest of our lives. I was sure this one particular teacher was saying stuff like that to other kids too. Most of my classmates didn't have a counterbalance at home or anyone saying, "I believe in you."

I was fortunate because I had a strong father who was present at home and a loving mom who always encouraged me. She was constantly telling me, "David, you were born to do great things."

My home was a little island of safety within the dangers of Lynn. I had stability. I knew I was lucky. And I didn't want to let my mom and dad down, my parents who had worked so hard to lift our family out of the chaos and poverty of Puerto Rico, and into a country where anything is possible. I didn't want to let my siblings down, knowing how much they'd given up for me growing up to make sure I had every opportunity to get an education and thrive.

Diana was in the United States now, and I was thrilled to have my second mom near me again. But she was struggling, trying to find her way as an unmarried Puerto Rican woman in her mid-twenties, which I knew was tough for her. In traditional Puerto Rican culture, unmarried women were called *jamonas*, and it was not a badge of honor by any means. She had earned a degree in accounting but the economy was awful in the early 1990s, and she was having a tough time. Dan and Diana moved in together into an apartment on Lewis Street, an area that was hot—lots of robberies and drugs. Dwayne was living a hard life on the streets, gone sometimes for days from our family home. He sporadically crashed on Diana's sofa to get rest or to hide.

While they had their own lives, I felt indebted to them. Even at a distance, I felt the weight of their sacrifices for me.

But I also knew that even with all of the opportunity ahead of them, and all the love my parents had for me, my family was working-class poor. We were Puerto Ricans. We were newcomers and we were struggling. I would change that. If I was really meant to do great things, as my mom said, I thought the greatest thing I could ever do was lift my family out of poverty. This thought overtook me every day: I *had* to figure out how to lift my family up and help them do better. For good. I would lay awake at night, staring at my popcorn ceiling and imagining a better life for myself and my family. I'd envision buying my parents a home, and my sister too. I thought often about the American dream and what it meant for us. I pictured myself with powerful connections to get my brothers good jobs. I imagined not just having money, but wealth. While I had no idea what career I'd need to get wealth and influence, I knew my future had to include both of those things in order to help my family and achieve my perception of the American dream. Money and influence were two things I didn't have, and I was determined to get.

Courage and grit? Damn straight. But money and influence? Not yet. I would, though. I would figure it out. I had to.

As eighth grade went on, I had a singular focus: be better than everyone around me at whatever I tried. I groomed my confidence into a swagger. My outer presence blossomed. While inside I was struggling with self-confidence and trying to mold myself to fit what was expected of me in different situations, outside, I walked like a young man who knew who he was and wasn't afraid to show it or test new things.

I started to ask my mother for nicer clothes, and she started using her credit card to buy them for me. I knew nothing about credit—all I knew was that Mom was finally buying me cool clothes that fit me to wear to school so I could look cool. My style was Hispanic all the way: shiny shirts, slicked-back hair full of gel. That year, I also got involved in a lot of different sports, including tennis, volleyball, and baseball. I'd played stick ball in Puerto Rico with broomsticks and cans. Now I was playing organized intermural sports in the United States.

Girls started treating me differently too in eighth grade. Natalie and Ive's teasing became flirting and wanting to hang out. The Pine Hill girls began inviting me to sit at their table at lunch and waving at me in the halls. It was like my world had flipped suddenly, from chubby, nobody David to fit, popular-with-the-ladies David. I was digging it.

I was self-aware, though, of the different environments around me, and my need to adapt in order to fit into each space. This single fact shook my self-confidence to my core, even if I didn't let it show. I realized quickly that I had to be a different David in different situations. If I was going to play ball with the Latino and black kids in Curwin Circle, I wasn't going to wear my shiny Puerto Rican-style shirts. I'd put on a T-shirt and basketball shorts so I would fit in. If I was going to a restaurant nicer than McDonald's or Taco Bell, I recognized that I needed to dress up a little bit, sit up straighter while I ate, and eat with manners. Similarly, when I hung around my Latino friends, who were mostly Dominican, I would listen to *salsa* and *merengue*, throw Spanish in the mix, and definitely wear a *guayabera* shirt to look as Puerto Rican as I could. Most of my friends in Lynn either didn't realize the need to adapt behaviors and how they dressed in certain situations, or didn't care—they were who they were no matter *where* they were. I respected that. But I didn't want to be put into a box; I didn't want people to see me as another Latino kid who dressed weird and could not adapt to the fabric of American life. Not me. People would respect me. I became aware that part of earning respect was showing up in a way people could relate to or appreciate, whether it was wearing a T-shirt and shorts on the court or a nice button-up for church, or saying a friendly hello at school.

Seventh grade was a year of self-awareness: I'm fat, I'm poor. Eighth grade was a year of exploration, a grand coming of age on the streets of Lynn and the halls of junior high school. I was figuring out my world on my bike, and going to hang out at places where I knew nobody—but saw that they were playing ball, and if there was a basketball involved, let's go! Eighth grade was the beginning of my expanding school of life, where my world turned from two streets to half the city. And I explored all of it. All except Pine Hill. At least not yet.

Silence stretched between my sons and me as I watched them process what I'd just shared. We'd had dinner and cleaned up, and now were sitting in the living room where the story began, with me in an easy chair this time and both boys on the couch.

I knew this part of my story would especially impact them because of the closeness to their ages. Anthony was deep in thought; Alexander was staring at his socks on the coffee table in front of him, wiggling his big toes. He sighed loudly and spoke first.

"So . . . you *lied*?" he said, still staring at his feet. "To Grandma and Grandpa?"

"I did."

Alexander looked up at me. "Why, Pa?"

"Yeah," Anthony said. "I mean, it's one thing to lie about a small thing, but it sounds like you were putting yourself in danger. You get mad at me if I'm home five minutes late! You could have been shot or hurt badly!"

I couldn't help but chuckle. He was right. But I could tell by their expressions that my laughter wasn't welcome. I cleared my throat, buying time to find the right words.

"I was tortured by my behavior back then," I finally said. "I'd lay awake at night and worry that your grandma and grandpa would find out what I was doing and who I was with."

"Then why did you do it?" Alexander said. "Why didn't you just stay away from all the bad stuff?"

"It's not so simple," I replied. "That was my environment. It was all around me. I couldn't avoid it altogether. But still, the guilt of my life on the streets, and the things I was exposed to every day, destroyed me inside.

"Your grandparents, aunt, and uncles had sacrificed so much for me. I was the youngest, the only child who would get most of my education in the US, the kid who had been spared a lot of the hardest stuff in the family. Dan, Diana, and Dwayne had it rough. They were exposed to more than me; they went through the worst of it with Grandpa and Grandma. My parents saw me as the family's hope, and I knew that if they ever found out the secret life I was leading, they'd be devastated."

"When you say 'secret life,' do you mean the people you were around, the dealers and stuff? The fighting?" Anthony said. When I nodded in reply, he added, "Were you drinking and doing drugs?"

"No," I said. "Well, not yet."

My boys looked at each other. "What do you mean?" Anthony asked.

I breathed in sharply. Even though I had already decided to tell them about my past, and had talked with my wife at length about what I would say, I was in unknown parenting territory. I knew I had to be straight with my boys, because I was finished with the lies. I'd had enough lying throughout my childhood and early adulthood, and I wanted to be an honest father. A good dad and a role model they could emulate, just like my father. I needed them to learn from my mistakes and understand the logic behind my decisions and actions.

"I didn't start drinking until high school," I told them. "And I smoked marijuana too."

My boys' eyes grew about three sizes. "Marijuana!" Anthony said. "Pa, really?"

"Really," I said.

"But you always tell us to never do drugs!" Alexander said.

"I know, and that's because I've seen what drugs can do to people," I responded. "Look, you live in a different world. I know there are drugs at your schools and you're smart enough to avoid them. But you have to understand where I came from in Puerto Rico, and where I moved to in the United States. Marijuana, drinking . . . both of those seemed mild compared with the strung-out dealers I saw on the corners with gats in their coats, or the drug addicts passed out in backyards with syringes hanging from their arms.

"But even when I did start experimenting with that stuff—and I'll tell you more about high school soon—I always knew I didn't want to be like Dad when he drank. My hero, your grandpa, was a changed man, but I had watched what alcohol did to him, and what it did to my family. I was extra aware of what substances could do to my mind and body. I also knew I was already an angry kid. Sometimes I felt like there was molten lava bubbling deep inside of me, ready to explode. All I had ever seen of alcohol was that it seemed to cause explosions. Yelling, breaking stuff—that's what I'd seen growing up. I didn't want that. I was observant and smart enough to realize that even though the drugs and alcohol I was surrounded with were normal, I didn't want them to be my future or to dictate the course of my life."

Another silence stretched between us. Finally, Alexander spoke. "Were you scared? Of the streets, I mean."

I pictured my gentle, intellectual Alexander riding his bike through my old neighborhood next to his tall, athletic brother. Of course, their bikes weren't cheap-ass bikes like mine; they had Giant mountain bikes that collectively cost almost as much as my monthly mortgage.

"To be honest with you? No. I wasn't scared."

"Why not?" Anthony said.

"Because I had been groomed for that life." I thought back to Puerto Rico, and the violence and death that was normal but outside my awareness as a child. "My brothers had beaten me up since I was a kid. I was getting strong, and I could fight. I wasn't worried about the dealers because I knew most were cool with Dwayne, and even afraid of him. Dwayne would have my back if I needed him. I was just a kid, riding around on his bike, exploring an expanding world. Now, would I let you two do that? Probably not. But that was my coming of age."

My mind snapped back to the image of them riding through my old streets. I shook my head. They'd probably never make it there. I was grateful they wouldn't have to.

"So what happened next?" Anthony asked.

"High school," I said. "High school happened next. And football. But first, I had an experience that shook me to my core. It's about Grandma."

I took a drink from a glass of water sitting on the coffee table, and began to share one of the most terrifying experiences of my life.

One weekend afternoon toward the end of eighth grade, I was playing basketball at Delwin's house. It was a pick-up game among a few of us fellas with a rubber basketball and the milk crate affixed to a wooden light pole with nails and screws.

My mother interrupted our game with her angelic Spanish tinge: "David!" My friends stopped playing as I turned to see my mom standing near our game, a big smile on her face.

"*Bendición, Mami*," I replied. In traditional Latin American families, it's customary to ask one's parents for blessings.

"*Dios te bendiga*," my mother responded, God bless you. She walked over to me and asked if I wanted to take a ride to the store. Panting and sweaty, I politely asked her if I could stay with my friends. She replied with a simple, "*Claro que sí, pero ten mucho cuidado.*" Of course you can, but be careful.

All good! Basketball was on and my mother was on her way toward our triple-decker across the street. I figured she would be back later to tell me dinner was ready, and then I'd be grubbing on rice, beans, and *plátanos maduros*.

A few minutes into the game there was the sound of metal-on-metal crashing in the distance, loud enough to stop our basketball game two blocks away. Then silence. We waited, a half dozen kids in shirts and skins on the court, straining our eyes in the direction of the sound we'd heard. Several minutes passed as we walked to the edge of the sidewalk, squinting into the distance.

Suddenly, yelling. People streamed from out of houses and businesses. Delwin walked over to me and stood to my right. More yelling. Then a figure running toward Delwin's house, like an ant in the distance, screaming something.

"What did they say?" I asked Delwin.

"I don't know, man," Delwin said. "Let's go check it out."

I tossed the basketball I was holding to my friend Jamal, and Delwin and I walked down the street. The person was closer now, yelling louder. "David!" I heard it this time.

Without thinking, I started to sprint. Delwin ran behind me.

"David!" the person called. "Your mom!"

I started running faster, my legs strong from riding my bicycle, my body breaking into a cold sweat as I willed myself to run faster. Delwin was long gone, huffing far behind me, but I didn't care. I wasn't going to wait for him.

I needed to find my mom.

As I approached the person who'd yelled for me, I noticed it was a woman who lived across the street from us. She was wearing a waitressing apron, and her face was tight with concern.

"Where?" I hollered as I ran past her.

She pointed wildly. "The corner! Straight ahead."

As I ran toward the corner, I called out, "What happened?"

"An accident!" she bellowed after me. "There was a car accident!"

The shock of this information caused my legs to become lead beneath me, but I kept running, shaking off the dragging feeling of dread until my feet were feather-light. By the time I arrived at the corner, I was breathing heavily. I saw our car immediately.

My mother's old white Nissan station wagon was wrapped around a tall wooden electric pole like crushed aluminum tin foil in the form of the letter U. The airbag had deployed. The driver's side door was deeply dented. I ran over to the deformed vehicle and saw my mom inside, her figure pressed back by the airbag and door, unable to get out of the car.

"Mom!" I yelled so she could hear me through the closed driver's side window. I tried to open the door, then braced my feet on the ground and tried again. It wouldn't budge. "Mom, are you OK?"

"David," my mom said, her voice barely audible through the glass. She turned her eyes in my direction but her head didn't move, and I could see how tightly pinned she was in the car. She looked terrified.

"Mom, what happened?" I yelled. "Can you get out?" I knew the answer before I asked it. My mom was stuck. We needed firefighters and paramedics. Now.

"A car . . ." my mom's voice trailed off, then back to me. I could barely make out her words. "A car . . . I . . . don't know what happened . . . I don't know."

"Help! Someone help!" I began screaming. I tugged at the door again, yanking it violently. The impact of the other car had pinned her door shut. When it didn't move, I ran to the other side of the car. I saw that the pole had violently crushed the side of the car, and the deep bend of the vehicle had pressed my mother's body against the passenger's side door.

I ran back around and placed my hands on the glass of my mom's window and stared at her, shock ebbing over my body from my head to my toes and back again. Was her neck broken? Had she hit her head? What if she had broken her legs or arms, or her ribs?

"Did someone call an ambulance?" I yelled into the crowd that had gathered around my mom's car. No one answered. "Did someone call an ambulance!" I screamed.

A man's voice called out, "They're on their way."

I turned back to my mom. "Help is coming. Just hold still, OK?"

"*Ay*, David," Mom said. She sounded weak. "Pray with me."

I quickly glanced at the crowd around me, then shook off my self-consciousness. Mom needed me. Mom needed God. I closed my eyes as Mom prayed for the next few minutes, my hand on the window, tears falling down my face as I begged God to let my mom be OK. By the time the ambulance arrived, roaring into our block and slowly navigating through the parting crowd, Mom was peaceful. But as much as I wanted to feel the same peace, the image of my mom in the mangled car, unable to move, and maybe paralyzed or worse—I couldn't be at peace. Not until I knew she was going to be OK.

I stood to the side as the paramedics brought out the Jaws of Life, and I watched as they took their giant metal tool and cut away the car door. After assessing my mom for several minutes and strapping her head to a board to hold her neck still, they finally got her out of the car like a jigsaw puzzle and onto a stretcher, and wheeled the stretcher up the waiting ramp to the ambulance. I stood at the back of the emergency vehicle as they laid her down and hooked her up to a blood pressure cuff.

"Are you her son?" the paramedic said to me from inside the ambulance.

I nodded. The adrenaline had worn off, and I felt emotion sweep over me. "Is my mom OK?"

"She seems to be, but we need to take her to the hospital to be sure. She was in a pretty bad crash." He patted the bench next to him. "Why don't you ride down to the hospital with us? We can call a family member when we get there."

I climbed into the back of the ambulance and took a seat on the bench. I held Mom's hand and didn't speak the entire ride to the hospital. I felt struck dumb with shock, the trauma of seeing my mom in that car, the helpless feeling of not being able to get her out. As she laid on the stretcher, the paramedics checking her eyes and attaching a heart rate monitor to her finger, I prayed silently.

Please let her be OK, God, I begged. Please. I'll do anything.

I thought of all my mom had sacrificed back in Puerto Rico, and all the love and patience she'd given my dad, siblings, and me. The hard work to support us. The prayer meetings and volunteer work at church. Before this accident, Mom had seemed invincible, a pillar of strength and stability that was always there for me, for my family.

As the ambulance stopped at a stoplight, the paramedic sitting across from me said, "Just a few more minutes. How you doing, Ana?"

Mom gave a weak smile. "Blessed." But the pain etched in her expression said otherwise.

Suddenly, guilt washed over me. I thought of my life on the streets, the violence I was around every day, the danger I put myself in on a daily basis. I pictured my mom sitting next to my injured body—or worse, attending my funeral. I shivered visibly, and the paramedic next to me patted my shoulder.

Here was my mom, who had barely escaped death, who had given so much for me, and I was letting her down. Daily. She would never know about my other life.

I would make her proud. I would make her life better. I would fulfill all the hopes and dreams she had for me, and for our family.

It was like my life stopped in the back of that ambulance. And the only way it would start again was if my mom was all right. I stared at my strong *ma'i*, lying on that stretcher, fragile and weak. I wondered why God chose her that day, why she was the one driving the car that got hit and smashed into that pole, why she was on her way to the hospital right now to get X-rays and prodded by doctors. Why my devout mom? Why?

As we pulled into the hospital, I made a promise to God and to myself. Get her through this, and I'll take care of her for the rest of my life. Please, please. I promise. Just let her be OK.

The doors to the ambulance swung open, and I stepped out and to the side, watching my mom's stretcher get lifted out and wheeled into the hospital, with me trailing behind, praying the entire way to the emergency room.

An hour and a half later, I was sitting with my mom when Dad arrived with Diana. They rushed to Mom's bed. She was separated from the other patients with a curtain.

Dad took Mom's hand. "Are you OK? What happened?"

"How do you feel?" Diana asked. She looked like she'd been crying. Dad's face was twisted in worry.

Mom was sitting up in bed now. She'd been checked for a neck fracture and a concussion but had neither. She had deep bruising on her ribs and arms, and a headache, but otherwise she would be OK. She'd been cleared to go home and was waiting to be discharged. We'd go home that night. After recounting the accident to my dad and sister, she turned toward me.

"I'm just fine," she said, reaching out with her right hand to take mine. She looked at my dad and sister. "David took care of me."

I smiled at Mom, tears finally falling down my face even though I'd tried hard to keep them away. I didn't care if Dad and Diana saw me cry. I wasn't too proud to love my mom. I leaned in and wrapped my arms around Mom, and held her for several seconds.

"I'll always take care of you," I said quietly, so only she could hear. "Always."

Chapter 6

YOU BE YOU

The measure of who we are is
what we do with what we have.

—VINCE LOMBARDI

My mom's car accident overwhelmed my thoughts for weeks, even months. And while I knew the memory would stick with me forever, its crispness faded as adolescence marched on. But my promise to her and to God never did. I was committed to her, to my family, and to living my purpose for a better future.

Soon, I was about to start ninth grade at Lynn Classical High School. Classical was located right across from the Lynn Common, a ten-acre city park shaped like a shoe, commemorating the city as the shoemaking capital of the world during its heyday. It was also a block away from Marian Gardens, which was publicly subsidized housing, and Huss Court, a hot spot for drugs and shootings. A few blocks down was Commercial Street, a haven for liquor, drugs, and random shootings. At the time, Classical was unaccredited and viewed as the worst and roughest high school in the city. It was the school you did *not* want to send your kids to. The building resembled a nine-teenth-century jail and was attended largely by blacks, Latinos, and all types of immigrants and newcomers.

My first few weeks of school were fascinating as I navigated new relationships, new teachers, new school rules, new ethnicities, and new social norms. I was also introduced to American football.

As I navigated the hallways, I noticed that the football players were treated differently by most of the students. They were revered by the girls. Teachers seemed to treat them a bit differently too, almost with a sort of camaraderie. Some of the players—towering figures of athletic prowess—wore green jackets with a large capital letter C on the front and Classical High School in bold white letters on the back with a large ram head in the middle. I was intrigued! What made football even more interesting was that George, the Greek kid I hung out with in junior high school, had tried out for the team and made it. Every day after school, I would walk home with George and several new friends who played football: Rob, Nicio, Antoine, Armstead, Delwin, and a few upperclassmen. My house on Henry Avenue was smack in the middle of the walk to football practice. Since I didn't play football, I just listened to their conversations about practice, girls, the coaches, and playing in front of large crowds under Friday night lights. I wanted in!

After some encouragement from George and Rob, Delwin and I tried out for the football team and made it alongside a group of tough dudes from my neighborhood. Practice was brutal, and the guys were worse. It seemed like everything I did was a shaming opportunity for the coach or one of my teammates, and I wanted to punch the breath out of everyone. But I knew I had to keep my cool at practice. To my surprise, most of the players had played Pop Warner football and knew the rules of the sport, how to hit, and how to run plays. But not me. This was all new terrain, and I was lost. Really lost.

I became a punching bag on the field. Within a few weeks, I was sick of the humiliation and screaming. I felt exhausted physically and mentally, and I became even more angry.

One afternoon, I sat in the locker room after practice, my football helmet on the bench next to me, still sweating in my pads. My body ached with a deep, throbbing, spiking pain from the top of my skull to the bones in my feet. A searing sensation in my temple made me dizzy. My upper back felt like it had been punched, point-blank, over and over. I picked up a water bottle full of Gatorade and took a long drink, wincing at the pang in my jaw. The lemony-salty liquid slid down my throat, which somehow also hurt. Must be from all that yelling, I thought.

I sat there for a long time, maybe an hour, maybe ten minutes. The guys had already left for their public housing and Section 8 homes.

My teammates were all like me: tough, working-class kids from poor areas. And also not like me: many from broken families, parents who were drug addicts. Lots of them were failing school and getting into trouble themselves. Football, for all its pain and glory, spoke to them and kept them off the streets.

And for some reason it had also spoken to me.

But in that moment, I was ready to be done. It had been a few long weeks of what I could only describe as torture. Coach Williams yelled at us for hours a day, barking obscenities and insults, telling us we needed to work harder. He constantly screamed at me that I sucked and that I needed a lot of work. The late summer weather was in the eighties and humid, and with an extra twenty pounds of football equipment it felt like 100 degrees. The coach had us out for hours every day, running until we puked, hitting each other hard with our bodies until the toughest guys I knew looked like they were about to pass out.

Until that afternoon, I had been certain I wouldn't let Coach Williams get to me. I'd go to practice and take my hits. I'd get better. This was the only way.

I was one of just a few guys who had never played before. Lots of my teammates had been playing for years and carried a dull acceptance of the game in their tense shoulders and stone expressions. After each drill, each hit, they slumped over like hunchbacks, hands on their knees catching their breaths. But then coach would scream at us to stop being weak, and get back at the starting line, let's do that again. We'd jog our tired bodies back to do it all over again, him screaming, me fighting every instinct within myself to hit him straight in the mouth.

Coach knew I had never played, and yet nobody took the time to train me on how to hit or how to take a hit. I'd go home with concussions and large, dark bruises. But I didn't say anything; I didn't want Coach to know he was getting to me. My anger was growing, and I was channeling it to get better at football.

My teammates were no better than the coach. They took advantage of my lack of experience. Sometimes, when I'd get knocked down, guys would surround me and hit me as I tried to stand, laughing as they knocked me down again. Coach said nothing. It was like he approved—like I should be punished for sucking at football. Everything inside of me wanted to lay each of them down, but I knew I couldn't. Not on the field. Not in front of Coach. It was almost like an unspoken rule that accepting my teammates' blows was the way to get better at football and earn his respect.

Each day, we ran. We tackled. We practiced plays over and over again in the heat and humidity, as the sweat drenched through our pads and jerseys and we felt light-headed. Several times each practice, I felt like I was going to pass out, the blackness creeping across my vision, but I would blink quickly and start jogging again, fighting back to consciousness. The worst were Thursdays, when Coach Williams would run a drill called "bull in the ring." He'd gather us into formation, a big ring of guys, all looking scared and angry.

Sitting in the locker room, my back involuntarily spasmed thinking about it. We had run the drill that afternoon, and my number had been called third. When Coach called me, I felt my body tighten, bile running its way up my throat. I hesitated a half second, and then strode into the middle of the circle confidently, my chin high, not wanting anyone to notice my fear. As soon as I got to the middle, I got into my ready stance: knees bent, arms suspended in front of me, ears alert, eyes scanning. I was like a gazelle being hunted by a ring of tigers, and I was ready.

"Martinez!" Coach bellowed.

Movement twitched over my right shoulder, and even though I was quick to move, I felt my teammate's body crash into mine, a sharp pain on my spine and shoulder, knocking me to the ground. He was on top of me, and as soon as he stood, I scrambled up quickly and resumed my place in the middle of the circle.

"Brown!"

I knew where Armstead Brown was standing this time, and I saw him move just in front of me and to my left, so I met him head on at full speed. We crashed together, our helmets hitting, my head dizzying, and we fell into a heap, neither of us victorious. We jumped up, Brown back to the circle, me back to the middle.

"Williams!"

"Gutierrez!"

"Jones!"

"Smith!"

The names kept coming, over and over, one by one for what seemed like eternity, until I was finally relieved of the middle. Everything in my body cried to limp out to the bench and lie down, but I knew better. I jogged to the edge of the circle as another teammate jogged to the center, and I waited for my name to be called, for me to be the one to annihilate him like he'd annihilated me.

After practice, as all my teammates walked toward the locker room to shower and change, Coach Williams barked my name across the field. He stood on the sidelines with his clipboard, sweat rings under his armpits and a dark, sweaty V on the chest of his gray shirt.

I ran over to him. "Yes, Coach?" I braced myself, because I knew what was coming. Deep inside I hoped this time would be different. Maybe he'd have something constructive to say, or even tell me I did a good job today.

"You suck, Morales!" he screamed. His eyes flared and spittle hit my nose.

I said nothing as he went on: I'd done terrible at practice, I needed to toughen up, I'd never make it on the field during a game unless I got better. Man up or get out.

I stood there, listening, my face stone. I knew better than to ask questions or argue. We were expected to take it. If we'd been on the streets, I'd have knocked him out a long time ago. But there on the field, I held my anger down, letting him scream.

"You got it?" he finally said. I nodded as he added, "Get out of my face."

Now, as I sat in the locker room, hunched over with my elbows on my knees, hands clasped, and head down, I remembered the pain of each hit during practice and the way I'd taken my teammate Pat out. I'd heard a little "oomph" escape from his lips, like I'd really hurt him. It felt different attacking on the field than when I was fighting on the streets. On the streets, there was a reason we were hurting each other. Someone had said or done something. It was on because someone had messed up. We were testing our manhood, defending our names and sorting out the street hierarchy. We were learning who we could trust and who would just start trouble.

Here, we were hitting each other over and over as Coach watched from the sidelines, seeming to enjoy the spectacle.

I was exhausted. I had bruises everywhere. My neck was sore, my legs were sore.

Screw this, I thought. I want out.

I felt something warm and wet slide down my face and drop onto my right hand. I lifted my head to glance around the locker room once more and held my breath to listen, but no one was there. When I was sure I was alone, I let the rest of my tears out, crying so hard my shoulders shook. I wiped a dirty hand across both cheeks and forced myself to breathe. Just then, I heard footsteps. My body tensed. My breath quickened. I didn't want to be alone with the coach, or for him to know I'd been crying.

I tugged my jersey up to wipe my face again, stood, and opened my locker, pretending like I was getting my things together to leave.

"What are you doing, Morales?" It was Coach Alicudo, the assistant coach for varsity football.

"Nothing, I'm good," I said. "Just leaving." My throat burned as I spoke.

He walked over to the bench near me, sat down, and motioned for me to sit next to him.

"Were you crying?"

"No," I said, but we both knew I had been. "I'm just tired."

"Look at me," he said. When I met his eyes, he went on. "You're going to be a killer. I can see it. Just stick with it. I'm telling you, Morales. You haven't passed out yet. You haven't quit. You haven't asked for help. You haven't told the freshman coach you're hurt or intimidated. I'm telling you, you've got football in you."

His words hovered over me as he spoke. I sat up straighter. "Are you serious?"

"You've got it in you, man. Stick with it. You're going to be a machine. Football is about toughness and heart. You have that. We have to teach you the rest."

I looked at Coach Alicudo, and he stared squarely back at me. His hulking six-foot-three frame overpowered the room. He was 250 pounds of pure muscle, a football star in his day. If he said I could do it, that I could become great at football, I believed him. Finally, he nodded and stood.

"I'll be watching you," he said, slapping a locker door shut on his way out.

The sound of the slamming locker reverberated through my ears like a soundtrack. Wow, I thought. Cool. Coach Alicudo thinks I have it in me.

I sat there for a long time, but I didn't cry anymore. Instead, I was forming a plan. I wouldn't let Coach Williams win. I wouldn't let other kids on the team know they'd gotten to me. I would prove to everyone that I could be an incredible football player. I finally stood, removed my drenched pads, and hung them in my locker along with my helmet.

Monday, I thought. I will show them. I will show up bigger, stronger, and meaner. I got this. It may take me longer, but I got this.

I walked out of the locker room with a deep rut of anger seared into my shoulder. But also, a sense of hope and a renewed interest in winning.

Anthony was stretched out on the couch, and Alexander was lying on the floor with a pillow under his head. It was late, and I knew I needed to wrap up for the night. I sat up, readying to head upstairs.

"We should get to bed," I said.

Alexander yawned. "Yeah, I'm about to fall asleep."

"Well, thanks," I teased.

"Not because of your story, Pa," he said with a laugh. As he sat up, I grabbed a throw pillow off the easy chair I'd been sitting on, and reached across the coffee table to playfully hit him. He dodged my second attempt.

"Football at your school sounds a lot rougher than at mine," Anthony said as he pushed himself off the couch.

I shook my head, thinking of those practices, remembering the physical and emotional pain. My boys would never know what that was like. For the first years of their life, I thought I had to teach that kind of toughness to them. I falsely believed that to eventually be strong men, they had to know what it was like to fight, to be fierce, to hit first. That they had to feel physical pain. But I was learning to be a different kind of dad now.

"Football isn't like that in most places anymore," I said. "At least in the United States."

"Were you scared?" Alexander said.

I looked at him and nodded. "You know, I was. I wouldn't have admitted it to anyone at the time, but I was. Not really scared physically. I knew I could handle myself. But scared of failing, and scared of showing weakness. Afraid of what others would say if I showed vulnerability. Funny, right?"

Alexander nodded. "But . . . you were beat up, basically. Every day."

"That's right. And that angered me for a long time."

"What do you mean?" Anthony asked.

"At school, if I saw people get made fun of, it lit me up because I experienced it on the field. I had anger issues for a long time. Even when you guys were little."

"Mom said you choked a guy once at a stoplight," Alexander said.

"I did. I reacted like that more than once. He was OK, but I still remember the fear in his eyes when I opened his door and reached in. I was haunted by anger. It followed me around, ready to burst out of me at any moment. It was like I had a torch inside of me, and in half a second I could go from fine to burning with fire.

"A lot of it stemmed from my struggles with perceived poverty and my freshman year of football. Thanks to Jesus, I am saved and am no longer that man, but for a long time, I was angry. I took a beating, not just on my body but inside of me too."

Anthony looked thoughtful as he asked, "So what changed? You're not like that anymore."

"I didn't fully change until I was an adult," I said. "Until after I became your dad. Becoming a better person, father, and husband would take years, and more importantly, God, to remake me, to save me, to change my heart and mindset. But that's a story for another time. Right now, I want you to know about the mistakes and lessons I learned growing up."

Anthony yawned this time, and I did too. "All right, you two. Let's head to bed."

The three of us walked upstairs, where I knew my wife was waiting for me. The next morning, I'd pick the story back up on our drive to church, assuming the boys weren't sick of hearing it by now. I yawned again as Anthony and Alexander called goodnight and shut off their lights.

Sticking it out in football paid off. I was losing more weight, gaining confidence, and getting more popular. And when it came to girls, it didn't hurt to be a football player either.

One afternoon toward the end of football season, I swaggered into the cafeteria wearing new Giorgio Brutini shoes, no-name stone-washed jeans, and a shiny silver button-up shirt from Ann & Hope, a department store where Mom would buy me clothes on layaway. My hair was combed up and back so I had a nice, smooth wave of hair, with a thick layer of Alberto VO5 gel, the same gel my father used, holding it in place. I scanned the cafeteria for the football table, looking for my teammates. I couldn't wait to talk to them about our win the night before.

I felt amazing in my new, flashy clothes like I'd seen the other Latino kids wearing. When I showed up, I *showed up*. But as great as I felt, the truth was that Mom had bought all these new clothes for me on her credit card and on layaway. Looking back, I now understand what a 22 percent interest rate can do to a person's finances, but back then, all I knew was Mom slapped down the plastic for me almost anytime I asked. I didn't ask much, but when I did, I knew she'd get it for me. I thought back to the JCPenney counter, with my pile of five pairs of pants and six brand new shirts, plus my $60 Giorgio Brutini shoes. I felt like a Puerto Rican rock star when I saw the triple-digit number on the cash register. It was a far cry from my sister's hand-me-down underwear and Dwayne's old shirts. I had no idea what it meant for

Mom financially to put the items on her card. I just knew that I was finally getting some new clothes, so my family must be good. And I was looking great.

The clothes were just one sign of something that was becoming clear to me: there was no obstacle when it came to my role in our family. I was the baby, the chosen one who would lift up the Morales name and do great things. My mom looked for every opportunity to support me, whether it was buying me new clothes or encouraging a hobby or sport. In spite of my parents struggling to make ends meet, they always made sure I was taken care of, and I had what I needed and wanted.

To my parents, I was special. I was going to be somebody. I was, in Mom's words, a calling from God.

As I spotted my teammates and strode across the cafeteria, head lifted, holding my government-subsidized free lunch tray, I thought of my mom. Every day since I was a kid, I'd heard from her: You're a conqueror, David. You have no idea how special you are. You are going to do great things.

But was I? And would I? Everyone in the family—Dad, Mom, Diana, Dan, Dwayne—had sacrificed. They had suffered. They'd struggled through my dad's alcoholism. They'd survived the violence and danger of Puerto Rico. They'd overcome the disruption of moving countries twice, and sacrificed years of their lives to make sure our family had a chance. I was the only one—the *only one*—whose suffering had been minimal, and in their eyes, almost nonexistent. To them, I was the chosen younger brother. I had the adoration of my family because I was the one who would help us.

Part of me rejected my role. I wanted to run away. I wanted to be a normal kid who played football and dated girls. I didn't want the burden of making my family's sacrifice worth it.

It was a lot of pressure. Man, was it a lot of pressure.

I shook away my thoughts as I walked up to the table where the guys sat, talking over each other and laughing. A couple of girls sat on the tabletop at one end; two guys slid over at the other end of the table to let me in. Voices cascaded toward me. A clap on the back.

"Yo, Morales."

"What's up, man?"

"Your play last night, bro. *Unreal*."

I laughed as I sat down. I took a bite of cheeseburger and dipped a fry in the generous portion of ketchup I'd dispensed onto my plate. We talked about the game, what was going on that weekend, and what Coach would do if we lost the next game. We agreed: we didn't want to find out.

When I was finished eating, I stood up. "See you guys," I said. They knew the drill. I come, I eat, I leave. Same every day.

From the football table, I floated to the other tables. Like most high schools, our lunch hall had specific tables where groups of kids sat. There were two entrances to the cafeteria, one that led to the gym, and the main entrance with two large green doors that swung open. The Latino kids sat together at two tables near the gym; the special needs kids sat over by the large windows that overlooked the parking lot behind the school; the social outcasts sat in the back of the cafeteria; the cool kids sat to the right of the main doors, near the front; and then a bunch of random stragglers sat at a mish-mash of tables toward the back edge, close to the outcasts.

I spent a lot of time moving between tables, talking with the Latino kids and the outcasts and everyone else. The Latino kids would usually call me a sellout for going to the white kids' tables. But I knew the white guys from football, and I knew the black guys and other kids on the team too. I didn't care about the color of people's skin or their background. My happy place was stopping at all the tables—moving around throughout the entire lunch period. And always asking different people for a quarter so I could gather enough to buy myself a cheeseburger, a warm cookie, or an ice cream sandwich.

"Hey, you got a quarter?" I'd ask the jocks.

"What have you got there, a quarter?" I'd ask the girls from Pine Hill. One of them would almost always giggle and hand me the twenty-five cents I was after.

"Got a quarter, man?" I'd ask my football teammates, to which I'd always get a laugh and a head shake. They didn't have quarters either.

But still, I was usually able to scrounge up a couple of bucks every lunch hour, enough to buy a cheeseburger or a piece of pizza and a cookie.

The other goal at lunch? Talk to the girls. There were a bunch of cute girls in my high school: Natalie and Ive, and also Kristen, Andrea, Jessica, and Dolly. There were girls at the Latino table I'd always talk to, and the Pine Hill girls, and some other white girls I used to try to talk to as well, including a cute girl name Rachel. I didn't have a girlfriend and didn't want one. But I had a lot of friends.

I focused on growing my social capital by watching what worked and what didn't, and popularity became a game. A game I was winning.

On the outside, other kids saw me as Mr. Confident. I'd strut into school and flash smiles at the girls and look teachers in the eyes. But on the inside, I still struggled with self-confidence. At home, I'd stand in front of the mirror, smoothing my hair for the hundredth time. I would leave school and head back home, walking past the strung-out used-to-be's, and remember—as if I could forget—that I was poor, and I was surrounded by people who were poor, and that most of the kids who grew up around me never made it out. I would not be one of them.

At home, I also picked up a secret hobby most would not know about until much later: singing and collecting records. Singing at church and in my bedroom was one of my escapes and one of the few places where I was free to dream of popularity and freedom of expression. I spent nearly every night of my high school life singing, learning harmony from old doo-wop records that my father used to listen to. I also memorized a ton of oldies by listening to Little Walter, a radio personality on Oldies 103.3 FM. I would imagine what it was like to sing on the street corners in the 1950s when groups like The Flamingos, The Robins, The Platters, The Five Keys, and The Drifters ruled the airwaves.

My quest for popularity compensated for the deep insecurity I felt. I knew my life journey would be harder and longer than the white kids from Pine Hill, and I recognized that I would have to show up bigger, badder, and bolder than any of them if I was going to have a different future. If I was going to get out.

I melded and molded, and tried to fit in while standing out and aiming to be better. Shape-shifting all the time began to eat at me. Deep within my gut, I began to wonder who I really was and what in the world I was actually going to do to get off that block and do something with my life. Mom said I could make it. That I could be somebody. Was she right? Or like the guys who came before me—hundreds of thousands, even millions, of them—would I continue on the path of poverty? Would I be another statistic, breaking my back every day for minimum wage at a burger joint? Or worse, strung out or dead?

No. I wouldn't. I would get out. I had to. God, I had to.

Being popular was my way out. If I was king, nobody could touch me, and people would look up to me instead of down on me. If I could wow them with my personality, maybe they wouldn't notice that I didn't have as nice of stuff or that I went home to the bad side of town. I would be step-in-step with the kids who had money. But my effort to be cool blew up in my face one afternoon in ninth grade.

I was at Delwin's house with our two friends Jamal and Seneca. Somebody had clippers. Somebody else had the bright idea to cut our hair all the same.

The style at the time was inspired by urban hip-hop culture: hair shaved on the sides, with lines cut into the shave, the top of the hair trimmed short and left wavy or curly. We took turns with the clippers: I did Delwin's hair, Seneca did Jamal's, Delwin did Seneca's, Jamal did mine. As I sat in front of the mirror, Jamal standing behind me, I was giddy at the thought of walking into school the next day, looking cool with the guys. At the time, hip-hop groups like N.W.A., Ice Cube, and Dr. Dre were all over the airwaves and they were gangsta' cool. My smooth, wavy hair would look awesome with this new cut. I imagined all the girls looking at me, from all the tables across the lunchroom, whispering, "Look at D. Love." I pictured my popularity skyrocketing and waving at kids like a celebrity as I sauntered through the halls.

Jamal shaved the sides of my head but didn't touch the top. He cut lines into the sides. It took him a long time to even out the cut, and when he was done, I turned side to side, admiring my new hairstyle. Then the four of us stood in front of the bathroom mirror, looking at our hair. We did mock album poses: N.W.A., Ice Cube, Boyz II Men. We couldn't wait to walk through school the next day.

It was getting dark, my signal to head home for dinner, so I said goodbye to the guys and walked across the street to my crib. I knew

Mom would be home but not Dad. When I walked in, Mom was in the kitchen. I smelled dinner: *chuletas* and rice. Suddenly, I was ravenous. Being cool worked up an appetite.

"What happened to your hair?" she asked, swatting my hand away as I tried to reach over her to steal some pork and protect my haircut.

"Do you like it?" I said, snatching a piece of meat and popping it in my mouth.

She tsked. "David, dinner isn't ready yet. Go wash up."

"My hair, Mom. What do you think?"

"I think you're handsome no matter what you do to your hair."

I laughed and walked to the bathroom to wash my hands as instructed. When I came back out, Dad had just arrived. He looked worn out from another long day on the job. His shoulders slumped. His button-up logo shirt had a dirt stain across the front. He had just set his lunchbox next to the kitchen sink when he noticed me—and then my hair.

"What the hell is that?" he asked.

I ran my hand up and down the newly shaven back of my head. "It's the new style."

"What's the style?"

"This haircut, *Papi*. Everyone's doing it."

"Everyone's doing it, huh?"

"It's cool."

"It's cool?"

"Yeah."

"OK." But I could tell it wasn't OK. His face had drawn tight, his eyebrows arched dangerously inward. It was the same face I'd seen when I'd stolen the milk out of the back of the truck in seventh grade. As Dad stomped past me toward the bathroom, I waited in the kitchen. Mom and I made eye contact and then she looked away, pretending to be preoccupied with dinner. I heard her mutter something about calling Diana to see how work was going at the new job Mom had just helped her land at the school department.

"David!" I heard Dad holler from the bathroom.

I walked down the hallway. When I arrived at the bathroom, I noticed Dad had clippers in his hands.

"Get in here," he said. "Sit down." He pointed toward the toilet.

"What are you going to do?"

"We're going to get rid of that haircut."

My hand reflexively went to my hair. "What? Why?"

"I said sit down." He flicked on the clippers. As I reluctantly sat, he began shaving my head.

"You be you," he said as he ran the clippers over my scalp. "You be you, not anyone else. You're not a follower, you're a leader. And if you have to stand by yourself alone, you do it, but you don't follow people or fads."

He adjusted the clipper length to the lowest setting and shaved the sides of my head. I could tell he was taking his time, even though he was angry.

"You're David Morales," he went on. "You're not David Black, David Dominican, David White. You're you." He flipped off the clippers and the buzzing stopped. He set the clippers down and walked out without another word. I sat there for several minutes, covered in hair and embarrassment. Finally, I stood, brushed the hair off my shirt, and walked into the kitchen to get the broom. I returned to the bathroom and swept up my hair slowly, thinking about school the next day and what I'd tell the guys.

Dad's words rang through my thoughts. What kind of person did I want to be? I didn't want to be a follower. I wanted to be a leader. I wanted to be the one setting the trends, not following them.

We ate dinner in silence that night. When I had finished, Mom stood and kissed me on the top of the head.

"Go do your homework," she said. "I'll do the dishes."

Dad didn't say a word as I retreated to my bedroom. I sat on the bed, my books strewn across my mattress, running my hand over my hair.

You be you. Got it, Dad, I thought. Point made. That was a life lesson I would never forget.

As we pulled into the church parking lot, I glanced in the rearview mirror at Anthony and Alexander. Both boys were subconsciously running their hands over their own hair. My wife gave me a knowing smile as she unbuckled her seatbelt and reached down for her purse.

"So Grandpa just shaved your head?" Alexander finally said.

"Yep. I was nearly bald. Dan called it a high and tight, like your Grandpa used to have in the Navy."

"And . . . what did your friends say when you went to school the next day?" Anthony asked.

"They asked me what the hell happened to my hair," I said, laughing.

In the rearview mirror, I saw Alexander and Anthony grin at each other as they unbuckled their seatbelts.

Anthony leaned forward. "I'd be so mad if you did that to me," Anthony said.

"I think I was too shocked to be mad," I replied. "And maybe Grandpa could have handled it better . . . but I learned an important lesson that day. It stuck with me. Even now, I remember the feeling of his words hitting me as he shaved my head, 'You be you.'"

I turned in my seat to look at them. "There are going to be a lot of times in your life where it's easier to blend in. You're going to be tempted to follow the crowd, to be cool, to fit in. But you weren't born to blend—you were born to be bold. You were born to lead and make a positive impact on others. Everyone is born that way. The problem is, some of us get lost along the way or cave to peer pressure. Don't let that happen to you. You were both born to lead and thrive."

Both of my sons were quiet. Usually these lesson-driven monologues get an eye roll. But that day, I could see they were listening.

"I get it, Pa," Anthony said. "Be myself."

"Lead, don't follow," Alexander added.

I nodded and smiled. "And I didn't even have to shave your heads to teach you that." I opened my door. "Let's head inside."

"Can we hear the rest after?" Anthony asked.

"You bet," I said.

We got out of the truck, and I grabbed my guitar from the back seat, pushed the button on my keys to lock the doors, and took my wife's hand, giving it a tight squeeze as we walked toward the church.

Chapter 7

GRIT MACHINE DNA

People don't have to believe what you say,
they have to believe what you do.

COACH DAVID DEMPSEY

The rest of ninth grade was about exploration. At home, I was still the apple of Mom's eye, the golden child, the one who would lift our family's name. I was performing in school, in large part because my mom was extremely aggressive about the fact that I had to be smart, had to excel in school, had to do better for our family. I learned quickly that she had all sorts of eyes watching me during the day—a perk of her job in the school system—and teachers and school staff reporting back to her if I did something out of line. She told me every day that I was intelligent and talented, and I was chosen by God. I wanted to show her I could be the David I needed to be for our family.

But on the streets, and in spite of the promise I'd made to God, I was still hanging with a tough crowd, fighting, and drinking. Nearly all my friends were from single-parent homes—their moms or dads had left long ago—and had a sibling or cousin who was dealing drugs, drinking heavily, and sometimes even involved in violent crime. While my brother Dwayne was in rough crowds and still home infrequently, Dad's commitment to work stabilized our family and set an example for me of what a strong, dedicated, principled family man and father represented.

Yet even with Dad's positive example, by now I was drinking. All around me were older guys saying, "Hey, give me five bucks, I'll get you a case," and my younger friends and I started listening to them. My curfew had extended to 10 p.m. by the end of my freshman year, and I took full advantage, staying out with my friends until I had to be home.

Even though I desperately wanted to succeed in school and life, I felt an invisible wall holding me back. I'd walk to school, or ride my bike around Lynn on the weekends, and pass by the used-to-be's. They were my constant visual reminder of what I didn't want for myself, and how I wouldn't end up. These guys had been heroes to us kids four or five years back, incredible athletes with promise of fame and fortune, or at least it seemed that way to us. We used to admire these dudes—and yet there they were, cracked out or drunk, bumming around at the Lynn Common or at basketball parks. They had beer guts, some wore dirty baseball caps, and they had torn baggy pants crawling down their butt cheeks. It took everything in me not to stare at their condition. On the outside they looked rough, mean, high. But inside, I knew they were in pain and lost.

What the hell happened to you? I'd wonder when I passed one of them on the streets. You used to be a star running back. You were the guy we looked up to.

George and Delwin also noticed how the used-to-be's fell from glory, and the three of us began to have long conversations about the kind of futures we wanted for ourselves. We saw what was happening to them and knew we never wanted to be like that. The sight of these former local superstars, now addicted and hanging out on street corners . . . well, it was all we needed to keep us in check. We saw who and what we didn't want to become.

But our environment wasn't exactly designed to help us succeed.

My freshman year was focused on making sure I set a precedent, that I remained cool. I needed to be seen as one of the tough guys but also one of the good guys. I had to emerge from high school victorious.

Ninth grade. That was a year of exposure, of testing boundaries, of noticing who I didn't want to become, of experiencing humiliation on the field, of seeing my mother's proud face and feeling shame at my behavior when she wasn't looking. Ninth grade was a departure from my boyhood years.

In tenth grade, I came into my own. I became a young man living in multiple worlds: Puerto Rican at home, football player, student, singer at church, loyal friend to my fellas.

My boys were quiet in the back seat, taking in the story of me as a kid about their age. We had finished church and decided to go on a drive to Lynn Beach. As tall trees whirred by, I tried to see the story I was sharing through their eyes.

I knew the picture I was painting of myself—the popular, angry guy—conflicted with the dad before them today. Because I was different. I had changed. God had changed me. I also remembered early in their childhood when I'd still been that angry guy, the one who believed toughness was the only way to survive, the dad who pushed his kids to man up, even as little children. I'd worried about them, especially Anthony, who in his own way was very much like me—tenderhearted with fierce intensity.

As I stared out the windshield and waited for their questions, I thanked God for the man I'd become, a man who understood better than nearly anyone on the planet just how vicious anger and poverty could be, how it could permeate your soul, how it could destroy you. Of course, I hadn't gotten to that point of the story yet. Soon.

"You seemed so . . . cool," Anthony said. He laughed as he added, "Puerto Rican cool."

"Yeah, the slicked-back hair and shiny shirts, Pa," Alexander added. "I can see it."

"I felt cool. Like I owned that high school," I said. "Even as a ninth-grader. In tenth grade, even more. But the truth is, I was always trying to be accepted."

"What do you mean?" Alexander asked.

I considered my words carefully. How could I explain it to them in a way they'd understand, in a way that might resonate? "I think on the outside I was building myself into an adaptable machine. I was trying to be as good looking as I could be, as strong as I could be . . . you know, all that teenage stuff. But deep down, I was insecure, frankly. I wanted to be accepted, and I yearned to be more than I was.

"I didn't realize all the students around me, even the Pine Hill kids, felt the same way. They wanted to fit in just like me. Only in the environment I was in, it was a different kind of fitting in. At your guys' schools, it's about who has the latest phone and wears the coolest brands, right?"

"Yeah, like when Billy got the new iPhone, everyone thought he was so cool," Anthony said. He rolled his eyes. "It's stupid. Who cares about cell phones?"

"Exactly," I replied. "Back then, and in my environment, I was navigating several worlds. I was navigating the streets, where I needed to show I was tough, and show up with aggression and . . . well, *big-ness*, all the time. I had to be on, constantly.

"At school, there were all kinds of different socioeconomic levels, and when I was around the wealthy white kids, I projected confidence to level myself with them. I was poor, but I could still be popular." I studied my sons' faces in the rearview mirror to see if they understood. As I pulled up to a stop sign and saw no traffic around, I held my foot on the brake and turned to look at both of them. "I think I had that mindset for a long time. I was always trying to be accepted, and I think part of it was the insecurity of my sixth- and seventh-grade years when I was always being made fun of by the girls. I wanted to make sure that never happened again."

I turned back around and checked for traffic before driving.

"I don't get it," Alexander said. He was staring out the window. "When I'm feeling uncool or something, I'm . . . quiet. You know? I don't talk. If you were really feeling that way, if you were feeling self-conscious, how did you act so confident?"

"I was insecure," I said. "But I was also proud, and I was taught by your *abuela* and *abuelo* that the Morales name is a proud name. They taught my brothers, sister, and me that the Moraleses came from warriors and workers. Even though I felt insecure, I wouldn't show it, and I had to make sure I was cool to everybody. That was important to me." I paused and let a grin stretch across my face. "On the outside, I swaggered; on the inside, I staggered."

"Pa, really?" Anthony said, rolling his eyes at my dad joke. Both of them couldn't help smiling at my terrible attempt at humor.

"I was insecure, and let me tell you, my friends used to laugh at my confidence. They'd say, 'Oh, here he comes, Mr. D. Love himself,' but deep down I wasn't a confident guy at all."

I measured my next words, really wanting Alexander and Anthony to hear what I had to say.

"I think most men wrestle with insecurity. Each one of us expresses ourselves differently, but we just try to hide from it. And a lot of young men don't have a role model to tell them, 'It's OK, man. You don't have to be perfect. Not everybody's going to like you.' But what matters most is that you understand that God made you unique and that He has a plan for you. Your job is to seek Him, treat others with respect and kindness, prepare yourself to do better, and give back to others in need. The more you give to others, the more God blesses you.

"I didn't learn that until I was an adult. In Latino culture, especially, if you show weakness, you're not a man. It's horrific, and it destroys kids. I grew up with that chip on my shoulder, and I became really good at hiding behind my anger and popularity."

My lane was clear and there was a wide shoulder, so I pulled the car over and unbuckled my seatbelt. I turned around in my seat to face them completely. I met my wife's eyes then surveyed my sons, making sure they were hearing me. I needed them to hear me.

"Look, guys. Men typically aren't taught to love. They aren't taught to show emotions to their children. Your *abuelo* never did. My dad never told me he loved me until my senior year in high school, and he only said it because I said it to him first."

"He never said he loved you?" Alexander looked confused. "But he says it to me all the time!"

Anthony nodded. "Yeah, Grandpa's an old softy now."

"He's changed a lot," my wife said.

"Sounds like it," Anthony said.

I reached out and took my wife's hand. I met Anthony's eyes, then Alexander's. They were growing so fast, becoming young men before my eyes. These days, I didn't get many opportunities like this, when I could tell they were really listening. Their world is full of social media, sports, friends, and school. There, in that car, I needed to say something that was on my heart. I took a deep breath, feeling emotion claw at my throat and threaten to spill out of my eyes.

"Boys, please listen," I began. "You are loved. You are chosen. We are deeply proud of who you are becoming: strong, smart, loving men. Regardless of your achievements, your skin color, your clothes, your ethnic heritage, we love you both.

"You don't have to be perfect. Not everybody's going to like you and you're going to make mistakes." I paused and leaned farther forward. "And guys, if there is anything you remember about this conversation it's this: one, God is real and He's always with you; two, your family always comes first—always; and three, your identity is not based on people's opinions of you. Your identity is given to you by God. Trust in *His* word always. We love you a ton—and no matter what, no matter the circumstances, we're here for you."

I let my words hang in the air for several minutes before I turned around, put the car into drive, and continued my story, this time in sophomore year of high school.

Sophomore year, like the year before, was about three main things: school, girls, and football. I was riding high on popularity as I got playing time in varsity football.

One day, the morning before a big game, I woke up the sickest I'd ever felt. I laid in bed, shivering under the covers as my mom took my temperature: 103. I stayed home from school, sleeping on and off all morning and early afternoon. I was weak, exhausted, and barely even able to eat the chicken soup my mom had made me that day.

As I lay there, too weak to get up and walk to the living room to watch TV, I looked around my room. We had moved to a small condominium my parents rented from a family friend at 404 Broadway, on the nice side of town. It had been weeks since we'd seen Dwayne. I wasn't sure where he was living, but I knew he was having a hard time—homeless, in a rough crowd. My mom desperately wanted him home, and worried over him constantly, but Dwayne was doing his own thing. He'd show up every once in a while; we'd play tennis in the back court of the apartment complex so I could work on my footwork and speed. But most of the time, it was just me in a small bedroom that had once been stuffed with three boys sleeping on the floor in Puerto Rico. Where I'd listened to my brothers sleeping and wondered what kind of lives we'd have when we were adults. Where I'd felt comforted by the proximity of their big bodies, knowing nobody could mess with the three of us.

Now it was just me, in a room decorated with posters of blues musicians and superheroes like Wolverine, with clothes strewn on the floor and a jar of hair gel on my dresser, a drawer stuck open. Where was Dwayne? I wondered. Here we were, living in a nice condominium in the good part of town, and my brothers weren't there to experience it with me. Diana either. She had her own life now; she was no longer around to mother me every day.

Suddenly, I missed Diana. Back in Puerto Rico, Diana was the one who cared for me when I was sick. She was the one who'd miss school to stay with me while our parents worked.

My fever swept across my body, chills coursing through me, and I shook, pulling the covers up over my head to block out daylight and warm my body. I drifted off and woke up to a soft knock on my door. When I pulled the comforter from my head, I saw that the sun had stretched its long rays across my bedroom. Mom was standing at the door with a cordless phone in her hands.

"David, it's Coach Dempsey."

My eyes snapped open, and I sat up, my head pounding. Dempsey was the varsity coach. Why was he calling me at home?

Mom handed me the phone. "Hi, Coach," I said, my voice gravelly.

"Morales. Why weren't you at practice today?"

My chills returned but not from sickness. "Coach, my mom called the school. I'm sick."

"How sick?"

"I can't get out of bed," I said.

"Is that it?"

"I have a fever. It's 103."

Silence echoed across the line for several seconds. "Look, Morales, we need you tomorrow. At the game against Beverly. You're our starting defensive tackle."

I glanced at my mom, who was still standing next to my bed. "I don't think I'm going to make it, Coach."

"Morales. I'm telling you we need you."

"I don't think I can." My voice was almost a whisper now. I felt ashamed of my sickness, my weakness. I cleared my throat. "I want to, Coach. But I can't even get out of bed."

The silence was back. I waited, my heavy breathing the only sound between us. Finally, he spoke. "Get some orange juice and fluids. Rest up."

"I will, Coach."

I pressed the off button and handed the phone back to my mom. She felt my forehead with the back of her hand, then picked up the empty water glass next to my bed to refill. "David, *bendito*, you're burning up. There's no way you can play a football game."

I smiled at my mom, grateful she was there. Then I scooted back down into my bed and laid my head on my pillow, feeling too sick to talk anymore. I was sweaty and cold, and spent the rest of the evening and night drifting in and out of sleep.

The next morning, I woke to the sound of voices in the living room: three men and my mother. Still weak, I propped myself up on my elbow to listen, casting a glance at my alarm clock: 8:00 a.m. I heard footsteps approaching my bedroom, and then my door swung open to reveal two massive, towering figures walking into my bedroom: Coach Dempsey, the head varsity coach, and Coach Alicudo, the assistant varsity coach and my strength trainer.

I took in the scene. My coaches, in my bedroom. Me, in bed, where I'd been for the past thirty-plus hours, wearing my pajamas. Coach Alicudo had a gallon of orange juice. Dempsey wore a stern look on his face.

"How are you feeling?" Dempsey asked.

I blinked and swallowed, making sense of the scene. I sat up, my arms shaky as I situated myself in bed. "I feel weak," I finally said.

"All right," Dempsey said. He walked out of my room and I heard him call out to my parents. Their conversation was muffled by the walls.

Coach Alicudo shut the door to my bedroom and walked over to my bed. He set the gallon of orange juice on my nightstand, bumping my alarm clock as he set it down. He kneeled so he was eye level with me.

"Sit up," he said. "You've got to play. I don't care what you do. You've got to get up, take a shower, and get some orange juice in you."

Another fever chill ran across my body, and I shivered it away. It suddenly sunk in what Alicudo was saying. "Now?" I asked.

"Now."

"Coach . . . I'm not sure I can play well. I feel weak."

"We'll shower you up with cold water. We'll put some orange juice and Advil in you. Water, liquids." He looked straight into my eyes, as if he was saying the most important words I'd ever hear. "You've got to get up. You've got to be a man. This is your moment. You either rise to the occasion or you don't."

Alicudo's words coursed through me just like my feverish chills, and something about his intensity clicked. I forced myself up, steadying myself on my bed frame. Alicudo helped me to the bathroom and waited outside as I showered in cold water. I put on a turtleneck. Mom had prepared clothes for me, and my father and Coach Dempsey were waiting for me in the front room when I walked out with Alicudo. As I got ready to leave with my coaches, Mom stopped me at the door.

"¿Estas bien?" she said. "You sure you want to do this?"

I nodded. "I'm all right."

"OK, David," she said. "But be careful." Behind her, Dad nodded with pride.

I went out that day and played with a 103-degree fever. I wobbled between plays, willing myself to stand straight, and finding energy I didn't know I had when the ball snapped.

By some miracle, we won the game.

In the locker room afterward, I heard things like "this guy showed up" and "David came through." I felt proud for pushing through to show up for my team. Each congratulation and slap on my back made me feel like I'd done something spectacular. I'd stepped up when all I wanted to do was sleep.

As I walked out of the locker room that day and felt a couple of claps on my shoulder on the way out, I thought, Damn, this is pretty cool. I came through for the team. I came through for myself.

Later that evening, I arrived home, showered, and collapsed into bed. As I drifted off, I thought of the game, of the coaches, of what

Coach Dempsey had said to me on my way out of the building: "We're building grit machine DNA. This is how winners are built, and you're a winner." I could see the seriousness in his eyes, hear deep respect in his words. My stock had risen, not just with my teammates but with my coaches.

From that day on, I started to see myself as someone who could rise up and deliver, no matter what. I was growing into an independent young man with a passion for winning, regardless of the situation or sacrifice.

That was fall of tenth grade, and it was the start of shaping my character: intense, fearless, resilient, and determined. I was physically fit, was developing a strong sense of self, and had a really good group of friends, including George Demoulias, Rob Jones, Nicio Echevarria, and Antoine Walker. Delwin had transferred to Lynn Tech, a vocational school, and since I had moved from Henry Avenue, we were still cool but didn't spend as much time together. Although I missed Delwin at school, I had my other friends to hang out with, and popularity to carry me through the hallways of Lynn Classical.

I was riding high. I was confident. Soaring.

My parents, however, were going through hard times. I didn't realize it at the time, but my dad was dealing with frequent job layoffs. My mom shielded me from what was going on, still buying me clothes and accessories on her JCPenney credit card when I asked for them, still chattering on about my purpose in life, how I'd go on to do great things. She didn't burden me with their worries. And amazingly, I never noticed what was happening. In my mind, my parents were always working, hardly home, and we were working-class poor—but financially stable enough that I didn't notice their concern.

Around this time, prayer meetings started up again at my house. These had been regular occurrences back in Puerto Rico, praying for Dad, and now church ladies were at my house for Dwayne. My brother had been gone for months now; we had no idea where he was, if he was even alive. We watched the news every night to see if his face would flash across the screen: Had he been arrested? Did he get shot? Was he wanted by the police? My mom prayed every day for his safe return; I laid in my empty room each night missing my brother. I worried about him and wondered where he was. I hoped he was safe.

I couldn't have known at the time that Dwayne was staying with a friend, and while he was safe, he was going through the hardest period of his life. My brother, *mi hermano*, my hero, was struggling. He wouldn't find himself for some time.

With Dwayne gone and Dan and Diana living their own lives, it was just Mom, Dad, and me. And the pressure of being the golden child was beginning to weigh on me even heavier than before.

As a sophomore in high school, I wanted to party and hang out with friends. And I did. On the weekends, I'd smoke, drink, and party. But at home, Mom saw me as her angel boy, the one who never did anything he wasn't supposed to do, her good-grades kid, the young man who would go to college and get us out of all this, the one who would make something of himself.

The pressure of my double life had started to get to me, and so had the intensity of my daily routine. I had a crazy schedule compared to my peers. I would wake up early, go to school, lift weights, listen (or not) in class, head to football practice, go home to eat, hang with friends, sing in my room, and then wake up early to do it all over again. It was intense, but it kept me off the street and instilled discipline.

On the field, I was getting angrier. Football trained me to become even more aggressive, to knock people out, to win no matter what. Grit machine DNA became my go-to, the default. I was developing a success mindset, a lay-it-all-out-on-the-field approach to everything I did. But deep inside my gut was a torrent of emotion and anger that swelled within me and broke out at the slightest provocation. If someone looked at me wrong, or said something I didn't like, I was in their face. I was no longer proving myself on the streets of Lynn; I was holding onto my top-dog position in high school and nobody would take that away from me. "I've got to show these people what I've got" became the mantra that ran through my head.

At the same time, I was developing my artistic side and singing was becoming more of an outlet for me. I started singing in the school glee club, just like I had sung in church choir years before back in Puerto Rico. I joined theatre. I continued listening to blues, oldies, and doo-wop. I also had long conversations with older adults my parents knew. I loved hearing about their lives, asking them questions, and learning about their experiences in high school.

I was a complex mash of selves: the good son, the fighter, the artist, the old soul, the football star. None seemed to fully mesh, and I felt internally pulled apart.

When I learned about the Great Divide in geography class, the term immediately resonated with me. Sure, it was talking about a mountain range, but I felt a great divide inside of me too. I wanted nothing more than to merge the many sides of myself, to feel complete and whole. But I had two pressures keeping me separate: on one side was my mom's adoration, my family's expectations, and my desire to be at the top, to be popular no matter the cost, and the other side of me just wanted to be alone in my bedroom with music.

But I needed to get the hell out of poverty, and I saw my only out as being at the top. If I had zero competition, I'd have the best shot at success.

The Great Divide was inside me: a divide between who I was at home and who I was on the streets; between the future I wanted for myself and the path I saw so many other guys around me follow; between who I was inside and how I showed up on the outside. I was constantly changing in different situations to be the "right" version of myself.

I didn't want to be divided, I wanted to be whole. Of course, I didn't know then that wholeness would take a long, long time.

I had parked at a trailhead at Lynn Beach, and my family and I were now walking a long trail overlooking the beach. The path stretched far into the distance, and I could hear my boys' breathing getting heavier. Alexander was in front, followed by Anthony, my wife, and then me.

"So, your coaches . . . they just made you play when you were that sick?" Alexander asked as he walked, looking over his shoulder at me.

I couldn't help but laugh at my son's concerned expression. Of all the things I'd just shared with him, that's what stuck. "He didn't make me. He encouraged me to be tough."

"Why?" Anthony said. "I mean, when we're sick you tell us to rest."

"You should rest when you're sick," my wife said. "But your dad had a different life growing up than you did."

I thought of how she'd worried over our sons' fevers and coughs when they were little, rocking them for hours when they were sick. I recalled a work trip I almost didn't cancel when Alexander had a 104-degree fever as a baby, until my wife demanded I stay home. I shook my head. I was such a different man back then.

I'm so lucky she stuck with me, I thought.

"Coach Dempsey was a tough dude," I finally said. "But he cared about us."

"If he cared, wouldn't he have wanted you to rest?" Anthony replied. "Get better?"

How could either of them fully grasp what it was like for me, and for all us guys? Growing up on the streets, being surrounded by such a different reality from them?

"I'm going to be real with you guys, OK?" When I saw the backs of both of my sons' heads nod, I went on. "At the time, our team was made up of a bunch of kids, mostly black and Latino, that everyone had given up on or looked down on. At least two-thirds of the team was considered a lost cause by everyone but Coach Dempsey. There's no other way to describe it.

"They were in remedial classes, they were getting Cs and Bs, nudge-nudge, wink-wink. They were coming from single-family homes, living in Curwin Circle and Marian Gardens, and surrounded by all kinds of violence, drugs, and crime every day. People gave up on most of these guys. They needed father figures, someone to take an interest in them, someone to say, 'You matter and you can do better.'

"And even though I did have two parents at home, they were working a lot and were hardly there, and I needed that attention and care too. I came from a loving family but I was in a transitional period in my life.

"And then there were the streets, where I was spending a lot of my time. There was no discipline on the streets. And here were these father figures like Coach Dempsey, who suddenly straightened all these guys up. We all respected Dempsey like a father. When we were away from home, he took care of us like sons. If we got in trouble at school, who was showing up to speak for us to the principal? Coach Dempsey. When one of my teammates did something stupid, who would show up? Not the parents. Coach Dempsey would show up."

I felt a tightness in my throat and blinked my eyes to keep the tears away. I thought of Dempsey sitting in the locker room, talking to Derrick, a quiet kid whose parents were absent, an incredible football player who could have been a stellar linebacker in the NFL but got lost along the way. I thought of Will, who came from a rough family but was a huge talent on the field. Dempsey's words to him after one game echoed in my thoughts: "You are a superstar. You have to see that in yourself." I thought of all the amazing guys we had lost along the way, the ones who ended up addicted or in jail, and then I remembered the ones who got out, the guys who made something of themselves and their lives. I knew why. It was Coach Dempsey who gave a damn about these kids everyone else had dismissed. He became like a father figure. Coaches like Dempsey and Alicudo, among others, offered the structure and discipline these kids needed to focus, to know someone was watching. That someone cared for and about them.

"Coach Dempsey treated us like we were better than the world around us," I told Anthony and Alexander. "He knew, because he'd had a tough upbringing too. I'd watch him talk to these rough kids, and they'd tear up because no one had ever talked to them like that before. I heard Coach say so many times, 'Come on, it's in you. You are better than what people say you are. You are a champion. You can win on the field and in life. But no one is going to do it for you.'"

It was emotional for me to revisit the past: remember my teammates, recall myself at that time. I was broken. I was angry. I was a different person. A boy, not yet a man.

"There was one other person my sophomore year, Mrs. Pappagianopoulos. That woman, I swear, she had a heart of gold. One day, she found me in the hallway, looked me straight in the eyes, and said, 'I've heard about you. I'm going to straighten you out.' I have no idea why, but she cared. Just like Dempsey and Alicudo, she invested in me. She saw past my anger and recognized something in me I couldn't see in myself."

Alexander and Anthony were still quiet. Finally, Alexander spoke. "Pa?"

"Yeah?"

"I'm hungry. Can we head back to the car and go get pizza?"

I couldn't help it: I burst out laughing and my wife did too. The two of us cracked up so hard tears ran down our cheeks. Our sons. I love them.

"Yeah, we can get pizza," I said when I caught my breath from laughing. "But only if I can keep telling my story."

"Deal," Anthony said.

"Deal," Alexander echoed.

We turned around and headed back to the car as I began to tell them about eleventh grade, and Abel Marquez.

My father, Antonio Morales, and my grandmother Estilita Morales in 1945 Dorado, Puerto Rico, sector Cuba Libre, barrio Espinosa

My paternal grandparents in Puerto Rico: Estilita Morales and Antonio Morales Vazquez in 1940s Dorado, Puerto Rico, sector Cuba Libre, barrio Espinosa

My grandmother Carmen Vale Roman sitting in my paternal grandfather's marquesina (porch) visiting from Moca, Puerto Rico, c. 1999

My maternal greatgrandmother Petra Roman Vale sitting in her marquesina (porch) in Moca, Puerto Rico, c. 1989

My parents, Ana and Tony Morales, in Gary Indiana, 1959

My siblings and I with our maternal great grandmother in
Moca, Puerto Rico. I'm the short, chubby one, c. 1984

My sophomore year of football at Lynn Classical High School.
I'm kneeling on the second row, number five from the right, c. 1990

At my junior prom with the fellas Nicio, Steve, and Rob, c. 1992

Senior year of college with some of my teammates, c. 1996

At my high school graduation with the family, c. 1993

At my college graduation with my parents,
sporting my new suit with Dad's tie, c. 1997

Samanda's high school graduation
picture. The same picture I carried
with me during college, c. 1998

Samanda's father (my father-in-
law), Cesar Cavallo in República
Dominicana, c. 1997

Samanda's mother, Ana Rosario, c. 1988

My American Familia

This is my America

This is my America

This is my America

And that's me . . . David A. Morales

Chapter 8

LEAVE IT
ALL ON THE FIELD

The final weapon is the brain,
all else is supplemental.

JOHN STEINBECK

I pulled the jersey over my head and stood in front of the locker room mirror. I was only a junior in high school, but in that moment, turning this way, that way, examining the number, I felt much older, a man in kid's clothing. The light fabric felt heavy like chain mail. I imagined Abel, wearing this number, 66, wowing the crowds with his bright smile and contagious energy.

Abel, who almost made it out and had been accepted to attend Bowdoin College. Abel, who was now dead. Me, who would be representing his memory in this game.

The tragedy was vivid in my mind: four guys from my high school in a car. An accident. Only one person survived, the other three died, including Abel. He had been a beacon of hope for so many guys. We had looked up to him, admired him, and wanted to be like him.

Abel had been a year ahead of me at school. He was Puerto Rican, one of Dempsey's projects. He'd lived on Commercial Street, a tough, *tough* area of Lynn. Abel came from a poor family and lived in subsidized housing; he'd witnessed violence and killings nearly every day. To most people, he was lost, one of the many kids who would slip through the educational system, who'd end up in cyclical poverty and prison.

But like so many of our teammates, Dempsey saw something in him. He mentored Abel, trained him up to be a football star and encouraged him to be an honorable young man. Coach Dempsey sent films of Abel's best plays to colleges; he wrote letters; he made phone calls. And Abel Marquez got a full ride to play football at Bowdoin College. We didn't know what the heck Bowdoin was, but we were happy to see Abel make it.

He was going to get out, play football, get a college degree, and make something of himself. He was going to break out of poverty and get off Commercial Street.

Before he'd even left for college, Abel had become a legend. He was a symbol and sign of what any of us could achieve, where any of us could go, if we just followed what our coaches said, stayed straight, stayed out of trouble, and played our hearts out on the field.

But then the car accident happened, and Abel was dead, and now I was wearing his number. My team would be coming in any minute, and I needed to pull myself together. This game was dedicated to Abel, and his family would be there to see his number passed on to me to carry for the rest of the season in Abel's honor. I had to do this for Abel. The weight and significance of that moment hung heavy in my mind and heart.

I leaned on the sink in front of me, both hands on the porcelain, my breath heavy, my eyes burning. When Coach Dempsey had initially told me Abel's family wanted me to wear his jersey in this game, I'd said no. Not because I didn't want to, but because I didn't feel worthy. Abel had been somebody; he'd been important to so many people. Now he was gone.

"I can't do it," I'd said to Dempsey. I didn't think I had it in me to represent him on the field.

Coach's words echoed in my ears: "Yes, you can. You and Abel had many things in common: your roots, your heritage, your confidence, your fighting spirit. You're the right leader to do this. The family is going to respect you for it. They want you to do this for Abel. They want Abel's memory to be carried on by someone as brave and as tough as he was, someone who understands his culture and can represent him well."

I'd felt the world of responsibility on my shoulders as I finally agreed.

Still hunched over the sink, I looked myself in the eyes in the mirror in front of me, giving myself a silent pep talk, cheering myself on, telling myself I could do this. I had to do this for Abel. And not just for him, for all the guys we'd lost along the way, ones who hadn't made it out. Our small community had lost many. I knew we'd lose more.

I stood up straight and pulled my shoulders back, jutting my chest out. If I was going to do this, if I was going to carry Abel's number on my chest and back for the rest of my junior year of football, I'd do it with pride and honor. I imagined his family in the stands that night, and hoped that for this one evening, they'd feel Abel with them. I couldn't bring him back, but I could show up for them and for the team with dignity.

Behind me, I heard voices in the hallway. The sound grew louder and rowdier as the team entered the locker room, our coaches behind them. I joined them on the benches, waiting for our pre-game talk from Coach Dempsey. When Coach spotted me, he nodded, and I nodded back. It was unspoken: let's do this.

That night, we won the game. Actually, we annihilated the other team. The jersey that had felt so heavy at the beginning of the game had become like a superhero cape. I felt Abel in each punt and hand-off, each fumble and field goal. As I jogged off the field that day, I saw Abel's mom, brother, and little sister in the stands. I waved at them, and they waved back, smiling through their grief. In that moment, I really did feel like a superhero. But more importantly, I felt like there was a bigger purpose for wearing Abel's jersey: a bright future, a new horizon, a new sense of self and leadership, and definitely a deeper level of responsibility and thought about my own future.

Soon, though, that feeling was confronted by the reality of the streets I roamed. I found myself sitting in a party at my friend William's house, smoke filtering through the room, beer bottles everywhere. I was relaxed, sprawled on the couch, my legs splayed wide and a bottle of beer in my hand. A girl named Yvonne sat next to me on the couch, telling me a story I couldn't quite focus on.

She touched my arm and laughed, and I smiled at her but had no idea what she was saying. Suddenly, my senses were on alert as I saw a few of my friends huddled in the back corner of the room together. I watched them walk across the room, fast. Their shoulders hunched forward as they pushed through the crowd. The music was so loud I could barely think.

Then I saw the looks of fury on their faces. I stood and, without a word to Yvonne, pushed through the crowd to follow them. As they went out the back door into the yard behind the house, I followed them. My buddy Matt was with them, and I walked toward him to ask what was happening. Just as I reached him, Matt started to run across the backyard, pushing people aside, the guys hustling after him. I followed as I tried to figure out what the hell was going on.

I heard a loud crack. Then two more. A girl's scream.

A figure fled through the crowd and out the open back gate. A car door slammed. Wheels screeched. I looked around wildly, trying to figure out what had just happened.

Suddenly, the place erupted with screams and yelling. The crowd fled, shoving and pushing to get out of there.

And then I saw.

Matt. Matt had been shot.

He lay on the grass, blood pouring from his chest. He choked as he struggled to breathe. As I rushed to him, I saw two bullet holes near his heart and lungs.

Someone called 911, but we knew he wouldn't make it. Matt was dying. He'd be dead before the ambulance got here. There was too much blood. His eyes were distant as he struggled to breathe.

I knelt down next to him and put my hand on his shoulder.

"Matt, man. It's OK," I told him. "You're safe now. You're safe."

I heard an ambulance roaring down the street. Minutes later, as paramedics flooded through the same back gate Matt's murderer had used, I stood, an observer. Most of the kids had run, but a dozen or so of us stayed. I took in the girls with wet eyes and mascara running down their faces. I noticed my friends standing to my left, the ones who had been with Matt, who knew what happened. I didn't ask. I didn't want to know. I wanted to go home. I wanted to kiss my mom on the cheek, to hug my dad even though we didn't really hug.

I knew the cops would be close behind the paramedics, and so I said a silent goodbye to Matt as they lifted his limp body onto their stretcher and pulled a sheet over his body and face. Then I crossed the backyard and went through the house, breaking into a jog once I was safely away. I didn't want to be questioned. I didn't want to be part of that story—it was too familiar and always had a bad ending.

But the truth is I was part of the story; we all were. The story of how we grow up—whether it's on urban streets, in tenement homes, in rural poverty, or in suburban America—is the story so many of us carry our entire lives, no matter if we get out or not. And Matt was a symbol of all of us, only he hadn't made it out. I'd seen it so many times before. It was part of life on the streets. The everyday reality we lived with. The fact that any day, we could die.

Abel. Matt. Antoine. They were names that echoed throughout our community. They were young lives that the greater Boston area, the country, the world would never know. Unless someone told the world about them.

I reached my house that night and walked inside, listening in the silence for my parents. When there was no noise, I walked straight into the bathroom. I stared into the sink, thinking of the blood and death, and then splashed cold water on my face once, twice, a third time. As I dried my face, I met my own eyes in the mirror. And I wondered: Could I be the one to tell these stories? Could I be the one who gets out, and then reaches back into the community to tell guys like Abel, Matt, and Antoine that there is a better way? There are people who care. There is a brighter future.

As I made my way to my bedroom and laid in the dark, I felt sadness and purpose mix strangely in my chest, replaying the party and Matt's death in my mind until I fell asleep.

If ninth grade were boyhood years, and tenth grade was when I came into my own, then eleventh grade is when I started to shine. Prom king, guitarist, singer—these events and activities kept me off the streets. While my other friends were smoking, drinking, doing pills, and taking harder drugs, I was spending most of my time in football and singing. Mom had bought me a $20 red guitar with black strings, and I'd spend hours trying to imitate Elmore James on the slide guitar until my fingers bled. I was spending time with lots of different girls. I made friends with kids from the nicer side of town from English High School, which was taboo because it was a rival school, but I didn't care. While I still rode my bike around looking for basketball games, I was now catching rides with friends whenever I could. George had gotten a used car, an old Pontiac Trans-Am, and when he wasn't working, we'd drive around, listening to blues, hip-hop, or classic rock, feeling like we owned the streets.

I had joined drama and glee club in tenth grade, and continued through senior year of high school, waving off the jokes from my teammates, and holding my own among all the white kids. I played Conrad Birdie in *Bye, Bye, Birdie* and sang to sold out shows. Drama and glee progressed to singing in the choir and the school band.

Once, Sonny Rollins, the renowned saxophone player, came to our high school, and heard me sing in a performance we did for him. Afterward, he said to me, "You can *sing.*"

Sonny's words impacted me. After that, teasing be damned, singing became a part of my life I'd never let go. His encouragement gave me the confidence to keep at it, and singing and guitar was a whole new side of myself I had never explored before. I practiced harmony and my guitar every night to develop my skill. Any free time and extra money I could scrape together went toward doo-wop records to learn harmony and soulful melodies. "I Only Have Eyes for You" by the Flamingos; "Diana" by Paul Anka; "In the Still of the Night" by the Five Satins; "There Goes My Baby" by The Drifters; and "It's So Hard to Say Goodbye to Yesterday" by Boyz II Men—I played these songs on repeat in my room. I listened over and over, partly because I loved them and partly because I was listening to the harmony, training myself to sing all parts of complex harmony.

I'd practice each night over and over in my bedroom after football, working out, doing push-ups and doing my homework, moving the needle on my record player to repeat sections of songs, practicing harmony. Each night, I'd stay up past eleven o'clock, singing and playing guitar for an hour or two, trying to understand every part of the song I was studying that night.

My goal, like in football, was to become indispensable, so that if our choir instructor needed someone to fill in, I was there. Lead, tenor, alto, baritone—I even did bass once. Dad, seeing my interest and work, began giving me $10 a week, a small fortune on his meager salary, to buy more records at a buck each. I'd collect 45s, neatly storing my records on a bookshelf in my room, selecting a new one to study each night. Music became my life outside of football. My hiding place.

Still, most people only paid attention to who I was on the field. As one of the leaders on the football team my junior year, I was constantly in the local newspapers—I was becoming somebody in my community.

I made the all-star team. I was riding high.

Where hope had shined on Abel, the one who was so close to getting out, Coach Dempsey's spotlight shifted to me. He started talking to me about college, and where I might play football. Both Dempsey and Coach Alicudo instilled in me, day after day, that football could be my ticket to college, my door to a better future for me and my family, and a tool to make something of myself. To lift my family and community up with me and change the trajectory of our family's story. To inspire other men to do the same. That I was serving as a role model for others, especially young Latino men. This was the message they preached every single day to me during my high school football career.

Every. Single. Day.

Football was never just a game to Coach Dempsey. Football was a classroom for life. Football was his way of teaching "his" kids how to adapt to society, overcome obstacles, and succeed in life despite barriers. Adapt, improvise, overcome—the US Marines approach—these were some of the values and life lessons he drilled into us. And just as importantly, how to maintain tenacity, integrity, and calm in the face of serious adversity.

Dempsey was the first person outside of my own family who believed in me and spoke profound words of encouragement. He talked to me about playing in top national college football programs.

He filmed every game and had started putting together a tape of my plays. He mentioned the college visits we'd go on, and the coaches I'd meet. For the first time, I began to imagine not just a better future but a bigger future. I always figured I'd just go to the nearest community college to get a degree. Just getting to college felt like an accomplishment. With Dempsey's encouragement, though, I was even beginning to dream beyond Boston. I was starting to believe maybe I could do big things in big places.

While I was proud of how far I'd come since the chubby kid in Puerto Rico, my family was prouder. I saw the look on my parents' faces at church, beaming with pride, my mom often with an arm hooked through mine. Dan had become a cop in Lynn, working in the gang unit, and part of his job required him to stay fit and tough. He started taking me to the gym with him for workouts in Beverly, Massachusetts, where I was surrounded by all these ripped white guys. When I lifted weights, Dan's expression shone with the same pride I'd seen on my parents' faces. I overheard him say to another guy, "I'll take my brother over anybody in a fight. He's a tank." Dan's admiration meant everything to me. My confidence shot through the clouds. I felt like I could conquer anything or anyone.

As my confidence grew throughout my junior year, I turned my gaze toward Pine Hill, what many of us referred to as the rich white neighborhood. The place I hadn't ventured to much. The area that was off-limits. I began to question why, to wonder about these ethnic, racial, and income divisions that had ruled my friends and me for so long. At school, I hung out with everyone, and it didn't matter if they were white, brown, black, male, female, whatever—but outside of school, there was still a dividing line between Pine Hill and everywhere else. A line I had never really crossed.

A line I was ready to cross. I refused to be put in a box—ever.

One day in April, as the trees began bursting into greens and flowers began unfolding around us, Nicio showed up at my house on Broadway with plans to find a game of basketball. We wanted to take advantage of the sunshine and nice weather. As we considered where to go, I mentioned Pine Hill. Nicio's eyes grew big and his eyebrows pulled into a distorted question mark.

"You want to go *there*?" he said. "To play with the white kids? Why the hell would we do that?"

"Man, why not?" I said. "I heard they have a nicer court up there."

"What if they don't want us there?"

I shook my head. "What are they gonna do?"

"I don't know. Tell us to leave?"

"We have just as much a right to be there as them. It's a public court."

"Yeah, but—"

"Trust me. We're good."

Nicio shook his head and grabbed his bicycle lying on the grass nearby. Mine was leaning on a stairwell, and I hopped on and took off, Nicio trailing behind me. We pedaled all the way to Pine Hill, which was a fifteen-minute bike ride but felt like the shortest ride of our lives. Before we knew it, we were leaning our bikes against a fence that over-looked beautiful fields of green, two baseball parks, and a new-looking basketball court. The court was surrounded by a sprawling green lawn. I ogled the park, taking in the color and tidiness of it all. And they had nets on their hoops! I noticed kids at a playground in the distance. And were those wooden bleachers and a concession stand?

Damn, I thought. This is *nice*.

As Nicio and I walked toward the court, it was like someone hit pause. Everyone stopped playing and talking, and the only sound was the ball bouncing after being dropped mid-play. Simon, a senior at our school, scooped it up. I noticed kids from the basketball team and foot-ball team, and others I didn't recognize. I saw Kristen and Jennifer, both sophomores at my school, sitting in the grass. All their faces stared back at us: Nicio and me, two Puerto Rican knuckleheads from the other side of town.

"Hey, Morales," Simon finally said. He held the basketball under his right arm, a question painted across this face.

"Hey," I said. Nicio nodded his head once but said nothing. I could sense his unease next to me, his body tense, his expression uncertain.

"What are you guys doing all the way over here?" Simon asked.

"We came to play ball," I said.

Simon looked at Shaun, another senior at our school, then to Matt, a junior. Finally, Simon shrugged and nodded.

"Cool," he said to me, then called to the rest of the guys, "I've got Morales!"

Simon turned back toward the court, and I met Nicio's eyes, my bottom lip pushed up and eyebrows lifted. I whispered, "See, man? I told you we're good."

But the truth was, I hadn't been so sure about what would happen. I'd played confident to Nicio, but I also knew we were doing something that felt awkward and new to both of us.

As I walked onto the court, I thought of the dividing line I'd placed between me and Pine Hill. I'd ridden by this road dozens, maybe hundreds of times, but I'd never once gone up here. All this time, I'd assumed I was unwelcome, that my presence would be rejected, that there'd be a fight or the discomfort of being here wouldn't be worth it. I thought I was safer in my neighborhood, and in that moment, surrounded by all the kids from my school, in an area I had avoided for so long, I recognized the irony. Because my area of Lynn was a whole lot less safe when it came to violence and drugs. Had I been scared of white people with money? If so, why? After all, they slept and ate just like I did.

We played basketball, passing and shooting, laughing at bad plays and high-fiving when our teams scored. The white kids didn't play street ball like the kids near my house, but they had skill. As Nicio and I called it a day and got on our bikes, I thought about all we'd missed by staying away. All this time I could have been up here, playing with them. But I had kept myself away.

Each pedal home brought with it greater confidence that I belonged in spaces I hadn't realized I had a place in before. I could show up how and where I wanted to. And the "rich white folk" areas I'd avoided, even feared, were just occupied by People. People like me. What did it matter if they were white or black, or whatever?

What did it matter if I wasn't? We all breathed the same air. We all put on pants the same way. We were all people.

As junior year came to a close, my nagging self-consciousness grew. Sure, I was popular at school and on the field, but inside I was still a complex teenager with all sorts of insecurities, especially when it came to my family's finances. No matter how cool I was, my high school social status couldn't make my family suddenly wealthy. I was still the kid who had grown up in a government-issued concrete home in Puerto Rico. My dad was still getting laid off every couple of years, and the older I got, the more I noticed the giant difference between where I lived in Lynn and where the white kids lived in Pine Hill. I couldn't shake the reality of my family being poor or working-class, no matter how hard I tried. But I vowed to improve my family's situation. I just wasn't sure how.

As my self-consciousness grew inside, I showed up bigger, bolder, tougher, more confident. And just as this internal storm was raging, as this inverted confidence grew, I met Samanda.

I was at my house when Ive showed up to give me a ride to get ice cream. I had just gotten out of the shower and answered the door shirtless, with my hair still wet. I knew she'd have friends with her and figured I'd show off.

I just wasn't prepared for what I saw when I opened the door.

There stood Ive, another girl named Yasmin, and the most beautiful girl I had ever seen in my life. She had luxurious long, dark hair, honey skin, and deep brown eyes. Ive introduced them as sisters as I led the girls into the living room and pulled Ive into my bedroom as I hunted for a clean shirt.

"Who is that?" I asked, rifling through my dresser drawer. I pulled out a rumpled blue T-shirt, smelled it, and tugged it over my head.

"Don't bother," she said, knowing exactly who I was talking about. "Their stepdad's a strict Cuban who doesn't let them out of his sight. I was surprised their parents let them come with me. If you so much as try to talk with her, he'll kill you."

"Who is she?" I pressed. I wasn't letting this go.

Ive sighed. "You're impossible. OK, look, their family just got here from the Dominican Republic. They're literally off the boat. She's Dominican and they have really strict parents."

"And?"

Eye roll this time. "And they're friends with my mom. I told her parents I'd take her out for a ride."

"What's her name?"

"Samanda."

"Samanda," I said, letting the word hang in the air between us.

"David, she's a kid. She's, like, *fifteen years old*."

"So? I'm seventeen. Age ain't nothing but a number."

Her eyelids dropped to half-mast. "Yeah, an old seventeen."

"What's that supposed to mean?"

"You know."

"I'm going to talk to her."

"Go ahead and try." Her smirk told me I wasn't getting too far with the pretty Dominican girl in my living room. But I had to give it a shot.

When we walked out to meet the girls, I was hit again by Samanda's beauty. She was stunning, but not in the loud, in-your-face way of the girls at school. Instead, she was peaceful, reserved, and quiet. Her long hair was pulled over the left half of her face and she was hugging her arms to her body like armor. She reminded me of a soap opera star I grew up seeing on TV back in Puerto Rico, Lucia Méndez, and my hard-won swagger turned into a puddle on the floor. I tried to talk to her but found myself struggling to come up with anything other than, "*Soy David*," and "*¿Donde vives?*" Since my parents had insisted on English at home, my Spanish was a bit rough, and she didn't know any English. She replied in clipped phrases but gave me a subtle smile that made me fall even harder.

I'm going to marry that girl, I thought to myself. She is unbelievably beautiful. I've never seen a girl with her beauty. Her smile. Her calmness. Her charm.

Minutes later, we were all piling into the car, Samanda and Yasmin in the back seat and me in the front. We rolled the windows down to let in the warm near-summer air, and Ive cranked the music. I guessed she was trying to stave off any conversation between Samanda and me.

Finally, we stopped in front of an apartment building. I watched the girls climb out and flashed my best smile.

"*Encantado de conocerte*, Samanda," I said. Pleased to meet you—really? I sounded like I was saying goodbye to someone's grandma. What was wrong with me? Where was my game?

Samanda said nothing but smiled a real smile for the first time all afternoon, and my jaw practically fell off my face. Whoa, I thought. She's stunning.

When the girls had finally disappeared from view, I spun around to Ive, who was messing with radio dial.

"You have to give me her number," I said.

"No way."

"What? Why not?"

"I told you! Her stepdad will kill you."

"So?"

Ive sighed loudly. "Look, I can't just give you her number. That's not how it works."

I could tell I wasn't getting anywhere with Ive, so I tried a different tactic. "Next time she's over, can you just call me? I'll just, you know, casually happen to stop by."

"Seriously, David?" Ive screwed her mouth up as she surveyed me. "What is up with you? You like her, huh? Like, *like her*, like her."

I nodded but said nothing, worried I'd mess up the moment. C'mon, Ive, I pleaded silently. This could be my future wife we're talking about here.

"Fine," she said, pushing the clutch and brake and shifting into first gear. "But you owe me."

I leaned across the car and planted a huge kiss on Ive's cheek. She quickly wiped her face, laughing.

As we drove away, I sat silently, listening to the music and wondering about Samanda.

Chapter 9

HOPE

You just can't beat the person
who never gives up.

BABE RUTH

I walked across the locker room to the small office with a window overlooking the football field. The air was drafty with a late-October chill, and I tugged my jacket closed over my long-sleeved athletic shirt. It was senior year football season, and practice had ended twenty minutes earlier. Coach Dempsey sat in his office, the door wide open, and I knocked lightly when I approached, rousing Dempsey from a film-reel trance. As usual, he was watching footage from the last game, a notepad on the desk next to him scrawled with notes. He grabbed the remote from his desk and hit pause.

"You asked for me, Coach?" I said from the doorway.

"Morales. Sit down." He motioned to a chair directly in front of his desk, and I sat, a growing uneasiness creeping through my body.

He swiveled his chair toward me. "It's your SAT."

I hung my head, feeling the weight of my poor test score. I had let him down. I'd let so many people down. The number flashed through my head: 880 out of 1600. It wasn't just bad. It was terrible. Embarrassing. In the second percentile.[1] This was my second time taking the SAT and I had bombed—again. I knew my score would keep me out of all the colleges Dempsey and I had dreamed about together. The visits we'd gone on during junior year, the relationships he'd nurtured at colleges on my behalf, the game tapes he'd sent in—pointless. Nobody would touch me with that test score. And with my senior season coming to a close, I had zero options for scholarships. I'd waged my entire future on playing football.

I knew Dempsey was waiting for a reply, but I had nothing. I stared at my knees and felt like someone had died—and in a way, someone had. I'd lost the future David Morales, the David Morales who would make the family proud. I couldn't do any of that if I couldn't get into college, and especially if I couldn't pay for college through a football scholarship or financial aid. The silence between us reeked of failure and disappointment.

"David, look at me."

Finally, I met Dempsey's eyes. He wasn't mad or sad. He looked determined. Something was in his hand, and he reached across the desk to hand it to me. I took it cautiously, a small bubble of hope rising in my chest.

I studied the brochure in my hands. Across the front were the words: BOWDOIN COLLEGE.

"Bowdoin?" I said, pronouncing it *bow-din* like I'd heard the coaches say it in the past. I knew this school. This was where Abel had been accepted to play football. Coach had mentioned it to me, but with our massive list of opportunities, I hadn't narrowed my focus on this obscure-sounding school. I wasn't even sure where Bowdoin was, but I thought maybe it was near a train stop off the Blue Line in Boston.

"David, this is an incredible school," he said. "Not just for football but for academics too. And guess what?"

I looked up from the brochure. "Yeah, Coach?"

"They don't require an SAT score to be admitted."

I sat fully upright this time, looking Dempsey straight in the eyes, suddenly on fire with the hope I'd had throughout my junior year, the hope of a football star who everyone said could play anywhere. I didn't need to play *anywhere* if I could play *somewhere*. My dreams and goals suddenly flooded back, but I held them away cautiously. I had already mourned the loss of a potential scholarship, and I didn't want to get too excited. I couldn't have my dreams crushed all over again.

"Do you think they'll accept me?"

"I've been working on them for a while, sending them tapes of you since last year," Dempsey said. He stood, walked around his desk, and sat in the chair next to me. I followed him with my entire body, turning to face him as he sat. "They know you're a good player with lots of potential. But I want us to visit so they can put a real, live human to the highlights I've sent them. If they like you, hopefully they'll send someone to one of our games to watch you play."

I thought for a moment, studying Dempsey's face. Could this be real? Of course it could. Dempsey was anti-bullshit. I knew that if he said it, it was true.

"OK," I finally said. "I'm in."

"How's Saturday?" he said, a grin stretching across his face.

I smiled, both at his eagerness and the joy bursting inside me. "Saturday's perfect."

As I left Dempsey's office, I thought about my SAT. My 880 score was an improvement on my first score of 770 but still nowhere near the number I needed. When I'd received that second score, my gut had knotted a thousand times thinking of what I'd say to my parents. I'd let them down. I'd let every single person who'd invested in me down: my brothers, my sister, my grandparents.

I had done terrible in the English section and bombed the math on both tests, and I knew partly why. For years now, I'd been passed along by teachers who wanted to make sure I could play. Some teachers did that for other football players too. No homework? Fail a test? No problem. Here's a B.

More than once, I received half-completed tests back with an A across the top and notes like "great play" or "saw your plays on Saturday." While I'd enjoyed the favors at the time, now I was seeing the results. I hadn't learned the math I needed to do well on an exam that could determine my future. I thought of the schools I'd applied to: Sacred Heart University, Notre Dame, Boston College, Penn State, Stanford, Trinity, and a few safety schools, about ten applications in total. Each had strict SAT requirements—or at least required that scores not scrape the bottom percentile. These colleges expected their football players to be scholar-athletes.

I walked down the now-empty school halls. Everyone had left for the day, and my steps clicked through the hallways, the dull sound echoing through my mind like a pattern: hope, hope, hope.

I had another chance. Bowdoin. I liked the sound of that: David Morales, starting middle linebacker for Bowdoin College. I reimagined my future, the one I'd almost let go of. David Morales, the guy who got out, the guy who made something of himself. The college graduate who got a good job. The man who bought his parents a house, who helped his siblings, who repaid all the sacrifices each and every person in the family had made for him, the youngest of the family, the one meant for a bright future.

I walked out the front entrance of the school and made my way to the same streets I had walked for three years. I thought of when I had brought the results of my second SAT attempt to Mrs. Pappagianopoulos, and the look of terror on her face. Her expression was panicked, her eyes wide, mouth open.

"You have to try harder," she'd told me, standing next to me in her office, eyeing the results I'd handed her. "Take it again."

"I can't," I'd said as I held back tears of anger and disappointment.

"You have to, David. You have to do better than this." Her expression had grown more alarmed by the minute. I understood: I had failed this life-altering test. And I'd taken it twice, with barely better results than before. My parents didn't have money for SAT prep; I didn't have the basic knowledge from high school I needed to do any better than my first two attempts. She'd sat then, as if she couldn't stand any longer.

"David," she'd finally said, "we'll find a way."

Her expression of resolve flashed through my mind as I walked home. I thought of Coach Alicudo, Coach Dempsey, Mrs. Pappagianopoulos, and Mrs. Duchesne, a Spanish teacher who went out of her way to encourage me daily—all these incredible adults who had spent so much time and energy trying to help me. Why, I wondered? Why me?

My thoughts drifted to the night before, sitting on the steps with George, Rob, and Nicio, drinking forties and talking about our futures. That night, less than twenty-four hours earlier, everything had been different. We'd commiserated about our destinies: becoming used-to-be's on Commercial Street and at the Lynn Common, with huge beer bellies, doing the same thing day in, day out.

"We're going to be bums for the rest of our lives," I'd said to George. He'd nodded. We had believed it, too. We had no vision and no exposure to what life could offer outside of the urban, gritty streets we grew up on. We knew violence, poverty, McDonald's, and the Lynn House of Roast Beef on the Lynn Common, but we had no exposure to the alternatives or possibilities that life offers, or even careers that enabled one to build a better life. We knew our city well. But we didn't know what lay beyond the streets, beyond our imagination. If you can't see it, you can't be it, or strive for it.

Buzzed and crushed from failed SAT and lost football dreams, I had bought the lie that we couldn't be more. The fiction that we were destined to fade into the background of existence until we died of alcoholism or violence. The untruth that our futures were written, and no matter what we did, our fate was to live the same lives as the guys on the street corners, the ones we'd pitied our entire lives. I thought of a few weekends back, sitting on the steps of Abel's house with George and Rob, half-joking that we'd be in the same spot in twenty years, hell even forty years, sitting on a step, drinking forties, and talking about our own kids. I thought of Dwayne telling me life was over after high school, and I'd better enjoy it now. That nothing good comes after high school.

And that had been my perspective since I'd screwed up my future with the SATs weeks earlier, since I'd let go of my dream to play college ball. I partied like my life was over, because I'd thought it was. All around me, guys were dropping out or dropping dead. There were many before me, all who had graduated in previous years. They were big guys, talented, athletic, with promising futures. There was Felix: six feet five inches and 260 pounds of pure grit and power, handed a full scholarship to Ohio State. He dropped out before the season ended. There was Jim: a huge white kid from a working-class family in Lynn. He was recruited to a Division I university and couldn't make it past his first year. There were dozens of stories like theirs, guys I knew, guys I had played with—all these folks had fallen. As soon as they stopped playing football, they collapsed. Heavy drinking, liquor, Ecstasy, acid, crack. At the height of their young lives, it was like they fell off a cliff. No vision, no ability to see beyond their circumstances.

Thankfully, I had the fear of God from Mom and Dad. I'd see my high school buddies on Commercial Street, and they'd offer me all kinds of ways to get high, but I'd always say, "Nah, I'm good." That was not the path I wanted. Although I couldn't see past the streets of my youth, I knew I did not want to end up on those same streets.

But I had still been drinking and smoking pot, and way more now that my future felt written. I'd staggered to my Dad's used Ford Escort and driven drunk and high more than once, George in the passenger seat, the two of us laughing with music blasting as we raced to make our 1 a.m. curfews. I'd risked my life and other people's lives to numb the ugly results of my SAT and the vicious cycle of life around me.

Of course, I made sure my parents never saw that side of me. I was more scared of letting them down than just about anything. Their pride, love, work ethic, and commitment kept me somewhat straight. Even with my failed SATs, my parents believed I had it in me to do great things. Mom insisted I could earn money for a year, enroll in community college, and work my way through. They'd help as much as they could. But I was broken inside, robbed of a future I had all but lived, and her words floated past me, incomprehensible through my pain.

But now, after my conversation with Dempsey, everything had changed again. I felt the wind on my face as I walked home and rebuilt my dreams, thinking of ways to execute a plan to succeed. I reached my building and flew up the steps to my apartment. No one was home yet. As I used my key to open the door, I remembered Dan and Diana were coming for dinner. I couldn't wait to tell them that their little brother might be playing football in college still. That I might get to live their dream and mine.

My boys were sitting up, alert, listening intently. It was Monday, and they had the day off for teacher-in-service. We'd spent much of Sunday talking before and after a family BBQ with my parents, and my wife's and my siblings and their extended families.

The boys had been gone all Monday morning, Anthony at a pickup basketball game at the YMCA, Alexander playing video games at a friend's house. I suspected they'd need a break from my storytelling, but after they both got home around one o'clock and devoured a large plate of rice and beans with chicken each, they'd asked to hear more.

Alexander looked at me in question. "What's the SAT again?" he asked.

"It's a test you take to get into college," Anthony said.

"It used to stand for Scholastic Aptitude Test," I added. "But they changed the name to Scholastic Achievement Test."

"It seems really unfair that a test would keep you out of college," Alexander said.

"It is unfair," I said. "And add on the fact that often Latinos do worse on the test than white students overall. Someone who is Latino and speaks Spanish and English will statistically do worse than someone who is a native English speaker and speaks only English. Odds are especially bad if that person learned Spanish first, then English, like I did. And if a student gets a fee waiver—meaning they can't afford the test fee—data shows that the test scores are way worse. I fit all those criteria back then.[2]

"Now, that doesn't mean you stop trying or make excuses for your results. You have to adapt, improvise, and overcome, no matter what life throws at you."

My boys considered this, and I could see them running through the information I had just shared.

"So . . . I'll be mostly good then?" Alexander asked.

I laughed. "I hope so. Your mom and I work hard to make sure you have access to as many opportunities as possible. We also want you to work hard and earn what you get. But the fact is, lots of kids aren't as fortunate. There are millions of Latinos, blacks, poor whites, Native Americans, and others who don't have a loving family or the opportunities you have." I met their eyes, wanting to make sure they were listening. "Before the door to opportunity even opens for them, those kids are shut out and have to work harder to get through that door."

Anthony, ever-analytical, seemed to be running a math equation in his head, his brows twisted in thought. "So what can we do?"

"You want to know the truth?" I said. They both nodded. "We need to tell our stories. We need to reach the guys and girls who don't have the opportunities you do, and share with them the hope for their futures. We need to show them that they have options. That they don't have to continue the path that's been laid out for them or limit themselves to the images or models they see on TV. They can aspire to be lawyers, company CEOs, investors. They need a vision of a different life, and to understand how our capitalist system works, and how to work within it, so they can overcome and live productive lives. Frankly, we need to teach others. There's a difference between educating and teaching. When we teach someone how to fish, we empower them to become self-reliant and productive.

"I got out. Do you understand me? *I got out.*" My throat caught as I allowed myself to feel, for the first time in a long time, that sense of hopelessness and anger that had overtaken me when I received my SAT score, and when all of those opportunities seemed to be slipping away, one by one. I had cried alone that night, sobbing quietly into my pillow, believing my life would amount to nothing.

With intensity in my eyes, I went on. "I remember sitting on those steps with George, Nicio, and Rob, and thinking that I was never going to get out of poverty, that I'd never do all those things my mom promised were in store for me. I sat on that porch, and I accepted my fate—that the door to my future, the door to opportunity, was closed. Until Dempsey opened a window. My life could have been completely different if Coach Dempsey hadn't done that. If God had not placed Coach Dempsey in my life."

I was getting emotional thinking of Dempsey, thinking of the fact that my life, *my boys*, might not exist if it weren't for people like him, and Mrs. Pappagianopoulos, and teachers, coaches, and mentors like them. That there were so many young men and women who didn't have what I had and never would. The system would eat them alive and spit them out.

While I had determination and grit, I didn't have exposure to understand what life was like outside my daily experience. While I had love from my parents, we didn't know anything beyond the walls of our small world. I didn't *see* the possibilities beyond the environment I'd been raised in and the streets I was so familiar with.

"We—all of us—have to share our stories beyond ourselves," I said. "And we have to reach back and open windows and doors for young men and women, and tell them that the only obstacle is in not know-ing how limitless their possibilities are. They need to know there is opportunity everywhere in America. There is always hope as long as you focus on your vision for a better life, a better future, and develop skills that command good wages and are in demand. There will always be obstacles. But grit, perseverance, vision, and faith are greater than any obstacle."

That weekend, Coach Dempsey took me to Bowdoin College, just like he promised. I dressed in my nicest button-up shirt and newest jeans, shined a pair of Giorgio Brutini shoes, and smoothed my hair with gel like always. I was determined to make an impression. Bowdoin was my last real hope for a college education. When Dempsey picked me up at our new apartment on the third floor of a beige triple-decker on Chestnut in Lynn, I was ready.

But as confident as I acted to Dempsey, I couldn't help but feel panic rise like bile in my throat as we sat in the parking lot of the campus. This college wasn't in Boston; it was in Brunswick, Maine, two and a half hours from my home. The campus was surrounded by lush pine trees and more green grass than I had seen since I was a kid in Puerto Rico. And it was whiter than a bag of marshmallows. Everywhere I looked was another white kid: preppy football players shoving each other and laughing as they walked into the entrance to athletic facil-ities; pretty girls in sweaters, their blonde and brunette hair swept back in headbands and shining in the autumn sun; even white cars in the parking lot, brand new Land Rovers, Jeeps, and Saabs. I looked at Dempsey and he looked at me, both of us knowing that this world was only 124 miles from Lynn but a million miles away from what I had ever experienced in my life.

I met the Bowdoin coach and stayed the night with another former Classical High student, a guy Dempsey had helped get admitted, to get a feel for the campus. But the entire time of my visit, it was like I floated above each exchange: shaking the coach's hand, meeting the football players, touring the campus with a student guide. When Dempsey picked me up the next day and we made the two-hour drive back to

Lynn, we talked about my future and upcoming football games, but I carefully avoided a long discussion about Bowdoin. I didn't want to get too invested in the school. It was a foreign world, there was no offer on the table, and I knew that while they didn't formally consider SATs, maybe they'd somehow think I wasn't college material. Maybe it wouldn't matter that I was the fiercest player on the field if I couldn't pass a damn test.

It was dark by the time we pulled up to my house. I waved goodbye to Dempsey and made my way up two flights of stairs to our place. Mom and Dad were watching television when I walked in, and Mom nearly leapt off the couch when she saw me. Dad clicked the TV off and stood.

"So? Did you get in?" Mom asked.

I laughed. "Mom, I told you, it's not like that."

She smiled and placed a hand on my cheek. "I know, but look at you. Of course you'll get in." She hurried over to the counter and grabbed a plate with aluminum foil over it. "Here. Eat. We already ate dinner so I kept this warm for you."

I lifted the edge of the aluminum and let the smell of rice and beans with fried tostones waft over me. "Thanks, Mom. I'm starving."

"Tell us about your visit," Dad said.

I told my parents the highlights of my trip between bites of my mom's dinner: the fantastic facilities, the beautiful campus, the team's win-loss record. My parents listened and nodded. They'd actually thought Bowdoin College was in Boston, just like I had!

I finally excused myself to shower and go to bed. But something hung with me that evening, the weight of responsibility, the hope in my parents' eyes as I told them about the school and football program. I also thought of how remote and different the college was. I did not fit, but at the same time, I was excited and anxious about the possibility of a new life.

As I fell asleep that night, all I could think was: I can't let them down. I can't let Coach down. I can't let myself down. But I knew it would be months before I found out anything. I'd have to wait and see if I would fulfill the legacy my parents laid out for me, or if I'd disappoint everyone I loved.

Winter came, its biting winds and white blanket covering the city of Lynn. With football season—and my entire high school football career—officially over and no longer a distraction from my impending future, all I could do now was wait. I distracted myself with parties and hanging out with girls. I drank and smoked and passed the time as best I could, but deep down I was overcome with worry, my stomach twisted and my brain a mish-mash of what would happen. Would I get into Bowdoin?

Soon, my concern for college took a sharp left turn.

It was a Tuesday night in late January. I was in bed and glanced at the clock: 12:03 a.m. School had just resumed from winter break, and although I needed to go to sleep, my stomach growled. I needed to eat something or I wouldn't be able to sleep. I got out of bed and walked out of my room, surprised to see the light on in the kitchen. A muffled sound came from the front of the house, and I walked quietly, not sure what was going on.

When I reached the kitchen, I saw my dad sitting at the table, his face in his hands. He was sobbing, papers spread around him on the table. I stepped closer, just behind Dad and to his right, and squinted my eyes to see what the pink and white pages were. The words "PAST DUE" screamed at me in red block letters from several of the papers, and I realized these were bills. Past due bills. What was going on?

"¿*Papi*?" I said. He jumped at the sound of my voice and quickly wiped his eyes.

He cleared his throat. "David," he said. He began gathering the papers up into a messy pile. "What are you doing awake?"

"What's going on? What's wrong?" I replied as I walked around the table to face him.

Dad looked too exhausted to be defensive or proud. His expression was open. Vulnerable. "I lost my job."

I knew Dad sometimes had trouble keeping jobs. Without a college degree, he was seen as a dispensable worker, always the first to get laid off. He usually got another job quickly, often within a few days and never more than a couple of weeks. This was normal, a part of life, so why was he so upset?

"You'll find another one," I said. "You always do."

Dad's voice cracked as he spoke, as if his pride was breaking with his words. "David, I've looked. There's no work."

I stood with my hands on a chair in front of me, leaning my weight and the burden of my parents' finances against it. Silence swarmed the space, choking out conversation, my dad and I each quiet in thought. My mind drifted to Puerto Rico. I remembered the house in Maguayo, and the chickens, and Spam, and my dad harvesting *ñame* and catching fish. I remembered, suddenly, his drinking, and the yelling and crying. The prayer meetings at our house. The women looking out for my mom. My grandfather looking out for our family when Mom and Dad were at work late at night. I remembered, and I ached, because sitting across from me was my hero, a man I had admired my whole life, a man who was not perfect and had been broken but put himself back together. A man who God rescued from alcoholism. A father who I knew worked hard every day to make sure I could have what I needed, and to make up for the mistakes he'd made, the pain he'd caused Mom. The person who left everything to come to the United States to earn money for us, for me, to bring us to America and give us an opportunity for a better life.

That man sat across from me, his eyes once again downcast, his shoulders slumped. He appeared broken but not like in Puerto Rico. He looked like a person who had tried his best and failed, and now he was baring his heart to his youngest son. Why? He had never shared this kind of thing with me before.

And suddenly it struck me. I was no longer the baby. I was nearly a man; I was almost done with high school. I could help. I could adapt and overcome.

I would find work. I'd help Dad and Mom. I'd fix this.

"Thank you for telling me," I said. "Everyone is going to be OK." It's all I could think of to say in that moment. My strong *papi* looked defeated, worried, and small. As I took in his slumped frame, I added, "Pa, I'll help. I'll skip college and get a job, and help you and Mom pay the bills."

My father gave me a stern look as he said softly, "David, no! You have to go to college. I don't want you to be like me. You have to do better than me."

"But Pa—"

"You'd better get to bed," Dad said. I was stunned and speechless. There was my hero, looking up at me with vulnerability and sadness, telling me he did not want me to be like him. Since I didn't know what to say, I went back to my room slowly, emotion overtaking me, forgetting all about the snack I'd come for. That night, I laid awake for another two hours boiling with anger, trying to come up with a plan to help my family. To help my father.

When my alarm went off the next morning, I got right out of bed. I needed to find Coach Dempsey before school started. As I walked to school that morning in the biting cold to clear my head, I thought through the options I'd come up with the night before, and reaffirmed what I would do. By the time I made it to school, my mind was made up: find after-school work, or drop out and get a job flipping burgers, like my brother Dan had done years before to help bring the family to the United States. I found Dempsey in the hallway; he taught special education during off-season, but I knew he didn't have a first period class.

"Can we talk, Coach?" I asked.

He studied me. "Sure. Let's go to my office."

I walked silently next to him. Finally, we made it to his office. He shut the door behind him. "What's going on?"

"Coach, I—" my voice cracked just like Dad's. I cleared my throat. "I'm quitting school."

"You're *what*?"

"I'm quitting, Coach."

"What do you mean, 'I'm quitting'? You mean you're dropping out?" I nodded but said nothing.

"David, that's crazy. You're not dropping out of school."

"Coach, my parents need me. I have to." I told him about the night before, and my parents' situation, and how much my father needed me. And by the time I was done talking, Coach was sitting on top of his desk, as if he needed it to hold him up. He looked determined.

"David," he said, his voice gentle. As I met his eyes, I was struck by how concerned he looked. "Listen to me. You are not quitting school. You can't, you hear me? You can't quit, because you're so close to changing your life . . . and your family's lives."

I was struck dumb, remembering the future I almost had but also fully accepting my fate. My parents had given me so much; now it was my turn to give back to them. My thoughts crowded out reason. After several minutes, Dempsey finally spoke. "We're going to go see your parents."

"Now?"

"Yes, now."

I followed him out of the school as he blew past the windowed office, the school secretary wearing a confused expression, and followed him to his car.

"Get in," he said.

We drove in silence to my house in his tiny dark gray Toyota Corolla, the heater blasting, my new future running through my head. If I quit now, I could find a job right away before all the other high school students graduated. I thought of my options, and suddenly I felt a brick in my chest, as the reality of my possibilities set in. I knew what I'd be doing: fast food, labor, some kind of menial job you can get with a young, strong body.

Dempsey flew up the stairs to our apartment, his hand on the railing to keep from slipping on the icy steps. As he knocked heavily on the door, my breath swirled around me and I worked up the nerve to look at Dempsey's face. Fear. That's what he wore: not anger, not disappointment, not determination. Fear. He was afraid. What was he afraid of?

Dad opened the door, Mom standing just behind him. I was surprised to see her there. Had she taken the day off work?

"Mr. Morales, Mrs. Morales," Dempsey said, "can I please come in?"

Dad opened the door wide, his expression tight and exhausted. Embarrassment weighed down his shoulders. I tried to meet his eyes, to apologize for whatever was about to happen, but Dad was already walking into the living room.

"Can I get you some coffee?" Mom asked.

"No thank you, Mrs. Morales. I won't be here long."

"What is this about?" Dad asked.

"You can't let David quit high school. I'm real sorry you lost your job, Mr. Morales. Real sorry. I know times are hard."

Dad's jaw clenched. He was a proud man, and I knew he didn't like this Irish guy in his living room lecturing him about his job situation.

"But look . . . David has an incredible future ahead of him. I'm telling you, if you let him drop out, it will be the worst mistake you'll make, because David has the opportunity to change his life and yours."

Dempsey, my tough coach, my other father figure, the man who had opened a window to Bowdoin when all the other doors were closed, was now standing in my living room arguing for my future. He sniffed loudly, his breath stuttering as he breathed, as if holding emotion tightly within his body, like it might erupt all over our living room.

My parents stood stiffly, my dad's chin lifted and shoulders back, his body language in faux pride. Mom sat down on the sofa, looking up at Dad, then Dempsey, then turning her gaze on me. I felt the weight of all the years growing up in our household, the times she'd told me God had big plans for me, the times I rejected her words. I thought of all my lost opportunities, the colleges I didn't get into, the teams I would never play on. Who even knew if Bowdoin would accept me? What if I didn't get into college at all? What if I stayed in high school and my family was ruined financially?

My parents had sacrificed. My siblings had sacrificed. My grandparents had sacrificed. And for what? For my Dad to be unemployed? For my parents to lose everything? No, I couldn't let that happen. I had to help.

"I'm telling you, you've got to let this kid stay in school," Dempsey said, his voice cutting through my thoughts, my parents' full attention on him now. "We're going to get him to college. I promise. I promise you we'll get him there."

Dempsey was looking at me now, his expression the most serious I had ever seen. "We'll get you into college. That is the best decision you can make, for both your short-term and long-term future."

Dad stepped forward and reached out a hand. Dempsey took it, and they shook for several seconds. As Dempsey and I left that morning, I looked back at my parents. I met my dad's eyes, then my mom's, and their expressions told me everything I needed to know.

Fight for a better future for yourself, David. For our family. Make the Morales name proud.

I wasn't sure what was in store for my family, but I let myself believe Dempsey was right. The hope that had been crushed by my SAT score, and had been rekindled briefly at the idea of Bowdoin, returned full force. I realized Bowdoin was more than just a college. It was a way out for my family. I just prayed Dempsey was right.

Over the following weeks, Coach Dempsey and I spent a lot of time together. He helped me fill out more college applications and he reviewed all of them, including my application to Bowdoin. Coach even had me shovel snow at the football field as a way to pay him back for the college application fee he paid for, and I knew he'd done the same for many others. He was giving back to me and others like me, in ways I would not comprehend until later in life.

A few months later, I walked up the stairs to our third-floor apartment on Chestnut Street and opened the front door. I headed straight to the kitchen for a snack, passing the kitchen table on the way. It was a chilly Saturday in March, and I was rubbing my hands together to warm up, and humming "Smokestack Lighting" by Howlin' Wolf. But I stopped abruptly when I saw a letter sitting in the middle of the table. As I walked to the wooden surface and leaned over to get a better look, I saw the words "Bowdoin College" in the top left corner. I grabbed the letter, holding it in front of me with both hands.

"¿*Mami*? ¿*Papi*?" I called into the apartment, but no answer came. Where were they? Clearly they'd been home, seen the letter, and put it on the table for me. I studied the envelope. It was small, certainly not the big scholarship packet I was expecting. Actually, I realized, it had the same lightness as the rejections I'd received. My heart thudded in my chest. Was Bowdoin rejecting me too?

"David?" I heard my mom say as she opened the back door to the apartment.

"In here!" I called.

"We're coming!" Mom said.

I listened to my parents' hurried footsteps as they made their way to the kitchen.

"What does it say?" Dad said.

"I don't know yet," I replied, still gripping the letter tightly in my hands. I thrust it at Mom. "You open it."

Mom didn't need me to ask twice. She tore the envelope along the top with her index finger, then slid out the single-page letter and opened it. I searched her expression, looking for clues, bracing myself. Sweat formed on my back and underarms. This was my last chance. My last hope.

Silently, I prayed, Please, Jesus. Let this be the one. Please help me.

Dad stood behind Mom, both hands resting on her shoulders as he peered over her to read the letter too. Their expressions were unreadable. I realized I'd been holding my breath and let it escape.

"What does it say?" I asked.

Mom and Dad looked at each other, then at me. Mom's reaction was indecipherable until she burst into tears.

"What is it, Mom?"

"David! You got accepted! You got in!" Mom practically threw the paper on the table and wrapped me in a tight hug. I felt her hair brush my cheek; her body shook with laughter and joy.

I got in? Shock ran through me, and then elation. After all the rejections, after all the waiting. After all the long nights in bed worried that I wouldn't get in. I gave my mom one more squeeze and picked the letter up from the counter and started reading it, examining each word.

"It says you also get significant financial aid, son," Dad said. "They're paying for most of your college."

I got in, almost fully paid, and I get to play football? I read the words myself: there it was, in plain English, that they were offering me a spot on the football team with financial assistance. Tuition, room, and board.

"David, honey, say something," Mom said.

But I couldn't speak. I could only read. I finished the letter, letting each word sink in, the weight of this chance—this *out*—echoing through my thoughts. Relief washed over me. Mom stood next to me, waiting. Dad cleared his throat. Finally, I turned to my mom. I hugged her again, this time lifting her up and twirling her once, twice, the letter still in my right hand, and then setting her down.

"I got in!" I said. "*I got in!*"

For a few minutes, standing in that kitchen with my proud parents, these two amazing people who had moved our family here for a better life, my dad whom God healed, my mom who was so loyal and sacrificial . . . in that moment, the anger within me parted like the Red Sea. I felt joy and relief. Pride. Gratitude to Diana, my second mom; to Dan, for working so hard to get us to the United States; to Dwayne, for protecting me and caring for me. I thought of my grandparents, the two people I missed fiercely. I thought of Sundays at Grandpa and Grandma's house and how much had changed from childhood to today. I knew they'd be proud. I thought of Coach Dempsey and Coach Alicudo and Mrs. Pappagianopoulos and all the people who had invested in me. I thought of my talks with George and Rob, and how we'd all accepted our fate and now mine was changing.

I couldn't wait to tell all these people who mattered to me that I, David Morales, was going to college. I wasn't going to be poor. I was going to rise up. And Bowdoin was the door of opportunity to my future.

"You got in," Mom said. "David, *mi amor. Que Dios te bendiga, mi hijo.* I told you. You're destined. You're designed for great things, David. God has plans for you. Plans to prosper you and to keep you."

Chapter 10

COLLEGE

Dejarse vencer por la vida es peor que dejarse vencer por la muerte. Lo último es inevitable. Lo primero es voluntario. (Allowing yourself defeat from life is worse than dying. The latter is inevitable. The first is a choice.)

JULIA DE BURGOS

My mother, father, and I made the two-and-a-half-hour drive to Brunswick in my parents' white Ford Escort. It was a silent trip, except for the music that played in the background: doo-wop, blues, and salsa. I sat in the back of the car, anxious and wondering about what lay ahead. What would the dorms be like? How about my roommate? What about girls? Could I actually make it through college?

As we arrived on the Bowdoin campus, I was in awe of the scenery. As Mom and Dad left to park the car and I stood on the main campus overwhelmed, I realized my first impression had been wrong. The campus was whiter than I remembered. I had figured there were probably some Latinos, blacks, or other people of color *somewhere* on campus. Maybe they were studying, in class, or at the dorms? Nope. As I stood on the campus lawn in late August of my freshman year, in 1993, I realized I was in Whiteville, USA.

There were the Jeeps and Saabs I'd seen during my visit, along with Audis, Mercedes-Benzes, and BMWs. A smiling blonde drove by in a Jeep Cherokee. Students were wearing these funny strappy leather sandals and polos, which I'd later learn were Birkenstocks and L.L.Bean shirts. Along with boxes of their belongings, I saw them carrying skis and poles into their dorms.

Skis? They brought skis? I had never seen skis in person . . . whoa!

I looked down at my own outfit: a tight, tie-dye T-Shirt my mom had bought at JCPenney that showed off my muscles, khaki shorts from Ann & Hope, and sneakers. I reached up and felt the black choker on my neck, then smoothed my hair. I had the same gelled hairstyle I'd worn since ninth grade, which had always felt cool but now felt out of place as I looked at the guys walking past me with loosely styled longish hair, parted down the middle or side, looking like they'd just walked off the beach. Or maybe the ski lift.

At five-foot-ten and 235 pounds, I was a sizeable dude, and all the guys around me looked to be 110 pounds wet. They flirted with petite girls wearing L.L.Bean shirts and tan pants.

I was a fish out of water. I had never seen anything like this before. It was like landing in a foreign country without a suitcase or a dictionary to help me speak the language.

It struck me suddenly that this felt even more shocking than moving to the United States as a kid. At least in Lynn, people looked like me, talked like me. They had real life struggles and street grit. These Bowdoin folks wouldn't last a day in my neighborhood.

Shaking my head, I searched the campus map in my hand for my dorm room, then spotted Mom and Dad in the distance, walking in my direction. I had a pile of belongings next to me: a large suitcase my parents planned to bring home empty, my guitar, a black trash bag full of shoes, my Triple F.A.T. Goose coat, and my music tapes. A grocery bag of snack food Mom had prepared for me, like she was dropping me off in Siberia. A cardboard box with my old sheets from home, two towels, and some toiletries. As I waited for my parents, I surveyed the campus.

Did that girl have a butler with her? I thought. I squinted my eyes. Yes, that was a uniformed man who carried boxes into the dorm as a pretty brunette girl walked up to a tall redhead and air kissed her on both cheeks. What the hell?

Where the hell am I?

Finally, Mom and Dad made it to where I stood.

"What's wrong?" Mom asked.

I corrected my incredulous expression and smiled. "Nothing, Ma. Let's go." I handed her the lightest item, my guitar, hoisted the trash bag with my belongings over my shoulders, and grabbed the handle of my suitcase. "You got that, Dad?"

Dad, already holding the cardboard box with the snack bag on top, nodded. "Where are we heading?"

I nodded in the direction of a red building set against tall pine trees. "That way. Second floor, room 3A."

Several minutes later, we arrived at my dorm room. The door was open, so I walked in. But then I stopped immediately.

Oh, hell no. I thought. *Hell no.*

Standing in front of me was another Latino. This was the first non-Anglo person I'd seen since I arrived. Seriously? Did Bowdoin room us together because we were the only Latinos on campus? Anger burst inside me. I felt like a pressure cooker about to explode. I was pissed.

"I'm Vern," my new roommate said.

"What the hell is this?" I replied.

Vern looked around the room, behind him, then back at me. "What do you mean?" he said. His face suddenly registered understanding. Mom and Dad looked at each other.

"Don't be rude, David. I'm Ana, David's mother," Mom said, reaching out her hand. "This is my husband, Tony." Vern shook both of their hands, one eye on me.

I said nothing but instead looked around the room. The space was small, with a fireplace in the middle of the wall opposite the door, and two beds pushed up against the walls on either side of the fireplace. I pointed to the bed to my left, farthest from the door. "I'll take this one."

I heaved the bags onto the floor, and stood the suitcase next to the bed to claim my space. Mom and Dad set their items at the foot of my bed. All the while, I eyed Vern. I was livid. It felt as if the two of us had been reduced to a label, to the color of our skin, to our ethnic boxes. The shock of the whiteness, juxtaposed with this categorization, pulsed within me. I was about to explode with anger and I needed to get out of that room.

"Let's go," I said to my parents.

As we walked out, I turned back to cast a warning look at Vern, who appeared dumbfounded. He met my eyes and quickly looked away, confused.

Soon, I was saying goodbye to my parents, waving at them as they drove away, and turning back to look again at my new home for the next four years. A sense of dread anchored within me, twisting my insides, clouding my thoughts. Around me, wealth and whiteness pulsed like a skipping record, playing over and over without relief. With my parents long out of view, I felt a deep sense of loneliness and distance. I was in a place I didn't belong, with people who I'd never connect with. What was I doing here?

Later, I'd learn that on the entire Bowdoin campus, there were twelve Latinos. Twelve, out of approximately 1,380. Twelve people who shared my ethnicity, if not my background. On the entire campus, only 6 percent were black or Latino, and 88 percent were white. No wonder it looked like a sea of white folks.

When I got back to the dorm that day, Vern was gone. Smart. At least he had that going for him. I unpacked my things, ate the sandwich Mom had left behind for me, and went to bed at nine o'clock, glad Vern wasn't back by then. I turned toward the wall and cried myself to sleep that night: angry, lonely sobs. I was woken a couple hours later by a creaking door and sliver of light from the hallway.

I felt Vern standing in the room, unmoving, as if considering something, and then finally the weighty sound of him getting into bed. I began to cry again, silently, letting the tears flow down my cheeks and onto my pillow.

The first weeks on campus were culture shock on overdrive. Football double sessions became the only time I felt some relief from my ever-present discomfort around all these students who were so different than me. On the field, all I had to think about was football, violence, and hitting. Helmet to helmet contact was definitely one way to take my frustrations out.

My third day on campus, I walked by a kid doing a "project on poverty," and as I watched him give away his belongings to "understand what it's like to be poor," all I could think was, This motherfucker. Seriously?

My classmates, the students who were supposed to be my peers, were studying people like me, trying to understand what it's like to be poor. As he handed out his jacket, coat, polos, and other belongings—most of which were L.L.Bean and looked brand new—I couldn't help but stare. I was incredulous. I walked away that day seething, barely holding myself back from punching him in the teeth.

Still, I stayed cordial to the other kids on campus. If I was going to make it at Bowdoin, I needed to understand how to fit in. I had to adapt and find my place in this environment that felt so foreign. But even conversation was hard. The other kids talked differently: When I'd say "What up?" they'd reply "How are you?" or "How was your summer?"

How are you? How was your summer? What *was* that? I had a lot to learn.

Vern, the roommate I'd rejected at first, soon became one of my closest friends on campus. He was a Puerto Rican-Ecuadorian kid from Brooklyn whose father had walked out when he was young. He'd grown up with his mom, sister, and grandma, and had to take odd jobs as a kid to support the family. All his life, Vern had been pressured by his mom and grandma to be the family's savior. Going to school, for him, was about obligation to help his family get out of poverty. I got that. Within days, it became clear what a wonderful human being he was. He didn't hold onto first impressions, and instead befriended me quickly and easily. He was soft-spoken, caring, and tender-hearted. To this day, I still believe God placed Vern in my life during my freshman year at Bowdoin.

When I asked him if he said, "How are you?" he laughed and said, "No, man. No. I don't say that."

Vern would make jokes about how people spoke on campus, mimicking the eye contact and giant smiles the white students wore when they talked. He'd crack me up telling stories about how he avoided interacting with other students and looked for ways to stay off campus. We also shared about our upbringings and the similarities of our family's trajectories: his grandmother's and mother's journey from Ecuador to New York compared with my grandparents' and parents' journey from Puerto Rico to Indiana, back to Puerto Rico, and finally to Massachusetts. We talked food, music, and girls.

I called my father at night during my first few weeks. Each time, I'd ask him how he and mom were doing. Then I'd tell him I was fine, I was doing OK, and that I wanted to come home.

But I wasn't fine. I had moved my bed into the closet—a walk-in about eight feet by three-and-a-half feet—so I could cry without Vern hearing me. I cried almost every night until my tears took me to sleep. I was crying out of anger and raw emotion. It was my way of coping with the dramatic changes I was facing. When double sessions for football ended in preparation for the start of the school year, I wondered, What am I going to do? Without the distraction of football, I knew I'd have way too much time with my thoughts. I'd be even more alone.

But even with my insecurity and feeling out of place, I started to make friends and kept reaching out to adapt and adjust. There was Vern, who was becoming an important part of my life: my inseparable brother, someone I looked out for and relied on. Then there were my teammates: Tony Teixeira, a Cape Verdean kid who had gone to Roxbury Latin, a private boys' school, but grew up on the poor side of Cambridge. Tex was smooth and knew how to play what he called the college game. He was my model for fitting in: he was polished, with khaki pants and the whole bit, but understood me and, in his own way, coached me. There was Bernie Owens, a burly Irish kid who grew up working-class and didn't give a flying rat's butt about anybody's opinion. There was Ryan Dunn from Westford, also in Massachusetts, who I had played against in an all-star high school game and started hanging out with on campus. There was Anthony Molinari, an Italian kid from Worcester.

This was my new family, my football guys. My brothers. These guys became crucial to my transition at Bowdoin and I learned a ton about college from them.

Still, I was calling Dad every night, telling him I wanted to leave Bowdoin. This place sucks, I'd tell him. Can I just come home?

By the third or fourth week, Dad was done.

"The calls are costing me money," he told me. "Stop crying. You're a man now. If you call me again complaining, you won't have a home to return to." He hung up abruptly, and I sat in my dorm room, stunned. His words ran through me, over and over. I'm a man now. But I was a man in transition. A man trying to understand the rapid change taking place in his life, trying to adapt to a new life in a completely unfamiliar place. I might be a football machine, but I was not made of stone. And this place, Bowdoin—this environment that was painfully foreign—was challenging every ounce of my mind and spirit.

The next night, I called Coach Dempsey. If I couldn't call my dad, I'd call my second dad. Dempsey picked up and listened for a long time. I told him about the Birkenstocks and the kid doing the poverty project. I told him I thought I was failing my classes. Just a few weeks in, and my teachers were already asking me to stay after class, giving me pep talks, and expressing concern.

Silence hung between us, and finally, I said, "Coach, what should I do?" I clutched the phone, waiting for wisdom from my coach.

"Bowdoin is one of the best things that's going to happen to you," Dempsey said. "It's going to change your life. It's transformational. If you quit, you're back on the streets of Lynn." His voice was tense, stilted. His breath heavy in the receiver. I imagined his shoulders hunched like they always were during games when he was explaining his strategy to the starting lineup. "You're going to end up at the Lynn Common with people who quit. If you finish Bowdoin, you will be prepared to soar in life, to help your family. If you quit, you won't. It's that simple. You quit, you lose. Is that what you want?"

"No, Coach," I replied, swallowing hard to hold back an explosion of emotions until I was off the phone.

"David, you can do this. It's in you. Dig deep and fight. I've seen you fight. Do it again." The line was silent for several seconds, and I held the receiver firmly in my hand as if it were a lifeline. Finally, he went on, "It's easy to give up and quit, but it's harder to fight, keep going, and overcome the challenge. The rewards will be unlike anything you can imagine right now if you stick with Bowdoin. Keep going. I'm proud of you. So are your dad and mom."

We hung up, and I sat on my bed in the closet and cried for what felt like the hundredth time since I'd arrived on campus. Maybe Dad and Dempsey were right. This was my shot. And I was trying to figure out how to approach it and change my mindset to overcome the challenges ahead: new life, new school, new people, new culture, new teams, new town, new outlook.

Around eleven that night, Vern opened the closet door to get his jacket before heading out to a party. I was sitting upright on the bed, leaning against the wall and staring at the clothes hanging in front of me. I quickly wiped away my tears.

"It's OK, man," he said. "Can I sit?"

I nodded, still wiping tears away. Vern sat next to me and leaned his back against the wall. "I'm going through the same shit."

I thought of all Vern had shared with me, about his family and the obligation he felt to succeed, not for himself but for them. If he could do it, why couldn't I? Here he was figuring it out and hanging out with kids on campus. He seemed fine. Happy. Why couldn't I be that way?

"I just can't get used to this place," I said.

"Me either," he said. "But we have to."

I thought of my family, each person flashing through my mind: Mom, Dad, Diana, Dan, Dwayne. Each face reminded me of why I was there. Of the sacrifices they'd all made. Vern might be his family's savior, but I had five saviors in my family, and it was my obligation to do my part, to follow through with this opportunity, this path that was paved by their sacrifice. It struck me that I felt out of place at Bowdoin, but I also hadn't fully tried to find my place yet.

I breathed in the smell of stale fabric softener and let out a heavy sigh. "You're right, bro. You're right."

We sat there for a long time, Vern and I, talking about our lives and what the next four years would be like. We shared our hopes for the future. I couldn't help but think of George, and remember those talks we'd had on so many porch steps: his, mine, Abel's. I thought of Rob and Nicio, and wondered what they were doing right then. I thought of Samanda, the beautiful girl I never got to speak to.

Vern missed his party, and it was one in the morning by the time we finished talking. As I lay in bed that night, I felt a new sense of resolve. I could do this. With Vern, and my football family, and whatever else I could find inside myself—courage, grit, faith in God—I could do this. Still, the chip on my shoulder, the one that had been deepening since adolescence, had gotten even bigger during those weeks. Acceptance of my circumstances didn't get rid of the anger. I wouldn't just make it in spite of where I came from, but because of it.

As I drifted off to sleep that night, Samanda's face overtook my thoughts. I hadn't stopped thinking of her since the day we met. I couldn't call her house because her stepdad might find out. In the dark of my closet bedroom, an idea struck me: I'll write her a letter under a pseudonym. I'll send it to her house as . . . Dina Mora. I fell asleep without tears, thinking of Samanda and my new mindset and approach to Bowdoin—adapt, adjust, ask for help, and overcome.

I stood up from the couch and stretched. Anthony and Alexander looked up at me from the two easy chairs. I figured if I stood, they would too. But they stayed put, so I sat back down.

"It seems like you cried a lot," Anthony said.

"Yeah, and in your bed too. It's like a theme or something," Alexander said.

I laughed. I had spent a lot of adolescent nights crying in the dark of my bedroom, away from the judgment of others.

"You're right, I did," I began. "Because I was raised in a traditional Puerto Rican culture, I was taught men aren't supposed to show emotion, much less cry. Crying was showing weakness, and it was not accepted. I was ashamed of my tears and how deeply I felt my isolation and loneliness. I could only really feel everything when I was alone, and since I always lived with people, the only truly private place to cry was in my bed under the cover of dark, where no one could see me."

My boys looked at each other, and for a second, I thought I saw a flash of humor in their expressions.

But then Anthony stood from where he was sitting opposite me and came over to sit next to me on the arm of the couch. He wrapped his arm around me in a side hug, squeezed me once, and let go. "I'm sorry, Dad. I'm sorry you were soft," he said, a witty look on his face.

I craned my head to look at him, then at Anthony, whose face was stretched into a big smile, and we all broke out laughing. My two boys. They were my legacy. They were proof of the cycle being broken, of young men who would go on to make a difference in this world. I could see my two boys opening up to the experiences of so many Latino, black, and poor white men and women, ones who didn't have a mom or dad who had broken free themselves, who didn't get the privilege of sitting on a couch in a two-story home in Lynnfield, Massachusetts, and wondering what life would have been like *if* . . .

"It was a long time ago," I said. "I am a different man today."

They were both staring hard at me now, and I felt emotion creep into my throat, but I took a breath to hold it down. I wanted to tell them the rest of the story with strength and clarity. I scooted over on the couch to make room for Anthony, and he slid next to me, leaning his head back on the fluffy built-in pillow on the armrest. With a deep breath, I went on.

First quarter of freshman year rolled on, and while I stopped crying myself to sleep, I started numbing my pain. Weed, booze, women, anything not to think about home or poverty or my insecurities. I began drinking almost every night, Wednesday through Sunday, and while I was performing on the field, I was failing in the classroom. I did anything I could to escape my own mind. On campus, I was becoming known much like I'd climbed the popularity ladder in high school. I started getting recruited for fraternities; guys would hunt me down to take me to parties. They knew I'd always be up for it.

I was struggling academically, not just because of partying but also because I wasn't prepared academically. I didn't understand the schoolwork. I'd never written a thirty-page paper. I'd never had to independently manage my coursework—and the reading! There was so much reading. I wasn't able to comprehend, let alone critically think about, the scholarly articles, essays, books, and assignments my professors gave me. Being one of twelve Latinos on the entire campus, and also from a low socioeconomic area, I wasn't prepared, and Bowdoin wasn't prepared for me. The college wasn't equipped to deal with low-income kids from inner cities or rural poverty. In the 1990s Bowdoin was an elite, small New England college, with a large percentage of the student body from small New England private schools.

At the same time, there was a tiny percentage of students who weren't wealthy white kids. Kids like me were failing, and the school noticed. We didn't know how to study effectively and hadn't been trained to think critically, at least not in the way Bowdoin appropriately required us to. So here I was, here *we* were, at this amazing institution that wasn't well equipped to support kids like me navigate the elite college experience.

There were kids like Johnny from northern Maine, near the border of Canada; he was a potato farmer who studied and worked hard but was also completely out of place. There was a black kid, Willie, from the inner city; like me, he was completely out of his depth. A good number of the kids at Bowdoin had gone to prep schools or had taken advanced placement classes in high school. They hadn't had teachers pass them so they could play in the game on Friday. The class load, the material, the way professors expected me to think critically—I wasn't ready. I didn't know how to catch up and I was afraid to admit it.

Along with my academics, I was still struggling to adapt socially and understand my identity and place in this new place. I had what felt like mental craziness every second of the day. Questions ran through my head: How can I make it here? Should I start talking like these people? I was stuck in a world of me versus them, and I knew that wasn't the right equation or the right analysis. But I had no idea how to address the cognitive dissonance.

Underneath my insecurities was a major mental dilemma I could not escape. I felt like I wasn't accepted. The chip on my shoulder became a deep crevice, something I carried with me to every party, every conversation. A rumor went around campus that I didn't like white people, but the truth was, I felt like I didn't belong, like an outsider, and that made me angry. Defensive. I had verbal run-ins at frat parties and got into dumb fights.

I'd walk up to people and say things like, "What are you looking at?" To which most of the white kids would say, "Nothing. I wasn't looking at you." I was proving myself and my worth, just like I'd done back in Lynn. But these weren't the streets of Lynn; this was Brunswick. I recognized the difference, but I didn't know how to handle this realization and wasn't adapting the way I perhaps should have. Instead, I got angrier, more insecure, and more paranoid about my "otherness"—my poverty and my ethnic background.

But even as my anger boiled, something else was shifting inside me. As a reading assignment for education class, I read *Hunger of Memory* by Richard Rodriguez. In it, Rodriguez details his journey as a Mexican American, and although our heritage was different, there was truth in his writing that I felt deep inside me. He writes:

> *The boy who first entered* a classroom barely able to speak English, twenty years later concluded his studies in the stately quiet of the reading room in the British Museum. Thus with one sentence I can summarize my academic career. It will be harder to summarize what sort of life connects the boy to the man.[1]

Although I did not agree with many of his points of view, I related to how he embraced education as a powerful tool for personal growth, how his family sacrificed to enable him to attend prestigious schools, and how he grew up surrounded by Spanish-speaking relatives who kept to themselves. His writing made me think of my own family.

> *I grew up in a* house where the only regular guests were my relations. For one day, enormous families of relatives would visit and there would be so many people that the noise and the bodies would spill out to the backyard and front porch.[2]

His education, faith, and family were powerful engines that shaped his life. My experience was similar: shaped by family, faith, education, and grit. But whereas he appeared to eventually reject his ethnicity and family, I fully embraced my heritage and my family. In college I was discovering more about my family's history and my heritage than ever before, and it served as an anchor in a sea of personal uncertainty.

As I read his words, I began to recognize that the turmoil inside me wasn't just because I was out of place. It was because I was changing. I was being tugged away from my life and transformed into something completely new, something that mirrored the people around me who didn't look and sound like me.

As I read Rodriguez's book, I started understanding my place. His words spoke to me: You are part of a longer historical identity. You're part of a family who is trying to make it in this country, and you're going to have to figure out how to adapt here. It was OK to adapt, embrace change, and experience something new. It was OK to engage in open dialogue to learn about "them" and help them understand and learn about me. The closed Latino family atmosphere I cherished was being disrupted by books, new friends, new vocabulary, new ways to analyze, new ways to absorb information, and a new environment I needed to adapt to and dominate.

About two months into my first semester, my student adviser, Professor Kaplan, asked to meet with me. She handed me two pink slips, warning that I was on the verge of failing two classes, and told me that if I continued to get bad grades, it could result in failure—or worse, going home. I was mortified. I didn't know what to say or how to respond. As I stared wordlessly at the pink papers in my hand, she said she'd already talked with the office of student affairs and this was my official warning.

As I walked out of Professor Kaplan's office, I thought of a fellow student I'd met in my government class, Herly, who had noticed I was struggling and offered to tutor me. These pink slips confirmed Herly's concern for my success at Bowdoin. I was afraid enough of failing to finally accept the help—scared of letting my family down, terrified of ending up on the streets like Coach told me I would if I couldn't make it at Bowdoin.

Shortly after my conversation with Professor Kaplan, I went to meet Herly at her dorm room. I knocked on her door and was greeted by two smiling women, and right behind them was Herly. The two women parted so Herly could step forward.

Herly was a Haitian American woman from Florida with a sharp intellect and commanding presence. A freshman like me, she exuded confidence and stood her ground on issues she cared about. While she was my height, somehow she seemed to tower over me—and everyone else too.

"Hey. Can we talk?" I said.

"I knew you'd come," she replied. I tried to read her expression. Was she still willing to help me? "Ladies, can you please give me a few minutes? I need to talk with David." I said goodbye to the girls as they left the room and then turned to face Herly, who had stepped aside to let me in.

Herly was no joke. She asked me point-blank if I knew how to study or comprehend what I read. I was stunned and embarrassed. There was no small talk; it was all business, like she had everything under control. She spoke eloquently, and I realized right away that she wasn't intimidated by me.

After a long, uncomfortable silence, I finally replied, "Herly, I need help. I don't know how to focus or study like I should. But I want to learn, and I'm willing to put in the time and the work to succeed."

"OK," Herly said. "We need to make a deal. No parties or drinking on weekdays. No staying at parties after midnight. Weeknights and weekend afternoons, we study." She paused and eyed me. "Deal?"

I gulped imperceptibly, considered my limited options, and finally said, "Deal."

We got to work that week. I kept my end of the bargain, and Herly kept hers, helping me study every day. Herly was caring but tough, just like the women in my family. And she also put me in my place like they did.

Herly was a force: outspoken, confident, smart, and quick-witted. To say that her academic confidence outpaced mine by miles is an understatement. I learned that she came from Haitian parents who had emigrated to New York and worked all of their lives to put their children through college. She knew how to walk, talk, and even sit like the kids at Bowdoin, but she seemed to do it without compromising her identity.

Pretty soon, Herly became one of my closest friends on campus, and with Vern and her, I now had allies who made sure I was OK. By mid-freshman year, my football buddies knew that when Herly showed up to a party, it meant David had to go. She would hunt me down, searching for me from party to party, and drag me home. I eventually stopped resisting and started relying on her as my third mom. My Mom, Diana, and now Herly.

She cared for me. She saw something in me that she wanted to protect. She saw goodness within me and a desire to grow. And she appreciated that my street grit needed refinement.

Herly was like a bridge between me and Bowdoin.

Slowly, my grades started improving. In our study sessions, Herly emphasized critical thinking, one of the fundamentals Bowdoin instills in students. Between my professors at Bowdoin and Herly's investment in me, I began to think critically and to question everything I read. Herly also challenged me to expand my vocabulary by learning a new word every day. I got organized with my classwork and developed study skills, as well as discipline and structure that resembled my football routines. My grades began climbing back up. I began devouring the assigned reading—thanks, especially, to the support and encouragement of Susan Bell, my sociology professor, and Penny Martin, my education professor—absorbing the information and ideas from my classes. Professors Bell and Martin were always on my case, asking me to come by after class, quizzing me with questions to test my comprehension and critical thinking.

My Spanish professor, John Turner, also took an interest in me. In his thick British accent, he'd encourage me: "You're a big, tense guy. Relax. This is a small moment in time. You'll see. You've got to embrace this and absorb as much as you can. Learn from everybody. Talk to people. Everyone is going through the same shit, Morales. *No seas tan pendejo* . . . just relax."

He helped me understand that all the white kids around me were dealing with similar issues that I was or worse. Some were poor and didn't want to show it. Others struggled from a lack of confidence, and their luxury cars and name-brand clothes were hiding a side of them they didn't want the world to see. Some were fighting mental health issues or came from broken homes. They, too, were trying to find their place, just like me.

I began connecting with more and more people. I learned about networking from my professors and turned it into a competition in my mind. "Who can I meet today?" became a sport. I also stopped calling people out at parties as often and began having more conversations with people who didn't look like me, or who were involved in activities or sports I knew nothing about. Though I still felt like I didn't belong, I at least felt like I might survive college. I might make it at Bowdoin. More importantly, I began to realize that most of us students had more in common than not. Each of us was in a period of transition in our lives, and while some were more prepared academically than others, we were all kids in college trying to figure life out. From my perspective, our race, color, and socioeconomic class didn't matter as much as our character and mindset.

Freshman year, I felt my identity evolving, shifting, metamorphizing. I also felt my brain expanding, thinking differently, and absorbing more data and information by the day. By the end of the school year, as I packed up my dorm room and said goodbye to Vern for the summer, I had adopted a new mindset.

"If, because of my schooling, I had grown culturally separated from my parents," Rodriguez writes in *Hunger of Memory*, "my education finally had given me ways of speaking and caring about that fact."[3] I wondered, Am I growing culturally separated from my family too?

That was something I could not accept nor would allow. But as my intellect and desire for more knowledge grew, the tug between life in Lynn and my new reality at Bowdoin was ever-present in my mind.

That summer put my transformation to the test.

I was home for break, working at Upward Bound, a program led by a wonderful individual we all respected growing up, Chris Hogan. Chris was from a fantastic family of hard-working Irish Americans. Older than me, Chris grew up near Marian Gardens and knew my brother Dwayne well. Ever since I was a young kid, he'd referred to me as "Dwayne's little brother."

Upward Bound helped to prepare young people of color and kids from low-income families for college by taking them out of the inner city and hosting them at a college campus for a week. As part of the program, I mentored juniors and seniors in high school, spending a week in the dorms at the University of Massachusetts Amherst, which was about two hours from Lynn and nothing like the city. It was such a cool program, and I couldn't help but think how different my own freshman year would have been if I'd attended something like it.

I spent those first weeks of summer as essentially a camp counselor helping Chris with whatever he needed to make the program successful. Watching Chris operate was impactful because it was the first time I saw an executive-type person who came off as relatable—one of us Lynn kids in a leadership position. Chris treated each of us like professionals and expected a lot from us, making sure we knew that we were instilling leadership as well as a passion for educational opportunity in these kids. As I watched Chris lead our group of counselors, I thought to myself, he looks like one of the kids from Bowdoin. If he can grow into a leader, maybe I can too.

While Upward Bound required a lot of my time that summer, I hung out with friends when I could. One hot August evening, I was with Rob at our friend Luke Morris's house. Luke was a poor Irish dude from a tough family who was fully immersed in urban culture and lived and breathed the television show "Yo! MTV Raps." We used to say that if you cut Luke with a knife, he'd bleed black. We'd been friends in high school and hadn't seen each other since the start of the school year. But while I'd gone off to my private college, Luke was in Lynn, partying, going down the life path George, Rob, and I were afraid of following. As I looked around the room at Luke's place, I realized most of the people there had done the same. They had never made it to college or had dropped out, and were spending their time partying, getting lit. I thought of my friend Antoine, who had been killed by his girlfriend just a couple months earlier; I remembered another friend, Joseph, who had been shot at a party over something to do with drugs and women.

Their lives were just gone. Poof. Erased from the streets. Mostly forgotten. Death was part of our lives. I didn't want it to be part of mine.

The party pulsed around us: alcohol, weed, cocaine, crack, pills. Rob and I were drinking and hanging out, enjoying the party and talking about college when Luke spoke over the noise of the party.

"You're a fucking sellout, Morales," he said. He was sitting on a couch near me, a beer in his hand.

"What did you say to me?" I said. Anger raged through me like someone had flipped a switch in my brain. I felt my knuckles clench into a fist.

Luke stood. "You sound like a white boy. You ain't the same anymore, dawg."

I stared at Luke, and everything inside of me wanted to destroy him. Shut him up. Prove that I was from the hood, that nothing had changed, and I could crush him in seconds.

But the truth was, I had changed. I was changing. I felt my body relax, and heard myself laugh. "Whatever, man. You're crazy."

Someone called Luke's name and he glared at me, then lifted his chin. "Fucking sellout," he said before walking away.

When Luke was out of earshot, I said to Rob, "Let's get out of here, bro."

Rob waved me off so he could finish a conversation, and as I waited for him, I processed what had just happened. Less than a year ago, I would have laid Luke out. I would have gotten high to prove I fit in. But for some reason, I didn't.

Damn, I thought. I'm changing. I don't belong here anymore.

I thought changing would feel wrong, like I was somehow betraying my community and culture, but the truth was I felt comfortable. I was at peace with who I was becoming. As the party hummed around me, and Luke eyed me from the other side of the room, I felt, for the first time, like I was becoming who I was meant to be. I didn't want this for my life: to become a used-to-be, fight at parties, and constantly prove myself as being tough enough, man enough, hood enough. It was a life of poverty and I feared poverty. I remembered a line from *Hunger of Memory*: "This is what matters to me: the story of the scholarship boy who returns home one summer from college to discover bewildering silence, facing his parents. This is my story."

At home, things were changing too. Dad had a job and Mom was struggling with a mild illness. Dwayne had landed a good job and was calming down. Dan was a police officer in Lynn, and Diana was studying to become a teacher. After my Upward Bound work, we spent a couple of weeks together in the evenings. I started using my new vocabulary with Dwayne, and he would laugh at me.

"Punk, I don't care how big or smart you are, I'll still kick your ass," he told me.

Meanwhile, I would talk to Mom and Dad about all the new things I was learning. It was funny to see how my brain was processing information differently. Prior to college, I wouldn't question my parents or siblings. Now, I would respond to them with logical explanations or dissertations. My mind was evolving, and so was I.

To my surprise, I wanted to be back at Bowdoin. I couldn't wait to return to my new friends and professors, and the college that was giving me the opportunity to discover new parts of my brain, and the qualities and skills I needed to develop and prepare for the future. The place that was offering me the keys to a whole new universe and doors to new places and opportunities I would explore later in life.

Sophomore year of college became a watershed experience for me, a big transition in my life at Bowdoin. While I'd spent the first year feeling like I didn't belong and struggling to adapt, I felt like I was finding my place sophomore year. I was becoming more popular, talking to more people. While my confidence had boosted during freshman year, it exploded sophomore year.

Nearly anywhere I went on campus, people knew me. I could walk into any situation—any party, any department, any gathering—and be welcomed. I'd go to other fraternities, off-campus apartments, and the dorms. I'd hang with frat guys, stoners, athletes, nerds. When I wasn't at parties, I'd play my guitar. I started a blues band and began singing on campus and at bars.

I was also seen as a leader among many of the younger people of color who were coming onto campus. I joined the Latin American Association and the African American Society. I was a fraternity member. Alongside football and schoolwork, I worked two on-campus jobs, at the library and the cafeteria, to help my father pay the modest amount left after my financial aid. Even with my two jobs, I didn't have much disposable income after splitting the school fees with my dad, about $1,200 per semester. I was able to buy myself an inexpensive electric guitar and small amp with the money I'd made, but I didn't have much extra. While most students spent spring break abroad, or in California or Florida, I didn't travel. I couldn't ask my dad for money to do something like that.

While Samanda and I had written sporadically freshman year, I lost touch with her sophomore year. Even though we hadn't communicated for a year and a half, I still kept the senior photo she had given me in my wallet. No matter what girl I was interested in at Bowdoin, or who was interested in me, deep in my chest was an inexplicable connection to that girl back home. The beauty who resembled a Mexican soap star, just like the ones I remembered watching on TV when I was in Puerto Rico.

I still called home to talk to Mom and Dad, but my siblings had their own things going on. I started to feel an intellectual divide with my family. I was learning all this new information at school and began to think I was really smart. I started speaking better, using bigger vocabulary, and phasing out my Boston-Puerto Rican accent. Deep down, I thought I was more intelligent than my family members.

My siblings didn't seem to notice, or probably laughed it off as they typically did, since I was still the baby brother. Diana was getting married. Dan was immersed in his work as a police officer, and every time I talked to him it was police department this, cops that. Dwayne still seemed to be on a better path, but he didn't give a crap about much other than women and his boys at La Grange Terrace.

I started coming home less frequently. I'd stay on campus during some breaks and began focusing on one quest: How do I get better? How do I get smarter? What do I need to do to get out of poverty and land a good job when I graduate?

I was still drinking. I was insecure, but acted confident. I continued wrestling with my identity, especially as I noticed myself breaking bread with all these white kids around me, beginning to adopt some of their mannerisms and ways of speaking.

Still, as I developed my identity as a sophomore, I noticed something different about this experience compared to high school. In high school, I was plagued by a deep lack of confidence; how I showed up on the outside was not how I felt on the inside. I was careful not to ruffle too many feathers because I wanted people to like me. I wanted to be accepted.

In college, I was learning to socialize in a new environment. I felt more confident in who I was, but I was navigating different social environments. I was observing, learning. It took time to reconcile the way I was taught to socialize in Lynn and how I was expected to interact at Bowdoin. The people around me, my mentors and close friends, helped me find my way: Vern, Herly, Penny Martin, Susan Bell, John Turner, Tex, Ryan, My Lam, Anthony, and my newer friends, Payne, Wihbey, Lorne, Devlin, Steve, Katie, Allison, Uyen, Besty, and Hart, among others.

One day, as I walked across campus on a bright spring afternoon, something clicked. I realized the networking I'd learned about in class was something I'd been doing most of my life. Going from table to table in high school, frat to frat in college—it was all networking. I had been forming relationships that became essentially social capital, without even realizing it. This realization blew my mind, and I started looking for even more opportunities to network. I focused on building relationships and connecting with as many people as possible, including my professors and even the college president, Bob Edwards.

Along with becoming more intentional with networking, I spent most of my time outside the fraternity I lived in. During my time on campus, frats were seen by many as enclaves that wouldn't associate with other folks on campus, and I wanted to do the opposite. I wanted to associate with many on campus because people didn't like football players at Bowdoin back then, and I wanted people to know we were just like everyone else. I wanted them to know that football players were human beings, and I also wanted to explore and experience everything Bowdoin had to offer because I was loving the discovery of new worlds.

My sons hadn't moved from their spots on the couch and chair, but now my wife was leaning against a wall in the kitchen, holding a mug of tea with both hands and listening to my story.

"What do you mean 'new world'?" Anthony asked. "Wasn't everything pretty much the same as freshman year? Same fraternity, same school, same football team?"

"Yes and no. Yes, it was the same. No, it wasn't. Because I wasn't the same anymore."

Alexander had a funny look on this face.

"Do you want to ask something?" I said with a smile.

He grinned. "Did you wear L.L.Bean?"

I couldn't help but laugh out loud. "Not yet," I replied.

My boys erupted in laughter, like this was the funniest thing they'd ever heard. I wasn't sure if they were laughing at the fact that I changed so much or picturing me in an L.L.Bean fleece.

"But in all seriousness," I began, waiting for them to compose themselves, "I learned a lot about myself that year, especially when it came to networking, which became crucially important for the next decade of my life, especially after college."

"Did you know what you wanted to do after you graduated?" Alexander asked.

"I had no idea what I was doing," I replied. "I just knew I wanted something better for my life. I wanted to run away from poverty. Looking back, I believe the hand of God was working. Back then, I was just taking small steps and learning by watching other people, both the students around me and the adults. I was adapting and learning as I went."

"Do you think other kids felt that way?" Alexander asked.

"I don't know. I don't think so, at least not the kids who grew up with money or resources, or exposure to elite colleges or prep schools, which was a large portion of the student body. I was part of a small group of kids who would either recognize the amazing opportunity of Bowdoin . . . or fail. Go back to the streets, or the farm, or wherever they'd come from."

"Did some fail?" Anthony asked.

"Some failed."

Alexander had reclined and now sat up straight. "What happened to them?"

"I don't know," I said, wishing I had a better answer.

Silence formed between us like a spiderweb, each of us spinning our own thoughts. I thought of Jaime, the Mexican American kid who didn't make it, dropped out freshman year. I remembered Shandra, the black girl who transferred to a community college. What had happened to them? Unlike most of the kids in my neighborhood growing up, they'd had a shot. They'd tasted possibility. Privilege. They'd had exposure to a different life. Had they made it out? Did they find their way?

"So what happened next?" Alexander said.

"The story gets even better my junior year." I stood. "How about we walk for a bit?"

We grabbed our jackets and walked out our front door. The sun was setting and the sky was awash in gold and red. We had a short window of daylight, and I was already hatching a plan. We'd walk, and then light a bonfire out back. The rest of the story seemed best told by firelight.

Chapter 11

MOMENTS THAT DEFINE YOU

*Be sure you put your feet in the
right place, then stand firm.*

ABRAHAM LINCOLN

I opened my eyes and looked around the unfamiliar room. It was the first semester of my junior year, and last I remembered, I had been with several friends. My head throbbed, and I shielded my eyes from the sun streaming through the windows.

Pushing myself up to sit, I realized I had been laying on the floor. I looked down and saw I was fully clothed, wearing the same thing I'd left the house in the night before, but my clothes were stained and rumpled. Where was I? I rubbed my temple as if that would bring back something, anything. As I stood my knees wobbled, and I gripped the desk next to me. Exhaustion swept over my body. A room—I was in a dorm room. I looked around. A cream sweater hung on the bed frame; a photo collage was above the bed with pictures of a smiling brunette hugging different people; a fuzzy pink pen sat on the nightstand; a J. Crew backpack was slung over the desk chair. I leaned forward to study the girl in the photos. She looked familiar . . . I rubbed my head again. It ached. My throat and mouth were bone dry, and suddenly I needed water more than I'd needed anything in my life.

An unopened plastic water bottle was on the desk. I grabbed it and twisted the cap off, drinking it within seconds. Then I walked over to the window and looked out. I was in the Coles Tower. The previous night started coming back to me: I'd been hanging with friends on campus. We'd been in one of their dorm rooms, and they'd had mushrooms, speed, marijuana, beer, and who knows what else. We started partying at eleven in the morning, me with weed and alcohol, and them with a cocktail of drugs and alcohol. At some point that night, I must have blacked out and wandered to whatever room this was and crashed.

Trying to orient myself, I walked to the door and opened it, peeking into the hallway to look at the dorm number: 500. Fifth floor. I had started on the eleventh floor. Where were my friends?

Feeling dizzy, I left the door open and walked back to where I'd been lying to sit on the floor, leaning my back against the bed and stretching out my legs. I glanced at the clock on the nightstand: 12:04 p.m. I dropped my head onto the mattress behind me and rubbed my head to soothe the headache. Everything in my body ached and I was exhausted.

"You're up," a voice chirped.

I lifted my head. It was the brunette from the photos.

"You OK?" she said, as she walked over to sit on the bed just above me and to my right.

"I think so," I said, surprised at the hoarseness of my voice. "What happened?"

"I don't really know," the girl said. "But you were wandering around the halls super late last night. You looked bad. So we put you in my room, and I went to stay with my roommate." When no reply came, she added, "You seemed pretty out of it . . . and we were worried about you. We brought you here and all you did was talk and ramble, so I locked the door and left you alone. When I came back later to bring you water, you were passed out on the floor."

A groan escaped my lips as I started having flashbacks of that night: wandering hallways, looking for my friends. Stairwells, elevators. Then my memory faded. I didn't remember this girl or this room, so I must have been pretty out of it by the time I made it here.

"Did I do anything stupid?" I asked.

"No," she said. "You just looked like you were in bad shape. So I let you sleep here."

"Well, thanks," I said, rubbing my neck, trying to alleviate the throbbing pain in my muscles.

"Sure," she said. "I'm Sue."

"David," I said. I needed to get out of there. "Thank you for letting me crash. I'd better go if I'm going to make it to lunch on time." I stood slowly. My body wobbled once more but I found every bit of strength to steady myself. It was bad enough to crash in a stranger's room; it was worse to still be a mess in front of that stranger the next day. When I was finally upright, I added, "Saturdays are the best days in the cafeteria."

"Saturdays?" she said, standing to walk to the door with me.

"Yeah, I think they're doing burgers today."

"David . . . it's Sunday."

I turned to face her. "What?"

"You definitely need food!" she said, biting her lip. "I finally found your friends this morning and asked them if I should call someone, but they said you were fine. To just let you sleep. I figured you were OK since you were breathing and everything."

"They didn't come to get me?"

"They said to leave you and let you rest."

My thoughts raced in spite of my sluggish brain, hangover, and full day of sleep in a stranger's room. "Thanks, again, Sue," I said as I walked out of her dorm. "Sorry to have crashed in your room for so long."

"Don't mention it," she said. When I was about halfway down the hallway, she called out, "And David?"

"Yeah?" I replied.

"Get better, OK?"

I lifted my hand to my brow and saluted, then turned and continued down the hallway, my legs heavy beneath me, my heart even heavier. My friends—guys I trusted, my buddies. Were they friends, though? They left me. They knew I was gone, out of it, and didn't try to find me; they knew I was passed out and didn't get help. That wasn't cool.

As I walked to my room, the crisp fall air struck my nostrils, waking up my brain, energizing my body. I needed food and headed in the direction of the cafeteria. A shower could wait. I was starving.

Walking alongside the golden oak trees and green pine trees that peppered campus, I realized: I could have died. I could have passed out on that floor and never woken up. According to Sue, I'd been there for more than twenty-four hours. Was it alcohol poisoning? Should I have been taken to the hospital? Was sleep my body's way of fighting for my life? Plus, I'd gone a long time without food or water—why hadn't my friends come to get me, make me drink something, check on me? Why hadn't they done *anything*?

I heard someone call out my name but I ignored them, my head down in thought. As much as I tried to fight the images away, I imagined my mom getting the news that I was in the hospital. That I was hospitalized or dead. I pictured my dad holding her up as she dropped the phone and wailed. I imagined my funeral, a memorial service like the ones held for so many of my friends back home.

I didn't die, but I could have. Or I could have done something stupid and lost my financial aid, or been kicked out. In some ways, that felt worse. I had so much to lose. My Bowdoin friends had parents they could call to get out of trouble; they could transfer to another school. I had this one shot, this one opportunity. I wasn't going to blow it.

No, I decided. That wouldn't be me: a failure, dead. I had been numbing myself with alcohol. I'd been escaping from a feeling that I didn't belong. That I'd never belong.

The life I had been living so far wasn't going to work. I couldn't party hard and succeed at Bowdoin. It wasn't just about grades; it was about my family and our legacy, and how I was preparing for a better future. Bowdoin was a chance to transform my life and my family, and to create a pathway for future success. I needed a clear head and strong body. I needed to change from the insecure young Latino kid from Lynn to the focused, resilient grit machine Coach Dempsey instilled in me. I needed to remember my father's words to me in ninth grade: "You be you."

For myself. For my family. For my community. And for the many kids like me who were given an opportunity to pursue a better future.

As I walked through campus that clear fall day, something struck me, a thought that seemed to come out of nowhere: maybe I could decide to belong, just like I'd decided that past summer to not belong on the streets anymore. Maybe I could make a choice. Maybe I could go down a different path, one that didn't involve partying and doing stupid stuff. One that didn't involve friends who leave me passed out.

I walked into the cafeteria, my body and mind suddenly clear, reenergized. No more hard drinking. No more hard partying. I was done.

My sons were quiet, taking in my story. We were sitting around the bonfire on our back patio, just like I'd planned earlier that night. The boys were wrapped in blankets; my wife was inside, giving me this moment one-on-one with our sons.

I looked at the kids and asked, "What are you two thinking about?"

"You could have died, Pa," Alexander said.

"Yeah, and you wouldn't be here," Anthony added. "We wouldn't be here."

"I know," I said. "And there were other times too, before that moment. Driving drunk and high, and getting pulled over by the cops in Maine. Doing all sorts of stupid things while I was intoxicated. Believe me, I've thought through the worst-case scenario about a million times."

"So what happened after that?" Alexander asked.

"Well," I said, leaning forward. I was about to share one of the most meaningful moments of my life. "What happens next is my favorite part of the story."

From the "Tower Incident," as I began to think of it, I spiraled into deep self-introspection and self-analysis. Even with my realization that fall day after leaving Sue's room, I had a lot to reconcile internally.

With football season over for the year, I would show up for classes and study with Herly, and then retreat to my room. I'd moved out of the frat house, into a single dorm room, and I would sit on my bed for hours most evenings after work, reading, studying, or playing guitar. I'd attempted to join the on-campus a capella group, the Meddiebempsters, freshman year, but I couldn't take the pop songs from the 1930s and 40s, so I had formed my own band sophomore year, Boot Hill. The band was still going strong, and I spent most of my free time rehearsing song after song for gigs I didn't have the energy to perform. I often played with my eyes closed, humming the lyrics, moving my fingers with precision on the strings of the used electric guitar I'd purchased at a local pawn shop.

It had been three weeks since I had blacked out. I'd changed. I no longer partied, no longer went out. I knew people were talking about me. Every day, someone stopped by my room to invite me to a party. I had a constant stream of knocks on my door and declined every invitation, saying I needed to rehearse. I didn't want to go out, and I didn't want them to come in because I was busy.

One Saturday night, I sat on my bed playing guitar as four different girls stopped by until about two in the morning. It was clear they'd each come to hang out, and I turned them all away, using a variety of excuses: I have to practice. I'm tired. I can't right now.

As the fourth girl left, I heard her call out "asshole!" as she walked away. I shook my head and shut my door, walking back over to my bed and sitting on the edge like I was readying for a medical exam: feet flat, spine straight.

I knew these girls didn't like me for me—they liked David the football player, the Puerto Rican with a chip on his shoulder, the lead singer in Boot Hill. I saw superficiality in some of my friendships too. They liked the outside; they didn't care about what was inside. Is this what relationships are about? I wondered. Is this how it will always be? Will I ever find someone who knows me, who truly cares for who I am, not all this surface stuff?

I wanted a relationship with someone who understood all the crazy thoughts running through my head about life, love, the future, career, intellect, music, football, anxiety, failure, poverty . . . and I wanted a woman who would love me for me, the real me. Did she exist?

Suddenly, a face crowded my thoughts: Samanda. She was the only woman I'd ever felt fully saw me and understood the real me. She was calm, sweet, and knew the poor David who had nothing to offer. The moment I met her way back in high school, I'd known there was something special about her.

I saw my wallet sitting on my desk and walked over, picking it up. I eyed the faux black leather for a half second before opening it and hastily sliding my fingers into one of the credit card slots, my heart dropping when I couldn't immediately feel the thick paper inside. But then I felt the worn edge of the photo and slid it out.

I walked back to my bed and held the picture in front of me. Samanda stared back with a subtle smile. Her beauty was transfixing. She had an innocent charm, long black hair, and deep, honey-colored skin offset with haunting brown eyes that shined like the sun.

But it had been years of infrequent letters from "Dina Mora." I wasn't even sure the address I had for her was current, or how to get in touch with her. I wondered what she was doing right then. Was she in college? Was she dating someone? I knew her stepdad didn't allow dating, but what if she had fallen for someone else?

Did Samanda ever think about me? Did she wonder about me? How was I going to find her?

I was determined to find her.

As junior year went on my self-analysis continued, and I focused on finding Samanda. I called Ive to get Samanda's current address and began writing letters, always signing Dina Mora. Samanda was still living at home, and although she was technically an adult, I knew enough about her stepdad not to mess with his rules. Plus, I didn't want to risk losing contact.

I still went to parties but always left by eleven and headed to stay at Herly's, or off-campus at a friend's apartment. Their couches were an escape from the parties and wildness of the fraternity or Coles Tower. Since there were no cell phones, once I left, no one could get in touch with me. I'd crash and then get up the next day and head to my dorm to shower. The system worked well: it let me still be social and hang with my friends but also shielded me from going too far. I'd have a casual beer or two, then peace out.

With my mind clear and body clean, I found myself even more focused on school and music. The finish line was so close I could feel it, and I doubled down on my classes. I'd be graduating with a major in sociology and a minor in archeology, and I began thinking about what career field I could go into after college. While some of my friends seemed nervous, even worried, about the next step, I was mostly excited. I was ready for the next part of my life.

I began observing the world around me even more than before. When I did go to parties, I stood in the corner of the room, watching the space. This was partly a deep-seated need to be able to scan the room, and partly a desire to study and learn, a quest to understand my place and the environment I was growing accustomed to and adapting to. I watched all the Bowdoin kids, some from elite, powerful families. I saw the ease with which they interacted, how they greeted each other, the way they talked about their future careers and seemed to assume everything would work out OK. They knew their futures were bright and they'd have opportunities when school was done. I was constantly observing and learning—and adapting.

What would it be like to feel that way? I often wondered as I sipped my one beer for the night. What was it like to grow up seeing endless possibility before you? And since I don't have the same upbringing and automatic opportunities, why not create them for myself? But *how*?

On my late-night walks to Herly's room or my friend's off-campus apartment, I'd run the parties I'd been to that night through my head. I was hanging with all sorts of crowds, from football players to computer nerds to weed heads. And still, no matter how different they were, with the exception of the few kids of color and poor white kids, they seemed to belong. They had a sense of place that money, stability, and opportunity appeared to bring. They had something I would never have, something I couldn't go back in time and create for myself.

But I could create it for my family in the future: for my mom, dad, sister, and brothers. The idea of my own family—wife, kids—felt far-off and unlikely, but what if? Could I raise kids who showed up to a place like Bowdoin and inherently belonged and thrived on day one? Kids who were prepared to tackle life and harness the opportunities that life in America—the greatest country in the world—offers? Absolutely.

Some nights, I thought of Rodriguez's book, and his journey from poverty to professorship. Education, for him, was a pathway to a better future for himself, a way to rise up and powerfully impact his family tree for generations. I could do that too. And for the first time, I wasn't just hearing Dempsey, Mom, and Mrs. Pappagianopoulos tell me I could make it. I wasn't doing something because I had talked myself into believing what adults were saying, or because I was competitive and just wanted to be the best. For the first time, I started to actually believe I could be greater than what I knew. When I believed in myself, my actions followed. My decisions changed. I didn't know where I was going, but I could at least recognize who I needed to become in order to get there. I was embracing who I could be in the future. I was finally visualizing a picture of endless possibilities.

By March of that school year, Susan Bell had become one of my go-to professors as well as a mentor. She found me on campus one afternoon, greeting me with her customary smile and energetic eyes.

"Hey. What are you doing this summer?" she asked me, straight to the point. She was clutching about a dozen folders in her right arm, a coffee thermos in her left, looking at me expectantly.

"I don't know," I said. "I'll probably go back home, work at Upward Bound again." She knew I'd worked in the program the past two summers, and what an impact it had made on the kids who attended.

"I have an idea," she said.

I tilted my head, confused. "What do you mean?"

"There's this epidemiology and public health internship at the Centers for Disease Control in Atlanta, Georgia," she said. "I think you're a perfect fit. Let's see if you can get into the program. I'll write you a letter and help you with the application. What do you think?"

I had learned by then that when Professor Bell says something, you don't ask questions, you just do it.

"I'm in," I said with a grin. While I had no clue what the program was about, I was excited about the idea of visiting Atlanta and venturing to a new state. I'd heard about kids working or studying away and desperately wanted to do the same but hadn't had the option—until now. I knew my mom would be disappointed to not have me home for the summer, but I figured I could at least visit for a couple of weeks. She'd understand. After all, I'd tell her, this was part of the plan for my future.

Professor Bell made good on her promise. She helped me prepare the application, drafted a letter of recommendation, and supported my candidacy. I was admitted a few months later to the summer internship program. The program was led by the CDC in conjunction with Emory University, Georgia's Department of Public Health, and Morehouse College, the all-black men's college. The summer program included students from all over the United States: about nine black women and men, and me. Wow, did I stand out! Each of us was required to select a project that focused on a public health issue facing the state of Georgia, and then leverage data, research, and interviews to complete a presentation. We were given a time line of about two months, during which we were required to travel around Georgia, researching and interviewing as much as we could.

That summer was profound for a number of reasons. Our mentor, Rolando Thorne, was from Panama: handsome, six-foot-six, with deep, dark skin. He was smart, kind, and professionally dressed in beautiful suits—a true gentleman. Seeing a black man who was fluent in Spanish in such an important professional position inspired me, just like when I'd seen Chris Hogan run Upward Bound. Rolando was eloquent, smooth, and nothing like all the urban kids I'd grown up around. His protégé, Carl Hill, was just as impressive: good-looking, articulate, athletic. He reminded me of the singer Billy Eckstein with a modern twist. I had never been exposed to black men like Rolando and Carl, and I soaked up everything they did and said, like I was attending lessons in a classroom.

Those two months were profound for me. We traveled all over the greater Atlanta region, as well as Clay County, meeting with people who were rich, poor, black, and white; seeing the effects of rural poverty firsthand; and understanding the impact minimal access to income or nutritious food has on one's personal and intellectual development. Many of these conversations reminded me of my upbringing in Puerto Rico. Here were folks, both white and black, many of whom had never been outside their two-mile area. They were stuck. Poverty largely impacted them the same way, regardless of their race. In Atlanta, I was also awed and inspired by the professionally dressed people, especially black men and women who welcomed me with open arms. They seemed just as eager as I was to exchange open dialogue about who we were as individuals, our backgrounds, and our unique purpose in life.

I experienced a different lifestyle, and I embraced it. I also had unforgettable moments, like meeting Toni Braxton and her sisters at a restaurant and hanging out at the 1996 Summer Olympics, standing just 100 yards away from the stage when a bomb exploded during the concert. I traveled on trains through metro Atlanta: through the ghettos, through the wealthy areas, and to Stone Mountain, one of the most segregated places I'd been to. I got to know Jamal, one of the other students in the program, and Stephen, the first Muslim American I had ever spoken with in my life.

What struck me most was the people. Here were all these black guys who could have shunned me and made me feel like an outsider. It would have been easy because I was different than them. I looked different, sounded different. But they welcomed me.

When I suggested we go into the traditionally black areas of Georgia for southern food and music, they surprised me. They pushed me to go into the Latino area of Atlanta, even asked *me* to come hang out with them in those parts of town where they had hardly ever ventured. They were curious about my culture and background because all they had been exposed to were Mexican immigrants who lived on the outskirts of Atlanta. They hungered to understand how Puerto Ricans were different from Mexican migrant farmers. That summer became a fusion of sharing culture and identity between black men and women and one guy from Indiana, Puerto Rico, Lynn, and Maine, my fusion of wonderfully complex environments rooted in family, work ethic, and a passion to build a better future for my family. We stayed up late every night talking about our lives and learning about each other's challenges and opportunities in a country that abounded with opportunity for all of us.

When I left the program, heading to Lynn for the last week of summer before returning to Bowdoin for senior year, I had grown as a person and as an American. I became truly convinced that the words in our nation's Declaration of Independence are alive and real for everyone:

We hold these truths to be self-evident, that all men are created equal, that they are endowed by their Creator with certain unalienable Rights, that among these are Life, Liberty and the pursuit of Happiness.

That summer helped me understand that for the most part, each one of us has the ability and opportunity to defy the path that has been laid out for us by others and pursue happiness, success, and a better life. And more importantly, to fulfill a life greater than what we can imagine. To do so, we must have an ability to see beyond our limitations, deep-seated faith, and endless perseverance.

As I hung out with my friends back in Lynn, our cultural divisions stood out to me like an open wound. I recognized that my friends could be open, inquisitive, and free. They could be like the guys I spent the summer with; we could be deliberative, inquisitive, analytical, caring, and curious about each other. Instead, we felt forced to prove our worth and manliness. We limited ourselves and our choices. What had happened to cause this? Where was the disconnect?

That summer gave way to a realization about my future. I knew what I needed to do. I had to cut through the divides, find a way to change the way things were, connect cultures, reach back into my community, teach others that there are different choices to be made, and try to make a difference. I was locked in on success; my view of what was possible for my life, for my community, even for my country, expanded. I just needed to figure out how to build my skill set, home in on my future, and serve as an example for others as to what was possible in America.

While my summer in Georgia was profound, something else monumental happened that summer: I saw Samanda. I had called Ive before arriving in Lynn to ask about her. Where was she? What was she doing? I knew from her letters that she had a job at TJ Maxx and asked Ive when she'd be working next. Since I couldn't just call her, I decided to show up.

When I arrived in the parking lot of the store, I surprised myself by how nervous I felt. I'd heard girls talk about butterflies for guys they liked, but I didn't think it could happen to me. Yet there I was, sitting in a TJ Maxx parking lot in Swampscott, in my dad's Ford Escort—the same one that had taken me to Maine, to a new life. That car was now bringing me to see the woman I'd grown to admire for more than her beauty. Samanda was resilient and resourceful. Through our letters, I learned of the hard childhood she'd experienced and how she had worked since she was a young child in the Dominican Republic. This woman . . . she was incredible. At her young age, she had already beaten the odds. I sat in the driver's seat in 90-degree weather, forcing myself to take deep, slow breaths to calm the jittery feeling in my stomach.

All year, I had thought about Samanda. I'd built her up in my head to a nearly goddess-like level. What if I had worked myself up too much? Worse yet, what if she didn't feel the same about me? There was only so much I could read in her letters, which were mostly about what was going on in her life: she was attending Salem State College, and spent her time studying and working to pay for college. Still living at her family home. Volunteering at her church.

Not dating.

I finally turned my car off and collected myself, looking in the mirror to check my hair, my hat, my nose, my ears. Then I opened the driver's side door and walked toward the store. As I entered the building, the cold blast from the AC punched me in the face. I wondered how long I'd have to look through the store to find her. What if she was unloading stock in the back room? Should I page her at the front? No, she might get in trouble with her boss. I'd wait around all day if I had to. As I walked around the women's section, I saw her. She was putting clothes back on their racks, restocking inventory. My heart jumped and my legs went numb.

Our eyes met. I froze, unsure of what to do. Should I run to her? Should I pick her up and twirl her around?

No, she was at work. And anyway, we were friends. Nothing more. And I had no idea how she felt about me.

But in that moment, standing across from her, I felt it again, all those feelings I'd had the first moment I saw her. She radiated beauty, strength, resilience, and intelligence.

Finally, it was like someone took a sledgehammer to time and both of us unfroze. I commanded my legs to move, to look like a normal, somewhat-cool human as I greeted her.

"David," she said as I walked up.

"Samanda, what's up?" I said. My heart thudded. I felt dampness in my palms. My feet were sweaty against my work boots.

She looked into the store, as if searching for her manager so she wouldn't get in trouble. Another employee stared at us, bored, from the faux jewelry counter.

"What are you doing here?" she asked.

"I'm . . . shopping for clothes."

"In the women's section?" she said with a smile.

"It's good to see you," I said. That smile. My thumping heart began to race as I added, "I'm back for a couple of weeks."

"Well, I'm surprised to see you," she said. Her expression dropped into a frown. "But I'm working. I don't have a break for another hour."

"I'll wait," I said too quickly.

"You'll wait? For an hour?"

"I have some shopping to do at Stop & Shop anyway," I lied, pointing in the direction of the store next to TJ Maxx.

"Do you?" She raised an eyebrow.

"Definitely," I said, a grin stretching across my face. I couldn't help it. "See you in an hour? Lunch?"

"See you then." She turned and walked toward the back of the store, then looked over her shoulder and gave me a low wave goodbye.

As I walked to Stop & Shop for no other reason than to pass the time, I smiled. I didn't know where things would lead, or if her flirtation was genuine, or if I even had a shot with her, but I knew something in that moment and nothing could change my mind: Samanda was the one. I couldn't imagine my life with any other woman than her at that point. I was certain. I hoped she felt it too.

Chapter 12

THERE'S NEVER AN END, ONLY BEGINNINGS

*"For I know the plans I have for you," declares the Lord,
"plans to prosper you and not to harm you, plans to
give you hope and a future."*

JEREMIAH 29:11, NIV

As much as I had fallen for Samanda, we were just friends. There was no "dating" in Samanda's world. Growing up in a traditional Dominican household, the concept of dating was strange to her. She didn't understand it, and she definitely didn't agree with the idea of casual dating. She was clear with me: this is what we are, and this is what we aren't. To Samanda, we were either "going together," as she put it, or not, and I was pretty sure going together really meant "going to get married." We weren't ready for that, so we were friends. We wrote letters. I was allowed to call her after several months.

To my surprise, Samanda agreed to visit Bowdoin during the first semester of my senior year. I wasn't sure how she'd gotten around her stepdad, but I didn't care: she was coming. I borrowed a friend's car and drove to Lynn to pick her up and bring her back to Bowdoin over a long weekend. The plan was for her to stay with me in my dorm room, and then I'd drive her back home. I knew beforehand not to try anything with her—she was clear, and I knew the boundaries. I promised to sleep on the floor so she could have my bed.

During the drive to campus, we talked about our lives and futures. We drove around Brunswick, grabbed a shake at Denny's, and headed back to my room around ten o'clock at night. My dorm room was filthy! Her face contorted with horror at the dirt and trash on the floor. I had warned her about the worst part: I had no furniture other than the sofa, desk, and bed we were provided . . . oh, and a small CD player Dwayne had given me as a gift. She was not impressed. But at least she stayed.

We sat and talked into the early hours of the morning in my dorm room. I played her a boleros CD of Trío Los Panchos, some of the most romantic music ever recorded. The music reminded me of home: my grandparents, my parents, and Delwin's father, Tomas; now I was the one swaying to their melodic voices and love-filled lyrics. Trío Los Panchos and their boleros called to me. Their music was passionate, full of poetry, and I wanted to share it with Samanda.

That night I played the guitar and sang her "Vida Mía," a song written by Osvaldo Fresedo and recorded by Trío Los Panchos in 1957.

When we finally went to sleep, I laid on my floor staring at the ceiling, feeling surer than ever that Samanda was the one for me. I really liked her. She understood me for who I was. She did not know me as a football player, or a jock, or a singer, or the kid from Lynn. She only knew me as the guy who wanted to be her friend and explore what a relationship with a real woman was like. She radiated beauty but commanded and demanded respect in a way I had not seen since I was growing up in Puerto Rico.

The next morning, I almost made a huge strategic mistake when I tried to sneak out to meet friends without waking her. I didn't really know how to treat a woman, and I was completely immature. I guess I also didn't want to look weak to the guys, especially over a girl.

Sunday mornings were reserved for breakfast with the fellas. I always met my buddies at the cafeteria for breakfast on Sundays— always! If I didn't show, they'd know why. "Bros before bras" was a familiar chant among some of us. I woke up before Samanda, brushed my teeth, threw on my jeans and T-shirt, and grabbed my boots quietly. Just as I was putting on my beanie and leaving the room, Samanda woke up.

"I'm heading out," I told her. "I have to meet the fellas for breakfast, but I'll be back in about an hour. It'll be quick."

Samanda sat up, her long, dark hair a cascade of waves around her. "What?"

She was stunning, and I had to catch my breath before replying. I reminded myself of what the guys would say if I missed breakfast because I was with a girl. "I'll come back and drop you off at the bus station later," I said. "Cool?"

"What?" she said again. She stood and walked across the room, tugging at her rumpled T-shirt and smoothing her hair.

"I said I'm heading out with my fel—"

"I heard you."

"O-OK . . ." I stammered, not sure what was going on. "So I'll see you later?"

"You'll '*see me later*'?"

"Um . . . yeah?"

Samanda was standing tall now, her chin lifted. "David Anthony Morales Brignoni, if you think I came all the way up here to be treated like one of your *girls*"—she poked me in the chest, hard—"then you're crazy. And you don't know a thing about me, or how to treat a woman. You are not going to 'drop me off at the bus station.'"

I hesitated before replying, "I'm not?"

"You're not. You *are* going to take me to breakfast," her eyes flared, her lips pursed. "And then you're going to drive me back home, just like you promised."

I looked at Samanda, stunned again, this time by her strength. If I took her to breakfast, I knew what my friends were going to think. They'd say I'd gone soft, that I was choosing a woman over my bros. But looking at her that morning, her hands on her hips and eyebrows lifted, my respect for her suddenly skyrocketed, and I thought, screw the guys. They can say what they want. Who cares what they think.

"That works," I finally said. I thought of my meager bank account. "How about Denny's?"

Samanda's usually shy smile was now confident, and I recognized a side of her I'd never seen. She was fierce. She'd put me in my place. Between the night we'd spent together, and that morning, my level of respect for her multiplied by a factor of a thousand. I suddenly wanted to make her feel like the most special woman on earth that morning, even if she was just a friend. A friend I was falling in love with.

After that morning—breakfast and the long drive back to Lynn, conversation and laughter and sharing our biggest hopes and dreams—a knowing was anchored deep in my chest. There was no dislodging Samanda from my future. Maybe "going together" wasn't so far off.

But as I dropped her off and drove back to Lynn that afternoon, a small seed of doubt crept in as I realized I had nothing to offer Samanda. I was about to graduate in less than half a year and still had no job offers. Other kids were getting recruited to private equity and venture capital firms, jobs and terms I had never even heard of before. Friends were getting paid internships at big companies. I hadn't had the exposure to even know those types of jobs and internships existed, let alone known early enough to apply and get selected, and now most of the jobs and internships had been filled. I suspected family connections were helping some of my buddies land their first jobs. Their parents and grandparents had all sorts of high-end, Ivy-educated connections in big places. I sure as hell did not.

Whenever one of my friends got a job or internship, I'd ask a bunch of questions, trying to understand how to do the same. I was doing my best to soak everything up and learn as much as I could. My mission was simple: learn, adapt, compete, and get out of poverty.

If I wanted to win Samanda over, and give her the life she deserved; if I wanted to lift my family out of poverty; if I wanted to have a better future, one that didn't involve hanging out on the streets but rather giving back to the community that had shaped me—if I wanted all those things, I knew I needed to graduate. And I needed to get a job.

Those were certainties. They were clear goals I needed to achieve.

Part of me felt confident, excited even. I was ready for that next step. Eager to leave Bowdoin and go out into the world to finally make some money and pursue the American dream.

My drive back to campus was full of visions of the future and a mental checklist of what I needed to do to execute my plan. I needed to build a résumé, so I would go to the career office the next day. I had to expand my network, so I would talk to the guys who had job offers.

I needed to write cover letters, so I would ask Herly to help edit my drafts. I had to have job references, so I would ask Professor Bell and Professor Turner. No problem, I thought. There's a plan for everything, or at least that's what I was learning from my class on practical economics with Professor Kent Chabotar, the college's treasurer.

The road curved before me, and I pulled onto Bowdoin's campus, taking in the stately scene: brick, grass, pine trees. It struck me as funny how a place that had felt so unfamiliar just a few years back now felt like home. But it was a temporary home, and one I would be saying goodbye to. Forever. I had no plans to return. This chapter of my life would close, and it would open to the next stage, whatever that might be.

I pulled into the dorm parking and locked the car. I needed to drop the keys off with my friend who'd lent me his ride. I fished $10 out of my pocket for gas, even though I knew he'd say not to worry about it. As I walked into the Winthrop dorms and ran up the stairs, I thought of Samanda that morning: wild hair, indignant expression. I laughed to myself, remembering how she'd softened once I'd agreed to skip breakfast with the guys. I was still laughing when I saw my buddies Tex and Tim at the top of the stairs.

"Where've you been?" Tex said, a smile stretched across his face. He knew where I'd been.

"Long day, bro," I said. But the truth was, it had been a great day.

My wife had made her way onto the back patio during my story and sat silently on a lounge chair diagonal from me with a smile on her face.

"That girl, Samanda," she said. "She sounds smart. I like her." Her eyes twinkled as they met mine and the boys looked at each other, at their mom, and then at me.

"What happened next, Pa?" Alexander asked.

"Yeah, no more sappy love stories," Anthony added, rolling his eyes.

I laughed. "All right, I'll spare you . . . for now." Both boys groaned as I went on. "So where was I? Oh, yes. Senior year."

—

Senior year continued unfolding like a plot twist of a confusing movie in which I couldn't for the life of me guess the ending. My mind continued expanding from classes in education, archeology, sociology, and practical economics. After finishing the class on practical economics with Professor Chabotar, I was now in his second semester course.

Simply being in his class was an accomplishment and honor—his courses were the only business-like classes on campus and only about twenty kids a year were selected to enroll. I had gone to him proactively in the fall semester of my junior year to ask to be one of those students. After lobbying him several times—and probably annoying him—he finally invited me to interview for his class. When I walked into his office for my interview the previous year, I was instantly intimidated—there I was, a 230-pound linebacker being interrogated by the school's treasurer, who had piercing eyes and dressed elegantly in pin stripe suits and bow ties.

Still, I had done well enough to get in. But sitting in his office that day, forcing confidence as I replied to question after question, I had no idea what I was in for in his classes: exposure to a whole new world—the world of finance, and the language of business.

Since Bowdoin was a liberal arts college, the main focus was to teach us how to think critically. And while that education was crucial for me, Chabotar's course was a game-changer because suddenly I was exposed to practical, real-world applications that were preparing me for life outside the walls of Bowdoin—and inside the walls of a company. I had never, ever been exposed to any of this business and finance stuff, but I knew from movies that business and finance was where money could be made. And I definitely needed to earn money.

My brain expanded; the landscape of post-college possibilities grew with it. I began reading publications like the *Financial Times, Wall Street Journal*, and *The Economist*.

I devoured books on history, military, and business. If it had a spine, pages, and interesting facts, I read it.

Yet even as I grew more confident in my knowledge and grasp of the business landscape, my concerns about the future increased. I continued to watch friend after friend get recruited for jobs, and during the first part of my second semester, I started to panic. All senior year, when I wasn't playing football, I'd been applying to jobs, internships . . . anything paid that would be a solid stepping-stone to my future. I kept up the pace of my applications into my second semester, sending as many as humanly possible, walking neatly sealed letters to the mailroom on campus nearly every day.

But I had no offers, not even one interview. Fear began rising in my throat again, underpinning every moment, every interaction. I tried to swallow it back, push it down, shut up the endless worry with a prayer-like chant: I will land a job. I will get out of poverty. I will get myself out of poverty. I will land a job.

Just like I'd done back in high school, I paid attention. I asked friends if I could read sample cover letters; I asked Herly to edit my résumé; I visited the library to look at jobs on the computer. I molded my writing and myself to fit the spaces I wanted to occupy, starting letters with phrases like "Dear Mr. Baxter" and writing things like "I would be honored to work at your company." But the truth was I didn't have the exposure to understand how to present myself and win a competitive internship or job, and no copycat flowery language could solve that problem.

By the middle of the second semester I was lying awake every single night, a knot in my stomach, tightness in my chest. What if I didn't get hired anywhere? What would I do? I couldn't go back to Lynn without a job. I couldn't leave the golden child and return the fallen angel. No. I repeated my chant and sharpened my mindset: I will land a job.

I doubled down, spending every second I could in the library, looking up jobs, printing off cover letters and résumés, stopping by the on-campus mailroom to drop off my stamped letters, sometimes sending two per day. The students working at the mail center began asking me if I'd heard anything or gotten any offers. The answer was always no.

One Saturday night, with just a couple months left of school, I sat in my dorm room, playing the guitar and singing a sad ballad, "Flor de Azalea" by Los Panchos.

As I sang the last line and set my guitar down on the bed, anger swept over me like a forest fire, overtaking my entire body. I leaned forward, put my hands over my face, and wept. All this opportunity.

This gift of Bowdoin, the exposure to a new way of life, the possibility afforded me by this education. And here I was about to graduate with nothing to show for it.

That night, I fell asleep feeling the exhaustion of months of worry and drafting cover letters, as well as a sense of resolve: I would figure this out. Just like I'd figured everything else out so far. Screw poverty. I'd get out. I had to get out. I said a prayer as I drifted off to sleep, speaking out loud in the quiet of my dorm room: "*Querido Dios, por favor ayúdame. Dame dirección y alumbra mi camino.*" Dear God, please help me. Direct me and light my path.

"**And did God help you,** Pa?" Alexander's expression was inquisitive and sad. "Did you get a job?"

"I did. My first real job after college."

"Was that the one at the Hispanic Federation?"

"That's the one. I was able to land an internship there."

Anthony sat up and leaned forward, his elbows on his knees and hands clasped like I'd seen him sit on the basketball bench. He looked older, like he had magically matured in the firelight. "In New York City? Wasn't it hard to go away again after being gone from home for so long?"

"It was. But it was the only job offer I received and the only opportunity I landed. I knew it was the first step to the future I needed to build, not just for me but for the family, but that's a story for another day."

"Then what happened?" Alexander asked.

"Isn't it about time for bed?" A grin stretched across my face as both boys groaned and I winked at my wife. "OK, OK. Let's see. Where was I? Oh, yes, I was about to tell you about graduation."

I sat on a folded chair at the Bowdoin quad, a long green lawn right in the middle of campus. It was a sunny day in May, not too hot or cold. Still, I was sweating in the nice clothes my mom had insisted I wear under my gown, a green suit from Macy's, a yellow button-up polyester shirt, and a tie I borrowed from my father. I reached up to my face, rubbing my fingers over the barely grown goatee on my chin, then shifted uncomfortably in my seat.

Yet in spite of my physical discomfort, I felt like I owned the world. I had made it to the college finish line. And I had an internship waiting for me in New York City.

And then there was Samanda. She'd driven up a couple more times to visit me on campus. In the weeks and months after her first visit, my feelings continued to grow. If you asked her, we weren't going together yet, but in my mind, she was my girl. Since I had no money, I'd take her to Taco Bell for their two tacos for a buck special, or we'd get the meal deal at KFC. When I'd gone home for Christmas break, we had donuts and hot chocolate at Mrs. Foster's Donuts in Lynn.

Sitting on the hardback chair that day, half-listening to the commencement address, I remembered Samanda's pink nose and cheeks one blustery day at Mrs. Foster's donut shop, how she'd curled her hands around the paper cup of hot cocoa, how I'd seen in her eyes confirmation of the way she felt for me. But still, she told me, we were just friends.

I heard clapping and looked up at the stage, then searched the crowd for Herly, my classmate, tutor, and friend. She sat tall, paying close attention to the speaker, wearing the same look of confidence and power as the day I'd come to her dorm room asking for help. Our journey at Bowdoin had been profound: she had helped me survive four years ago, and now we were about to leave this place and go out into the real world. As for me, I was a street-built American football player brought to an elite college who had finally made it to graduation. I had crossed paths with all kinds of dissimilar students, from all walks of life and all types of families, and now here we were, sitting together, graduating. And the same woman who, like me, was considered a student of color, from a different background, ethnic heritage, and race turned out to be one of my biggest anchors. The American dream was becoming our realities. From many, one . . . powerful.

I craned my neck to look for my friends: Tex, Vern, Ryan, Payne Cave, Devlin, Jason, Katie, Alison, and Nina, among others. They were all sitting up straight, just as I imagined them sitting in their cubicles or offices their first day on the job.

The speaker finished and walked off the stage to the sound of clapping and cheering, as the president and dean of the college stepped up to the mic. It was time to hand out diplomas. I sat up straighter, wishing I could see my family from where I sat. It was a big day for me, and I knew it was a big day for them too. As I listened to the last names called: As, then Bs . . . Fs and Gs . . . and finally, my row was instructed to line up to the right of the stage. As I followed my classmates, I adjusted the neck on my black gown and reached up to make sure the tassel was on the correct side of my hat. I knew we'd be instructed as a group to move the tassel from right to left, signifying our transition from student to graduate.

The Ls and early Ms were called one by one, and finally, I was next. My heart raced, booming in my ears. I felt like I'd been plugged into an electric socket, with my body and mind completely alert, all of my senses on overdrive.

"David Morales," the dean called, his voice booming. I began walking on stage as he added, "Bachelor's in sociology, minor in archeology. Magna Cum Laude."

The president of the college, Robert H. Edwards, extended the diploma. I reached to take it with my left hand and shook his right.

"Congratulations, David." His smile was warm and genuine.

"I did it!" I said.

I walked across the stage, scanning the crowd. There, in the audience, in the first-row seats I knew they'd gotten there early to reserve, sat my family and friends: Mom, Dad, Dan, George, Dwayne, and Samanda.

I turned toward them and lifted my diploma up as their cheers erupted.

I had done it! I had graduated college!

As I made my way back to my seat, my mom continued standing, her hands clasped to her chest. I couldn't see her expression, but I knew. Mom would be crying, nearly weeping, over this achievement. Proud tears.

I realized, as I waved to Mom and took my seat, that Mom would only ever cry proud tears for me. Mom would never cry over my body, lost to violence on the streets. She'd never cry on the other side of prison glass, phone in her hand and hand pressed to the separating glass. She'd never cry over my wasted potential as she passed me on the street corners, a lost man who'd had such a bright future.

So many moms, dads, grandmas, and grandpas in urban and rural poor America had cried different tears. Tears of loss. Tears of pain. Tears of a future their children never got to see because of drugs, alcohol, or violence. Unnecessary tears.

I looked up to the sky to thank God. The clouds above me were bright, a puffy mass to quiet my swirling thoughts. The ceremony went on, and soon the emcee was calling us to stand.

"We offer our sincere congratulations to this year's graduates," he said. "Bowdoin College class of 1997, you may now change your tassels from right to left!"

In one motion, the entire graduating class moved our tassels, tossed our hats in the air, and entered the next stage of our lives.

After the ceremony, I walked across the grass toward the tree my family and I had agreed on as our post-ceremony meeting place. George strode out from the group to greet me, wearing a big smile. He wrapped me in a hug, clapping me solidly on the back as he embraced me.

"You did it, man," he said.

"*We* did it," I said. George had recently graduated from Bentley College.

"Remember all those conversations we had as kids?" he said.

I nodded, remembering our long discussions: on porch steps, in his Trans-Am. Sober, not sober. It was hard to believe that there had been a point in our young lives that we'd believed we wouldn't make it past senior year of high school. Standing in front of me was my Greek brother, also from the streets of Lynn, one of the guys who dared to not become a statistic and made it. We would never become used-to-be's. We were on our way to becoming successful, productive men.

Mom, Dad, Dwayne, and Dan caught up with us. My parents were beaming. Their entire bodies emanated pride.

I couldn't help but notice how out of place they were, in their TJ Maxx clothes and sun-kissed skin among a sea of white people in Ann Taylor and L.L.Bean. We were anomalies on campus, but my parents didn't care. They were happy and deeply proud. It didn't matter what they were wearing, what car they'd driven to the ceremony, or who was around them. To them, no one was there but me. This was a historic day for all of us.

My dad, the stoic, the one who always held it together no matter what, was taking a deep breath as if not to cry. He reached out his hand as if to shake it, then clasped my hand and pulled me into a hug.

He pulled away and placed both hands on my shoulders. "I'm proud of you, son," he said.

"Thanks, Dad," I said. "Thank you for everything." It was unspoken, but he knew what I meant. Dad's transformation and sacrifice was instrumental in our family's journey to a better life and one of the key steps to making college possible for me. He'd paved the pathway for our family to get out of poverty. It was my job to see his effort through and to pay it forward. To be his legacy.

Dad nodded, swallowed hard, and stepped aside for my mom.

I had never seen Mom so euphoric. Not when we'd walked into church after an especially good football play the Friday before. Not when I'd gotten the acceptance letter. Not when I graduated high school.

"David," she said. She hugged me tightly, holding on for at least a half minute. "I told you. Didn't I? You're going to be somebody, David. It's God's plan for you." She let go and withdrew a tissue from her purse, dabbing at her eyes. "*Que Dios te bendiga mil veces, David.*" May God bless you a thousand times.

"*Te quiero, Ma'i,*" I said. "Don't make me cry too."

I couldn't help but smile as I hugged her again—she would use any opportunity to bring up God's plan. All this time, I'd rejected what Mom said was my calling. She had insisted I was on this earth to do great things.

Yet as I hugged my mom again that afternoon, I started to think maybe she was right. But maybe she was missing a detail. Maybe all of us are ordained, maybe each one of us has a special calling. I was figuring mine out. So many of my friends back home never would, unless they were given an opportunity to see beyond their poverty, beyond their borders, beyond their real and imaginary limitations. If they couldn't see it, they couldn't be it. And many would never experience a family who cared: loving parents who were selfless and dedicated to the long term, not just the short term, with daily messages of aspiration, faith, forgiveness, and love.

I always had my mom and dad, these two amazing, sacrificial people, to counter the messages I received on the streets—that I was always going to be poor, that I'd never amount to anything, that I might not even make it out alive. There were times I'd let myself believe those lies, but my mom's voice was always in the back of my head:

"God has a plan for you, David. Plans to prosper you and not to harm you, plans to give you hope and a future."

"You were chosen to make a difference in this world."

"Inside of you is a light waiting to come out."

"You're meant for goodness and greatness."

Mom was dabbing at her eyes fiercely now. I put my arm around her as Dan stood in front of us.

"I'm proud of you, kiddo," he said. He wrapped my mom and me in a hug, then drew back as if to study me. "You did it, bro. You did it."

If I wasn't careful, I knew I'd start crying. I took a deep breath, tightened my grip around Mom. "Thanks, man," I said. "You and Dad, Diana and Dwayne. You guys made all this possible for me."

"No, David," Dan said. "You made this possible for you. You did the work. You put in the effort. You fought. You persevered. You got the acceptance letter. You believed you could, and you did it. You made the right choices and decisions, and you stayed true to yourself and to our family. That's what Americans do."

I considered his words and knew he was partly right. I had a fighting spirit and a ton of street-built grit. But I also had a lot of help from people who believed in me. Not everyone had that. Most of the kids I grew up with would never have a mentor like Coach Dempsey. They'd definitely never have people in their lives like Vern, Herly, Penny Martin, Susan Bell, and John Turner. And yet those kids I grew up with and played basketball and football with, the students I had classes with—they couldn't see beyond their four walls. Like me, they needed an opportunity to author a different future for themselves. They had to fight hard and intentionally seek help, guidance, and advice to pursue a better outcome and better life for themselves.

My thoughts stopped abruptly as I noticed Samanda. She was still standing by the tree, smiling in my direction: that sweet, mysterious smile that had drawn me all those years ago.

"Excuse me, guys," I said to my family and George. I handed my diploma to my mom.

"Go right ahead," Dan laughed.

"It's about time," George added.

I walked toward Samanda. She followed me with her eyes as I made my way to stand in front of her.

"Congratulations," she said. Her hair had fallen over her eyes, so I gently tucked it behind her ear. She blushed, looking at her feet, then back at me. "How does it feel to be done?"

"Crazy. Unreal."

"What's next for you? Hispanic Federation, New York . . . then what?" her eyes searched mine. I knew the question behind her questions.

I stared straight into her eyes, and she stared back at me. We both knew the answer. It was standing right in front of us. I took her hand, and the two of us walked back to the group. As I looked around at my family, this unit I loved so dearly, and thought of Diana, I felt peace. Prosperity. Unity. Love.

In many ways, I felt like I'd lived so much of my story already. But really, my story was just beginning.

Alexander was curled up on the patio sofa with my wife; Anthony had taken her place on the lounger. My boys' expressions were unreadable in the firelight.

I had shared so much of my teenage story with them: growing up in poverty, seeing violence and death all around me in Puerto Rico, but also still feeling happiness and love. Getting rocks thrown at me while walking down the street with my mom. Entering elementary school in the United States and learning to speak English. Growing up around drugs, violence, and death. Rejecting the false characterizations that TV shows portrayed about people like me. Fighting through the lies that street life was all I'd ever know and all I could ever be. Learning to adapt and overcome. Building a resilient mindset and a passion to live a better life.

Anthony yawned one of his infectious yawns and stretched his legs out in front of him.

"All that, and it's only the beginning?" He grinned at me, the firelight flickering across his young face.

"It'll take weeks to hear the rest," Alexander added with a smile. He yawned too.

"A lifetime is hard to tell over a few days," I said. "And I think this is what you need to hear for now, anyway."

"What do you mean?" Anthony asked.

"At each stage of our lives, we can only understand so much," I said. "Right now, you're growing into young men. You have high school graduation and your first year of college to look forward to. I told you the part of my story that will help you understand more about me at your ages and yourselves as you get a bit older."

My sons were silent, and my wife was too. I knew what she was thinking about. There was much more to tell: my internship at the Hispanic Federation, and how my anger and pride butted with the head of the organization, and I abruptly quit. Looking for jobs in Miami, Florida, coaching football at Lynn Classical High School with George. Walking to my first job at the Ways and Means Committee in the Massachusetts State House, a government job I never, in my wildest dreams, would have imagined I would get. Working at the highest levels of state government, serving a Speaker of the House, a Senate President, and a Governor, serving as a commissioner of healthcare finance, working as an executive of a national company, starting my own company, leading a health benefits company, starting a nonprofit organization, serving at my church, leading a Latin music band, producing two CDs. There was so much more.

"There is one more thing," I said. "Remember how I told you about when Grandma and I had stones thrown at us on our way to my elementary school?"

"Yeah, and that guy came out to help you," Alexander said.

"Right. Well, many years later, before your mom and I got married, I was walking to catch the commuter train my first day on the job at Ways and Means, at the State House in Boston. It was October, so I'd bought an Inspector Gadget-style raincoat, beige with big buttons down the front, from K&G Fashion Superstore in their men's department with a credit card. Underneath the coat was a nice new navy-blue suit I'd also bought at K&G.

"I walked to work that morning down the same exact street I'd gotten those rocks thrown at me as a kid. I passed a couple of strung-out Dominican guys standing on a street corner, and they had looked at me suspiciously, as if I were a cop coming to bust them. I remember thinking to myself, Wow. They don't even know that I could have been right where they are, had I made different choices. This is crazy."

"Crazy how?" Alexander said.

"I felt like I was wearing a costume. And as I continued to walk to work every day, I recognized that I felt like a stranger in my own community. But this feeling was completely different than what I'd felt growing up. As a kid and teen, we were somehow raised to believe that it was the kids from the streets versus everyone else. Blacks, Latinos, poor whites versus affluent white people. Urban poor versus suburban rich. Puerto Rican American versus Americans who bleed red, white, and blue. Me versus them. Not fitting in. Not belonging.

"But that day, walking to catch my train, to arrive at my fancy government job where I would influence public policy in the state of Massachusetts, it felt like coming full circle, only arriving at a very different place than where I'd started. Belonging to a different world entirely, separated from the world I'd known all my life. It took me a long time to reconcile those two worlds within myself. Frankly, those worlds had much more in common than I ever imagined."

My boys were lost in thought, and I let the chorus of crickets take over as I reflected on the past several days we'd spent together while I told them my story. I could tell that all I had shared with them would take weeks, months—maybe a lifetime—to process. They wouldn't fully understand until they had lived their own lessons, but I hoped my story—our family's journey—would stick with them. I prayed they wouldn't develop a chip on their shoulder like me, and that they would thrive in the big, wide world. They had all the opportunity I'd ever dreamed of for them.

But we couldn't overlook the others who were out there, living in cycles of poverty and struggling through life. I would never forget them, because their story and mine are intimately intertwined. A story that belongs to my sons also.

I touched the screen on my phone sitting on the side table next to my patio chair to check the clock: 12:17 a.m. It was time to wrap up for good and head to bed. I stood and reached a hand across to Anthony to pull him out of his chair as Alexander and my wife stood too.

We gathered our glasses, mugs, and the two empty bags of chips my sons had eaten. As we made our way inside, profound peace swept over me. Telling my story to my boys was like living it all over again. I had felt, deep within my marrow, the fear of poverty all over again. I had experienced, through the retelling, the deep insecurities and uncertainties that had plagued me for so much of my life. Now, here, in this place: peace, family, grace.

My wife walked up the stairs with my sons, and I stayed downstairs to wash the dishes, throw out the chip bags, and turn off the lights.

As I switched off the back porchlight, I thought of Diana, who had married and was now a teacher, impacting so many young lives like she'd impacted me. With kids of her own now, and a quick wit, Diana was my sister, my second mom, and now a big part of my kids' lives.

I walked into the living room, and as I flipped the switch off, I thought of Dan, and his work in the gang unit, and how he'd essentially devoted his life to helping kids and adults who had taken the wrong path. Today, he's an executive and a father. Dan is still tough, fearless. Still someone I admire and look up to.

As I switched off the entryway lights, I thought of Dwayne, and the incredible transformation he had undergone. There were so many nights as a teen and young adult that I laid in bed, praying Dwayne would come home alive. And he did. Today, he has steady work and lives a peaceful life. He's got a big heart and I respect the hell out of him.

The lights now out, I walked up the lit stairs and thought of Mom, our family's conscience, the rock of our family, the reason all four of her kids ended up living solid, stable lives. Her strength was unbendable through all those years; she dug deep to show up for all of us, and her faith in God saw her—and us—through some difficult days. Today, she's living a comfortable life in a house Samanda and I were able to buy in Lynn, a city that has grown and changed for the better, just like me. It was my biggest dream come true to provide a home for my parents. With sweat, hard work, and commitment, I kept my promise to her. She would never, ever struggle financially . . . ever again.

As I turned the stairway light off behind me, I thought of my father, the man who sacrificed so much, who battled away his demons to become the dad and grandpa he is today. He changed so much, humbled himself, transformed his heart to serve our family. He's still my hero. A man I pray someday I can come close to resembling in honor, humility, and integrity.

I stood in the upstairs hallway for several minutes, thinking about all I'd shared with my sons. For a long time, I hadn't believed my story was important, or even worth sharing. And in some ways, it's not unique, because a similar history has been felt and lived by men and women across America. For so many, my journey and the Latino experience is a shared experience. My story is only extraordinary because I made it out of poverty by God's grace, a strong family unit, solid education, hard work, and perseverance.

Like others who came before me and will come after me, my story is one of resilience, and the power of the desire to want something better for yourself, the power of knowing that better is, indeed, possible. Even though I hadn't known what the future looked like, I knew I wanted more for my family and would fight with every fiber in my body to get there.

The desire to be better and do better, if acted upon, is a powerful force.

I poked my head inside Anthony's room. He was already in bed with the lights out.

"Goodnight. I love you," I said.

"'Night, Pa. Love you too."

I walked across the hall to Alexander's room. He was standing in front of his window, looking at the lit street below. Seeing his young frame brought me right back to my adolescence in Lynn, looking out the window of our first apartment on Henry Avenue.

"Love you, bub," I said.

Alexander looked over his shoulder when he heard me, then closed his blinds and got into bed, flipping off the lamp on his nightstand. "Goodnight, Pa. Love you too," he said.

As I shut his door, I heard him say, "Pa?"

I opened the door partway. "Yeah?"

"Thanks," he said.

"For what?"

"Sharing with us. You know . . . telling your story and our family's story."

I smiled. "You bet. Now get some rest. I love you."

As I shut his door, I thought of how fortunate he was to be safe in his bed in a secure home with both of his parents, a father and a mother who cared. Growing up, there were so many times I didn't think I was going to make it home alive. I'd be drunk or high, in a dangerous situation, and pray silently, Dear Lord, help me through this shit.

I'd wondered so many times: Why was I born? Why did God put me here?

I used to hope that I could make it out of there, that I could do better, that I could raise a family, that I could give my children a better life someday. All I wanted was to get out. I didn't have the exposure to understand what lay on the other side of my reality or the visibility to see beyond the cement sidewalks I traversed in Lynn. My sons, I knew now, would have exposure and access to a lot more than I did. Access to opportunities and the ability to dream big and become way more than they could ever imagine. That they were part of a long legacy of men and women who sacrificed to provide for their families, no matter the circumstances or difficulty.

But what about all those other boys and young men? The girls and young women? What about the mothers and fathers? What about the grandparents? What about them?

As I walked toward the bedroom, I thought of all the children and adults who had ever felt insecure, anxious, less than, beat down, and unsure of the future—whether their skin is white, black, brown, yellow, or any tone under the sun. I wanted to say to them: No matter how bad it gets, no matter how scared you feel, no matter how many nights you lay awake wondering about the future, it gets better. I promise you.

If you embrace faith, family, grit, personal responsibility, and integrity, it gets better. There is always a path to better, no matter how hard the road ahead. Embrace family. Don't compromise your values. Learn from, embrace, and celebrate American history. Learn how to critically think. Develop a passion for life. Have empathy. Cherish time with your family. Strive to do better for yourself, regardless of your circumstances.

Pensive and deeply grateful, I walked down the hallway to the master bedroom and opened the door. Samanda looked up at me from her book, still as beautiful, charming, and full of strength in her forties as she was at fifteen.

"You good, honey?" she asked.

I looked at her with a huge smile, the woman who had stuck by me, the compassionate pillar who forgave me, the person who I relied on and trusted more than anyone in the world, who helped me become the man I am today.

"*Claro mi vida*. God is good, all the time."

REFLECTIONS FROM TODAY

*Trust in the Lord with all your heart and lean not on
your own understanding; in all your ways submit to
Him, and He will make your paths straight.*

PROVERBS 3:5-6, NIV

Sometime during late January of 2018, Samanda said to me, "I think
you should share your story." I had gone through profound personal
transformation that led me to kneel before God in gratitude, asking
for His forgiveness and grace. He saved me. And with her encouragement, I felt compelled to share my personal and family history in the
hope that it might help others.

Over the span of forty-six years, my journey has thus far tran-
scended rural life in mountainous Puerto Rico and urban poverty in
the United States to reach success as a scholar-athlete in American
football, engage in deep discovery at an elite college, and have a highly
successful career across the halls of Massachusetts government and
corporate America.

Bowdoin College was the place where I discovered that wealthy
white people were not my enemy, and that as an American citizen
from Puerto Rico, I shared many things in common with poor, working-class white people from northern Maine and rural Tennessee than
I did with wealthy people of color from elite private schools. My college experience was transformational, not just because I discovered
truths about myself but also because I had access to opportunity,

and exposure to people with differing opinions and from different backgrounds. The ability to understand other's perspectives and lived experiences, and to engage in free exchange of ideas without prejudice or judgement, was transformational. And the opportunity to see firsthand the many possibilities available to me was equally powerful. After all, if you can't see it, you can't be it.

My family's life was transformed in one generation due, in large part, to my education, my street-earned degree during high school, and the lifelong lessons I learned in college, especially outside the classroom. As difficult as my first two years were in college, they were richly rewarding. But my personal growth was a two-way street: Bowdoin accepted me and offered me a once-in-a-lifetime chance. What I had to do was open my heart and mind to learn, adapt, accept or reject, and leverage the opportunity. My bitterness, my lack of exposure in high school, and how I perceived myself as a student of color in college were obstacles I had to overcome at that time. Along with my personal growth on and off campus, my college degree enabled me to compete professionally and sit at many tables of prestige and power I once thought impossible. I have come to learn that few things are as empowering as a job or career that empowers one to attain financial freedom and the confidence in one's ability to provide for his or her family's needs.

After college, I spent twenty years in a remarkable career that I never could have envisioned as a teenager drinking 40-ounce beers with friends on the streets. But one day, I decided to leave my job and money—lots of money—to save my family, rebuild my marriage, and raise my two young sons. Like my father and grandfather before him, I chose family.

The drive, determination, and relentless pursuit of success had separated me from my source of truth and the purpose for my life. Over time, escaping poverty became an addicting obsession. I lost all sense of what was truly important in life. I made many decisions based on a deep-seated fear of poverty, which led me to pursue money and professional advancement with reckless abandon, and at the expense of my family and my faith.

Money, power, exclusive dinners, private jets, and professional accomplishments blinded me. My career and how much money I could earn became the most important objective. I assumed that *mi familia*—Samanda, Anthony, and Alexander—were benefitting from materialistic goods, but the reality was that they were not. My kids were being raised largely by Samanda and my parents. Their father was consumed by work, influence, and travel. I was absent. I had ignored the values that my parents and grandparents had drilled into me: faith, love, family, honor, integrity, and gratitude. Ironically, the professional accomplishments and success I intensely pursued became the very reasons I was failing my family.

During 2017, I turned my life over to God. His compassion led to unimaginable prosperity and riches. Not materialistic riches—personal and spiritual wealth beyond my wildest dreams. Through *Him*, I am renewed in my passion for His truth and for sharing *His* promise with my family. By *His* grace, I am becoming a better father to Anthony and Alexander, and a loving and caring husband to Samanda. By *His* mercy, I am forgiven.

This book is one of the many ways in which I will share truth with my sons and anyone willing to read. It is a personal testimony of how God used challenging circumstances in my life for good. It is a message that advances the beliefs and values that my family and I live by.

But it is not just a memoir. This book is a collective representation of my family's values and a journey that transcends three generations of American men and women who put faith and family first. My personal history dates back to my grandfathers and grandmothers who toiled in the tropical island of Puerto Rico under duress and conditions that bred grit, perseverance, honor, and faith. My family—like so many other families—came to the United States to pursue better. A better future, a better tomorrow. My family's story is the story of America, a nation rooted in faith, tenacity, innovation, redemption, and the common good.

Anthony and Alexander, like millions of other young men and women, need to know their family's story and embrace the incredible blessing and opportunity they possess in America. They have to leverage their great-grandparents', grandparents', and parents' journey from Puerto Rico to the United States in search of better. They must adopt a winning mindset and approach all challenges with fearlessness. It is important that they understand that their lives are shaped by a legacy of hardworking Americans who wanted a better life and who would stop at nothing to work toward better.

My grandparents had a burning desire to better their situation and support their family. My grandfather knew intimately that Los Estados Unidos was the land of opportunity. He made a conscious decision to leave his family in search of work in America. With just a sixth-grade education, he worked incessantly and developed the necessary skills to grow, build, thrive, and prosper.

In the same way, my father battled his demons, left his family and a dead-end job to come to America and find better, be better, and pursue a better life for his family. My mother did the same. Her selfless tenacity and unshakable faith, coupled with my father's resilient discipline, produced values that live deep within my soul: faith, family, tenacity, and gratitude.

Now it's my turn.

As a father, it is my responsibility to infuse my two sons with the same values my grandparents and parents instilled in me.

Every day, Samanda and I tangibly demonstrate to our sons what love between a man and a woman should look like, with compromise, selflessness, commitment, and forgiveness. We tell them how much they are loved and that God has a special plan for each of them, and that they were created to do great things. We encourage them to think critically, foster their curiosity, and develop their analytical skills by discussing current affairs. We want them to know *how* to think, not *what* to think. We want them to compete and thrive in America.

We discuss American history, Puerto Rican history, Dominican history, and the American Constitution, and push them to think objectively about differing perspectives and a range of social issues. We encourage them to keep an open mind at all times but also to stand firmly for what they believe. These are all the ways in which we aim to build faith, character, culture, intellectual curiosity, grit, and family—all foundational ingredients that will serve them well as they grow up.

Our sons will also fully understand that the freedoms and opportunities they enjoy in America will not come from the color of their skin, or their ethnic heritage, but rather from their faith, work ethic, grit, skill, and their willingness to assume personal responsibility. Anthony and Alexander know well that character matters more than skin color or ethnicity. That they enjoy constitutional freedoms not available in any other country. That as Americans, they can live, pray, and learn freely, as well as pursue better for themselves with self-reliance, perseverance, and faith.

Only in America can one go from living on the third floor of a triple-decker in a small, working-class urban city to a successful career and prosperous life in one generation.

I believe in the promise of the United States of America.

I have deep faith in the values that my Christian upbringing instilled in me since my earliest days. And I am proud to celebrate America's constitutional freedoms, which are endowed by God to *all* Americans: the right to life, liberty, and the *pursuit* of happiness.

I am Puerto Rican by heritage. I know the history and music of Puerto Rico as well as the inhabitants of the island—yet I am 100 percent American. For the Morales family, every day is July 4th because we are free to think, live, worship God, love, and laugh without fear. Free to transcend poverty. Free to stretch beyond our current circumstances. Free to achieve our highest potential. Free to fail. Free to prosper. Free to reach back and bring others with us. Free to share the history of one family in the hope that it might impact others. Maybe even you.

ACKNOWLEDGMENTS

I have hundreds of people to thank, both for helping me become the man I am today and for their support, loyalty, and friendship.

Thank you to Jesus Christ for rescuing me and for having mercy on my life and my family. Through Him, all things are possible, and without him, nothing is possible.

Thank you to my familia. Samanda, my life partner. She has been my constant source of love, strength, compassion, and light. Mom, my conscience and the woman who sacrificed her future for her family. My mother taught us how to live a life of faith, prayer, and devotion to Jesus Christ and family. Dad, my hero. My guardian angel, my friend and life mentor. Because of his integrity, humility, and unspoken life lessons, I am who I am today. His actions always spoke louder than his words. Diana, my second mom. Dan, my big brother. Dwayne, my brother. My sons for teaching me how to love and for the honor of being their Dad.

Thank you to my friends and mentors. Coach Dempsey for the Xs and Os of life, both on and off the field. George Demoulias for his constant friendship and loyalty. Herlande Rosemond for her patience, friendship, and loyalty. Pastor Ed Marston for demonstrating compassion for a sinner like me and for guiding hundreds like me to Christ and to a life of service to Jesus. Professor Susan Bell for her patience and guidance. Professor John Turner for his friendship and understanding. Professors Penny Martin and Craig McEwen for their support. Damon Patton, My Lam, John Wihbey, Tim Ryan, and Lorne Norton for their friendship and insights.

Thank you to the team that helped get this book out into the world. The team at Greenleaf, including Lindsey, Lindsay, Anne, and Justin. Finally, a special and heartfelt thank you to Stacy Ennis for her empathy, kindness, and for believing in me; and for using her incredible gift of writing to help tell my story, the story of a humble American familia rooted in Christ.

NOTES

CHAPTER 1

1. United States Commission on Civil Rights, Indiana Advisory Committee, *Fair Housing Enforcement in Northwest Indiana: A Report* (Ann Arbor: University of Michigan Library, 1983), 14; James B. Lane and Edward J. Escobar, *Forging a Community: The Latino Experience in Northwest Indiana, 1919-1975* (Bloomington: Indiana University Press, 1987), 294.

2. Hilda Lloréns, *Imaging the Great Puerto Rican Family: Framing Nation, Race, and Gender during the American Century* (Washington DC: Lexington Books, 2016), 190.

CHAPTER 2

1. "Puerto Rican Emigration: Why the 1950s?" Lehman College, http://lcw.lehman.edu/lehman/depts/latinampuertorican/latinoweb/PuertoRico/1950s.htm; data for 1900-1970 are from José L. Vázquez Calzada, "La población de Puerto Rico y su trayectoria histórica" (Río Piedras, PR: Escuela Graduada de Salud Pública, Recinto de Ciencias Médicas, Universidad de Puerto Rico, 1988), 286; data for 1970-1990 are from Francisco L. Rivera Batiz and Carlos Santiago, *Island Paradox: Puerto Rico in the 1990s* (New York: Russell Sage Foundation, 1996), 45.

2. "Puerto Rican Emigration: Why the 1950s?"

CHAPTER 9

1. Dr. Fred Zhang, "SAT Score Percentiles (High-Precision Version)," SAT/ACT Prep Online Guides and Tips (blog), PrepScholar, January 3, 2020, https://blog.prepscholar.com/sat-percentiles-high-precision-2016.

2. Total Group, "2018 SAT Suite of Assessments Annual Report," October 25, 2018, https://reports.collegeboard.org/pdf/2018-total-group-sat-suite-assessments-annual-report.pdf.

CHAPTER 10

1. Richard Rodriguez, *Hunger of Memory: The Education of Richard Rodriguez* (New York: Dial Press), page 45.

2. Rodriguez, *Hunger of Memory*, page 11.

3. Rodriguez, Hunger of Memory, page 77.

ABOUT THE AUTHOR

Growing up in a poor, mountainous region of Puerto Rico, David Morales had no idea he would end up where he is today: an executive shaping the future of healthcare and public policy in America and a father dedicated to faith, family, and community. Over the last two decades, he has had an accomplished career in government, corporate America, and the not-for-profit sector. In addition to leading the UniCare-Anthem business, he served as chief strategy officer for Steward Health Care, founded his own consulting company, and enjoyed a rewarding career in public service. Alongside his wife, Samanda, he co-founded Ahora Inc., a not-for-profit dedicated to empowering working-class families and low-income individuals to build self-reliance through financial literacy, money management, and wealth building. His proudest accomplishment, by far, is raising two strong, God-fearing boys and getting them started on their own journeys toward self-reliance and prosperity. Learn more at www. davidamorales.com.